MURTY CLASSICAL
LIBRARY OF INDIA

Sheldon Pollock, General Editor

ALLASANI PEDDANA
THE STORY OF MANU

MCLI 4

ALLASANI PEDDANA

అల్లసాని పెద్దన

THE
STORY OF MANU

Translated by
VELCHERU NARAYANA RAO
DAVID SHULMAN

MURTY CLASSICAL LIBRARY OF INDIA

HARVARD UNIVERSITY PRESS

Cambridge, Massachusetts

London, England

2015

SERIES DESIGN BY M9DESIGN

Library of Congress Cataloging-in-Publication Data

Allasani Peddana, active 16th century, author.
[Manucaritramu. English]
The Story of Manu / Allasani Peddana ; translated by
Velcheru Narayana Rao and David Shulman.
p. cm. — (Murty Classical Library of India ; 4)
Includes bibliographical references and index.
ISBN 978-0-674-42776-1 (cloth : alk. paper)
1. Svarocisa Manu (Hindu mythology)—Poetry.
2. Telugu poetry—1500–1800—Translations into English.
I. Narayana Rao, Velcheru, 1932– translator.
II. Shulman, David Dean, 1949– translator. III. Title.
PL4780.9.A43M313 2014
894.8′2712—dc23   2014016315

CONTENTS

INTRODUCTION

1

Allasani Peddana confidently calls himself the "Creator of Telugu Poetry" (*āndhrakavitāpitāmaha*),[1] and generations of his readers, including his own patron, King Krishnadevaraya, accepted this description. We know for sure, as did Peddana himself, that poetry in Telugu had existed for nearly half a millennium before him. The classical starting point of the tradition is linked with the name of Nannayya at the court of the Eastern Chalukya king, Rajaraja Narendra, in the eleventh century; many standard features of poetic praxis were already in place in Nannayya's unfinished Telugu *Mahābhārata*.[2] Why, then, does Peddana think that he created poetry where none existed before? What does he mean by this title, and why was it so readily accepted?

We know when this poet lived and worked—roughly around 1520, at the height of the power of Krishnadevaraya, who ruled from 1509 to 1529 in Vijayanagara, the capital of the last imperial state system in premodern south India. In his introductory section Peddana describes several of Krishnadevaraya's well-known military campaigns, including a major expedition to the Gajapati kingdom on the Orissa coast. Krishnadevaraya himself quoted Peddana's description of the royal family in the preface to his own great work, the *Āmuktamālyada* (The Girl Who Gave the Garland She Wore). These two figures, king and poet, were thus very closely intertwined. We can think of Peddana as

Krishnadevaraya's primary court poet and his book, the *Story of Manu,* as the epitome of this vital, expansive moment in all cultural and political domains. To no small degree, Peddana's book embodies the ethos and creative vision of Vijayanagara at its height.

"Creator"—*pitāmaha,* literally "grandfather"—is a word applied to Brahma, the god who creates the world in the sense of forming and shaping in his imagination the stuff of potential reality. In some sense, every poet could be described as such a creator.[3] But Peddana's appropriation of the term has a different, far more specific connotation. He crafted a new kind of poetry and a new kind of book, one never seen before in Telugu. He clearly knew that he had achieved this and that after him Telugu poetry would be changed forever.

Our task is to try to define the essential features of this new departure. Observe, first, what Peddana inherited directly. There is a story, available in Sanskrit sources; there is a patron who says he wants to hear that story and therefore commissions the work. This template exists from Nannayya onward. A certain style also exists, including the *campū* genre, a mix of verse and prose, the richly Sanskritized diction, and a set of available meters, some south Indian, some borrowed from classical Sanskrit. Metrical praxis in *kāvya*-style Telugu differs from classical Sanskrit metrics, on the one hand, and from oral composition in Telugu, on the other, in that in elevated *kāvya* verses the semantic-syntactical segments usually do not coincide with metrical segments. In other words, each verse has a built-in contrapuntal structure, immediately recognizable by an ear attuned to musical recitation of poetry. (Further distinctions from the epic-oral style will be discussed shortly.)

There is also a conventional frame for the text, with the patron slotted as a listener to whom the poem is addressed, but who normally hears it as the story was originally told to another, embedded listener by another, embedded speaker (or set of speakers and listeners). In the present case, Krishnadevaraya listens to a story originally told by the sage Markandeya to another sage, Kroshti; this narration was then repeated by a group of learned and articulate birds speaking to the sage Jaimini. This doubled inner frame, along with the narrative itself, is taken from the Sanskrit *Mārkaṇḍeyapurāṇa,* where it forms part of a longer sequence of stories about the first Manus, who ruled the world for long cosmic periods known as *manvantaras.*[4] The same prototype of the story was translated into Telugu by an earlier poet, Marana (early fourteenth century), and it is very likely that Peddana knew this Telugu version.

So, formally speaking, Krishnadevaraya is actually overhearing a story told (twice at least) to others—as in all *purāṇic* narratives, including the Mahabharata. No one ever tells the story for the first time. In another sense, there are always two and only two roles—narrator and listener—sequentially occupied over several generations and dialogically linked. We ourselves overhear the story as Krishnadevaraya was hearing it. We have highlighted this frame by putting it in italics in our translation at the opening and closing of each chapter. All this is familiar and adapted from the earlier models. What, then, is new enough to explain Peddana's claim to have created Telugu poetry?

We can definitely speak of an unprecedented style, marked by distinctive qualities of complexity and intensity on all levels—thematic, lexical, syntactic, metrical, musical, and so on. But to understand these features, we have to look back to Peddana's immediate predecessors and to the literary genealogy that he himself offers his readers. Such a genealogy is yet another inherited element: from Nannayya on, poets describe their forerunners and praise them (Telugu commentators call this *pūrvakaviprasaṃśā*, "praise of earlier poets").[5] Tikkana, the second Telugu *Mahābhārata* poet (thirteenth century), added another feature, the *kukavininda* or "denunciation of bad poets," which became standard. Nannayya mentions only one model, that of Vyasa, the author of the epic he is re-creating. Tikkana refers both to famous Sanskrit poets and, with particular fervor, to Nannayya, the first Telugu poet (*āndhrakavitvaviśāraduṇḍu*). When we come to Peddana, we find a long series of Sanskrit poets honorably mentioned: Valmiki, Vyasa, Bhatta Bana, Bhasa, Bhavabhuti, Bharati, Subandhu, Bilhana, Kalidasa, Magha, Shivabhadra, Malhana, Chora,[6] Murari, Mayura, Saumilli, and Dandin (the list ends with an "etc."). Only three Telugu poets are named: Nannayya, Tikkana, and Errana, the three Mahabharata authors.

The denunciation, a general statement, follows:

A rogue poet, for want of any other means to feed his
    family,
steals, in desperation, from the vast forest of palm-
    leaf manuscripts.

But scholars catch him at it, his poetry loses its charm,
and he's put in the stocks under the gaze of the king.

Note the central image of graphic literacy—the palm-leaf
manuscripts—and, with the existence of such manuscripts,
the claim for intellectual-property rights. This verse is the
first occurrence in Telugu of the notion of plagiarism in the
specific meaning of stealing a poem as uniquely articulated
by the poet who created and therefore owns it (an earlier,
more general statement about plagiarism as imitating a
certain style comes from Annamayya, a generation or so
before Peddana[7]). This kind of claim fits well with the sense
of personal originality and innovation that we are exploring.

Who is missing from Peddana's list of Telugu poets? At
least three major names: Nanne Coda, the author of the
Telugu *Kumārasambhava* (Birth of Kumara); Nachana
Somanatha, who composed the *Uttaraharivaṃśamu* (Later
History of Krishna); and the great maverick and innovator,
Srinatha.[8] All three of them produced what Srinatha called
a *mahāprabandha,* a "great composition" comparable to
a *mahākāvya* in Sanskrit. We have argued that Srinatha,
in particular, reinvented the notion of a Telugu book as a
self-contained, sustained, well-integrated, thematically
coherent, stylistically ornate poem. In a way, Peddana was
doing something very much akin to these precedents, espe-
cially to Srinatha's great works. Modern Telugu literary crit-
ics have thus asked, with good reason, why it is that Peddana
fails to refer to these predecessors and above all to Srinatha,
who was also closest to him in time (late fourteenth and early
fifteenth centuries).[9] This silence gives us an important clue.

Peddana was perfectly aware that he was doing something very different from what Srinatha had done.

We can define the difference, on the level of style and texture, in the following way. Srinatha's poems are extravagant, full-throated, and orally compelling; each word forces each subsequent word to fit its rhythmic and musical pattern and rarely allows the reader-reciter to stop and think. Although they sound like orally produced poems, they were unquestionably fully "written" in the sense of being fixed, not improvised, with no empty spaces for filler words (unlike the standard oral style). We have called the Srinatha mode a "second-order orality."[10] It has the sweep and flow of full-blown oral recitation, though we know it was premeditated and carefully crafted. Srinatha was imitating oral composition even as he actually wrote his books. By contrast, Peddana shows us a first-order "written-ness." His poems are syntactically complex, with carefully chiseled phrases that do not force the reader to move on to the next word. The adjective "lyrical" comes to mind: a musical tuning that results from contemplative crafting of the line. We find repetition, but of a much more complex type than in Srinatha. Listen, for example, to the following single line of Peddana's:

kanaka-naga-sīma kalpa-vṛkṣamula nīḍa
pacca rācaṭṭu gami racca paṭṭu māku

We perform
on stages set with emeralds, in the shade
of wishing trees on Golden Mountain. . . .

(This is the divine courtesan Varuthini introducing herself to the innocent Brahman Pravara, 2.43)

We have a profusion of alliterative sounds—*kanakana*... *kalpa, rācaṭṭu*... *raccapaṭṭu*.... But this kind of chiming is unpredictable and nonrepeatable, also a little asymmetrical, off balance; the poet has to work hard to produce it. For contrast, look at a Srinatha line such as:

kāla-kaṇṭha-kaṭhora-kaṇṭha-huṅkārambu
cĕvulu sokkani nāṭi cittabhavuḍu

He's like the Love God before the angry yell of black-throat Shiva reached his ears.[11]

The alliteration comes naturally with a predictable repetitiveness: *kāla-kaṇṭha* leads inexorably to another *kaṇṭha,* and the whole line rolls off the tongue before you have even considered what it says. In fact, you know what it says just by listening to it. In Peddana's verse, semantic density slows you down and makes you re-read or re-recite the phrase before you can make sense of it, and the music itself demands attention and surprises you with its fresh, or exotic, combinations and cadences. Note, please, that we are not belittling the greatness of Srinatha's achievement; we have two very distinct forms of aesthetic excellence, each with its particular effects.

And we have not yet even addressed the question of theme and meaning.

We are, perhaps, beginning to understand why Peddana

has no wish or need to mention Srinatha as a formative influence upon him—even though without Srinatha's literary revolution, Peddana himself could not have existed as we know him. For a poet committed to crafting every syllable, every metrical rise and fall, every semantic nuance, Srinatha's verses hardly count as poetry. A new perspective on what a poem should be has emerged. Srinatha might even be dangerously close, in his own way, to this novel experiment—and capable of destroying it. To pass over him in silence is thus, for Peddana, an artistic necessity.

Here is another example of Peddana's extreme lyricism, in a compacted style that one only very rarely, if ever, finds in Srinatha:

vālārum gŏnagoḷḷan īv' alasatan vāyiñcu co nāṭakun
meḷamb' aina vipañci ninna mŏdalun nīv' aṇṭamin jesiy
āy-
ālāpambĕy avela palkĕḍu prabhātâyāta-vātâhatā-
lolat-tantrula meḷavimpa gadave lolākṣi deśākṣikin

Last evening you were idly playing your vina,
which you tuned to an evening raga.
Since then you haven't touched it.
Now it's playing the same raga
when the dawn breeze strikes the strings.
It's the wrong time. Dear friend
with dancing eyes, won't you tune it
to a morning mode?

Varuthini is lovesick, and her girlfriends are doing their best to distract her from her obsession. They would like her to resume playing her vina, and they tell her that, since she has not touched it since the previous afternoon, it is still tuned to a musical raga inappropriate for the dawn hour in which they are speaking. The morning breeze is playing the strings and producing sounds in the wrong scale, inappropriate for early morning, unbearable for sensitive ears.

But what about *our* ears? No Telugu listener can fail to be ravished by the sheer music and its gentle repetitions, much like when one listens to a raga unfolding. The notes repeat—but in this case, once again, the repetitions are unexpected and infra-semantic. The initial *v* of *vālārum* chimes with *īv' alasatan,* but the second *v* is a pure phenomenon of sandhi, or euphonic combination, not part of any word. It is music for music's sake alone. And by the time we reach the critical Sanskrit compound that stretches from line 3 into line 4, we are swept away by a gentle breeze of the long *ā*'s with their open consonants and liquids, intensifying like the resonance of a string plucked precisely, over and over. Each *ā* fuses with the previous one, creating a seamless movement. The music is inside the verse, in no way described by it. The final cadence gives us the name of the raga we should have been listening to, and two *kṣa*'s crown the verse and allow it to end, like the final notes of a concert. This breathtaking musicality moves the listener/reader intensely as he or she begins to grasp its full meaning and its implicit figure. The verse also bears, even demands, re-reading. Only repeated reading can reveal how the meaning is entirely enveloped by the sounds that trigger it. One could even go further and say that the verse generates in the reader, by its very perfection, something of the longing that the heroine, Varuthini, is experiencing and that her girlfriends know and feel together with her. On top of the sheer lyricism, there is a touching intimacy in the way these girls speak to their friend in second-person singular: *meḷavimpa gadave,* "Won't you tune it. . . ." English, sadly, lacks this expressive register.

No less intensely lyrical are Peddana's prose passages, which often appear at critical moments and serve to deepen the music and the mood. The poet resorts to prose when even a series of single verses cannot adequately convey the density of sound and feeling. In fact, this intensification is itself sometimes explicitly thematized, as in the hallucinatory depiction of moonlight, continuously heightened by reflections, in 2.28. Such passages go far beyond the compelling, universally influential precedent of Bana's Sanskrit prose, a stable presence in *kāvya* production from the seventh century on. They shape the aesthetic perception both aurally and visually by long, "thick" clauses that fuse into one another, leaving the reader, who is enunciating the sentences out loud, breathless, searching for a place of rest. Such prose cannot be captured by the mind. It is supra-semantic; the reader knows the meaning in his or her skin as a palpable, tangible reality. Such a physical sensation, induced by linguistic means, cannot be contained or explained by the traditional Sanskrit poetics of *bhāva,* "feeling/mood." Indeed, this kind of aesthetic experience, a regular feature of sixteenth-century Telugu literature, has never been theorized in South Asian poetics.

2

It is not, of course, enough to look closely at the novel texture of the poetic line or of the stanza, or to explicate the nature of the lyrical moves that pervade the work as a whole, or to identify structural innovation derived from or concomitant with these changes. With Peddana we find an entirely new mode of reception in which the reader, still reading aloud, experiences the work for herself or himself in a private manner. Again, we can delineate a historical sequence with three major stages, the earlier ones continuing to exist in tandem with the later ones. The three Telugu Mahabharata poets belong to the *paurāṇika* paradigm: the person who publicly recites the poem is, in effect, a second author who makes a selection from the original, restructures it, explicates the text with his or her own commentary, leaves out verses here and there at will, and always coincides fully with the internal narrator, as in the frame discussed above. The *paurāṇika* re-creates the poem together with the audience who listens to it and who coincides with the internal listener of the inner frame. We are, of course, talking about public, oral, musical (sung) articulation. This *paurāṇika* paradigm survives in the fifteenth-century *Mahābhāgav-atamu* of Potana (among other authors), a classic *purāṇa*, loosely constructed, not meant for silent reading. A second prototype was invented by Srinatha, who has dispensed with the need for a second author. Indeed, this poet allows no interference with his work. He has created a tight narrative, each verse indispensable, with narrative suspense carrying over into powerful prose passages somewhat reminiscent, as we have said, of Bana's Sanskrit style. The tight narrative generates a coherent book meant to be read through as a whole, without a break. Srinatha's major works are, we have argued, proto-novellas with unified themes and an interest in the depths of character. Still, these books are public texts meant to be read aloud by a reciter who articulates their beauty, with proper cadences and emphases, while the listeners give themselves to the collective experience of listening to and appreciating the poetry. The reciter makes no changes in the text; his job is to perform it in its completeness. In a sense, given this new mode of reading and performing, Srinatha invented the very notion of a modern Telugu book. The poet who most closely followed him in this quality of tight, masterful construction was Viswanatha Satyanarayana in the twentieth century, although in other respects Viswanatha is very different from Srinatha (he does not share the second-order orality of which we have spoken). Both poets produced works marked by a pronounced symphonic quality, every note in the right place and all parts cohering, in their varying heights and depths, toward a total aesthetic statement.

Peddana's poem, however, cannot be read out to a group. It still has to be *heard*—but now by the individual reader. Poetry, from this point on, is a matter of personal, private experience. One reads the book for oneself. We could call such poetry *pāṭhya,* "to be read for oneself," as opposed to the classical Sanskrit division into *dṛśya,* "visible" (that is, dramatic literature) and *śravya,* "audible" (that is, publicly read).[12] The new category has a thematic implication, since the *Manucaritramu,* like most of the other major Telugu poetic works of the sixteenth century, is powerfully focused on human interiority—the working and contents of the human mind and the expression and exploration of self. It is perhaps not surprising that books that investigate, above all else, the nature of awareness, including unconscious awareness, should be read primarily for oneself and by oneself.

Such individual connoisseur-readers undoubtedly constituted a group. A new literary community must have developed by this time if such a book were to come into existence and to survive. We can imagine an elite group of this sort living at places like Vijayanagara or Penugonda or other sites in Krishnadevaraya's vast empire in southern India. The existence of such a collective also helps to explain the profound intertextuality of sixteenth-century Telugu large-scale literary texts, which were composed for the same kind of readership and for one another. Such readers had an investment in the imperial political structure, and some of them, at least, were active players in the political domain— not least among them Krishnadevaraya himself. A dimension of leisure is necessary if one is to savor books like these. A well-known *cāṭu* (orally circulating) verse, attributed to Peddana, describes the context of composition-cum-appreciation in detail:

nirupahati-sthalambu ramaṇī-priya-dūtika tĕcci yiccu
    kap-
pūraviḍĕm' ātmak' impayina bhojanam' ūyĕla mañcam'
    ŏppu tap
p' arayu rasajñul' ūha tĕliyaṅgala
    lekhakapāṭhakottamul
dŏrikinagāni yūraka kṛtul raciyimpum'aṭanna śakyame

> Without a quiet place, without betel nut flavored
> with camphor sent by my lover through her
> dear friend as messenger, without a good meal
> that I find delicious, and a swinging cot,
> and men of sensibility who can tell what
> is good from what is bad, and the best of
> scribes and performers who will understand the intent
> of my work—unless I have all of these—
> can anyone possibly ask me to compose poetry?[13]

One important qualification has to be made to what we have said so far. Even a book like Peddana's, meant for private enjoyment, could have verses excerpted from it and quoted independently. In this way such verses, and their authors, enter the oral *cāṭu* tradition. We mentioned at the outset that a set of verses from Peddana's introduction was lifted verbatim and recycled by Krishnadevaraya in his preface.[14] One can easily imagine such laudatory verses quoted by literati and circulated widely within the empire. The new *mahākāvya* works show us the same distinction we see elsewhere between the recorded text—that is, the work as copied or, today, printed as a whole—and the received text, that is, those verses circulating freely and universally known and loved.

3

Having come this far, we might now ask ourselves what this book is about. The very selection of its theme—the birth of Manu/Man—is an eloquent statement about what seemed crucial to the early sixteenth-century literati and what the poet himself wanted to say to them and to his king. The story, as we have said, was known before, both in Sanskrit and in Telugu, but its elaboration and reconceptualization belong to this historical moment. Suddenly it matters very much to know what makes a human being human, and how such a being comes to be.

Let us make no mistake: being human is, for Peddana, a kind of achievement. When Varuthini, the ravishing and immortal courtesan, first sees the radiant but mortal Brahman Pravara and falls in love with him, the poet tells us that her immortality has become a burden:

Fluttering glances healed
her inability to blink, and for the first time
she was sweating. Even her surpassing
understanding was healed by the new
confusion of desire. Like the beetle that,
from concentrating on the bee, *becomes*
a bee, by taking in that human being
she achieved humanity
with her own body.

A little later, when Pravara has left her in an agony of love-sickness, she actually curses her immortality and wishes she were human:

Human women are lucky.
If their lover rejects them, they die.
But me—I'm immortal! I have to suffer

this shameless sorrow. My beauty
that cannot die is a lamp lit
in an empty house.

But there is more to being human than dying, and Peddana
has found in his Sanskrit source an opportunity to make a
wider statement. He even has his patron and friend, the king,
suggest to him, in the introduction, that this one story, "The
Birth of Svarochisha," is "particularly good to listen to" and,
in addition, offers scope for skillful writing (*caturaracanak'
anukūlambu*, 1.16)—that is, for interpreting the meaning of
the core narrative in novel ways. The whole book, on one
level, is an extended essay on the making of a full human
being and, by the end, of a fully human king.

Look at the way the story unfolds. An innocent but restless
Brahman is transported to the Himalayas, where a divine
woman falls in love with him and offers herself to him in
vain. The human lover departs. His image, however, remains
fixed, indeed burning like fire, in her mind. A gandharva, a
semidivine singer-magician, who had once loved this same
woman and been rejected by her, assumes the form of her
now-absent beloved and makes love to her, leaving her with
the all-too-real illusion that she is in the arms of the man
she loves. She conceives a child. What enables this moment
of conception?

We will take a close look at this question a little later, but
already one element can be clearly stated. Nothing will work
without the operation of cognitive error or illusion—again,
a pragmatically effective illusion that is, in that sense, real.
Human beings, that is, are conceived by means of a reality

that looks like illusion. Indeed, the later stages in the generation of Svarochisha Manu are no less pregnant with indirection. Varuthini's son, Svarochi (Sanskrit Svarochis), an avid hunter, saves a girl, Manorama, from an ogre who happens to be her father. Svarochi marries her and her two girlfriends in chapters 5 and 6. As wedding gifts the two friends bestow upon him the ability to understand the language of birds and animals and a mantra that fulfills all desires. After hundreds of years of making love more or less continuously with all three wives in the forest, Svarochi embraces a doe who turns out to be the Forest Goddess herself. He marries her too. Their child is Svarochisha, the Manu of one long cosmic cycle. So the birth of one Manu requires both the initial slippage—the loss of a concrete, direct reality and its reconstitution in the imagination—and the subsequent transformation of the Forest from animal into woman. The human being is thus balanced somewhere between the heavenly mother, Varuthini, and the earth mother, both of whom have to produce a real child by an imaginative act.

There is more. A complete human life has certain essential ingredients, all present in the trajectory that eventually generates Manu. The first father, Pravara, is a beautiful man (*alekhyatanūvilāsuḍu,* 1.51). Beauty matters. He is also learned, a great grammarian (*bhāṣāparaśeṣabhogi*), and devoted to Vedic ritual. The first mother, as we know, is a passionate creature, given to all the agonies of desire. Intense love and longing are intrinsic to the human. Interestingly, in this book they are also fulfilled, although in somewhat convoluted ways. First-generation desire proceeds via severe displacement and disjunction. The next generation, that of

Svarochi, experiences much greater and more stable satisfaction. Svarochi also becomes a great physician and, like his father, a proficient linguist (in fact, he outdoes his father in this respect, since he can understand animals and birds). At the same time, there is something shallow, or missing, in Svarochi. He lacks the depth of humanity. Unending sexual fulfillment, while not a bad thing in itself, is not quite enough. Fortunately, Svarochi's unusual linguistic abilities bring about a change. He overhears a ruddy goose (*cakravākī*) speaking about him with disgust:

> It's impossible for one man to love many women
> or for many women to love one man. There's no
> real love here. . . .

> If a man is attached to one woman,
> and a woman loves one man,
> that, one can say, is a good thing.
> But a man loving more than one woman
> is a lie.

This homily in praise of monogamy is reiterated, with different emphasis, many years later by a stag, whom Svarochi overhears indignantly turning away from a crowd of amorous does:

> Get away from me! Do you think I'm Svarochi,
> who makes love to women all the time, proud of his
>   vigor? It seems
> you've given up all shame. I've lost my taste for this.

Go find some other stag. I've put an end
to my desire.

This man has easily gathered women around him.
It's nothing but an excess of lust. As for his wealth,
he got it from the women. So he has no honor in this
    world
nor a place in the next. Don't let me become
like him.

Do not assume Svarochi assimilates this insulting message
right away. It takes him another six hundred years of love-
making before he embraces the Forest, at her request, and
begets Svarochisha. But the poet's point is made with the
birth of that third-generation child, who is "naturally calm,
controlled, kind, pure, and truthful" (6.99). This boy wants
only one thing: *sālokya,* to live in the same world as Vishnu,
whom he praises in a series of beautiful and unconventional
verses. The god asks him to wait:

I'll let you come into my world
in good time. Meanwhile, rule the earth
as the second king of men, with an unshaken
mind rooted in what is right and what is wise.
Make gods, sages, and the creator happy.

It impossible to read this verse without thinking that the
poet is speaking directly to his good friend and patron, the
king (he has made Krishnadevaraya actually call him his
friend, *hita,* in the introduction to the book, 1.15). These

two men are on intimate terms, and the poet seems to have no compunction about offering advice. It is by no means merely a matter of monogamy, though the fact that the theme emerges so powerfully in this early sixteenth-century courtly text, at a time when royal courts were full of wealth and women, is of interest.[15] Rather, the poet's imagination of what a good king should be includes an aspect of renunciation and control that follows in the wake of satiety. The progression as a whole makes sense. There is no denial of desire—quite the contrary, desire is articulated, explored, mapped, intensified, fully enjoyed, and satisfied. Then it can be put aside. Such is the royal path to discipline, wisdom, and self-realization.

This conclusion to the book conforms to the religious preference both of the author—who mentions his Shrivaishnava guru, Shathakopa Yati, at the onset (1.6)—and of his royal companion. Krishnadevaraya's personal choice was also Shrivaishnavism, as we know from his long poem, the *Āmuktamālyada,* which tells the story of the Alvar Antal or Goda. Note that Vishnu's parting words to Svarochisha envisage a king active and engaged in the world without being affectively involved in it. There is a strong tradition to the effect that Krishnadevaraya himself never wanted to become king and that he had yogic inclinations;[16] the final verses of the *Manucaritramu* may hint at this idea. In effect, both major Telugu works of the early sixteenth century, Peddana's and Krishnadevaraya's, coincide in their view of what kingship should be and what sort of moral and metaphysical stance it requires. It is as if both poets were striving to lay down a new basis for political authority at a time of imperial success.

Here is Krishnadevaraya's somewhat paradoxical way of articulating this highly specific vision (from the *rājanīti* section of the *Āmuktamālyada*, 4.278):

> The king is nonviolent, though he kills.
> Chaste, though he has women.
> Truthful, though he lies.
> Ever-fasting, though he eats well.
> A hero, though he uses trickery.
> Rich, though he gives away.
> Kingship is rather strange.

Like Krishnadevaraya himself in the latter's explicit self-portrait, Svarochisha Manu—the end product of all the intricate erotic illusions, projections, hallucinations, and cumulative bodily experience—does *not* want to be a king, though rule he must, at the god's direct command. This is the kind of king Peddana wants, one equipped to rule but not tempted by power and its pleasures.

4

Peddana and Krishnadevaraya invented a new genre, which has no clear name. Usually, these days, it is called *prabandha*, "composition," as distinct from *purāṇa*, for example. The sixteenth-century poets sometimes call it a *mahāprabandha* or "large-scale composition."[17] In all cases these are relatively unified works, by a single author who takes responsibility for his text, on some definable theme, with a meaning that can be expressly articulated by the end. We have already discussed the distinction from earlier works in structural settings and modes of reading, and we can now add to these formal features another one drawn from classical Sanskrit poetics but, like other such borrowings, radically reconceived. *Varṇana,* "description," occurs in Dandin's well-known definition of a *mahākāvya*[18] and is applied there to a long list of conventional topics (sunrise and sunset, weddings, battles, and so on). But the mode of description that we find in Peddana and Krishnadevaraya and that can be traced back to Srinatha a century earlier is of an entirely different order. Here we see a realistic fascination with real things that make up the world and shape life in the world, meticulously observed and reported by the poet at a level of high resolution. Nothing like this kind of hyperrealistic description had ever been seen before in Sanskrit or, for that matter, in other south Indian languages. Look, for example, at Peddana's remarkable depiction of the royal hunt in chapter 4. He tells us about all the kinds of falcons used in hunting, the way they are kept and fed, the different sorts of hunting dogs with their personal names and idiosyncrasies, the complex practice of cordoning off a part of the wilderness and setting a trap for wild animals, the names of trees and flowers the hunters encounter, the language they use, their elaborate arrangements for cooking the meat in the forest and apportioning it according to rank, and hundreds of other small details. In Krishnadevaraya's poem we find even more precise naturalistic description, as we have noted elsewhere; indeed, this kind of attention is one major aspect of the strong intertextual relations between Peddana and his patron-poet.[19] Such total commitment to a rather modern realism coexists with an interest in the fantastic and the magical, including boldly imagined events in the worlds of gods and gandharvas. Indeed, we would posit an intrinsic relation between the discovery of the natural world in all its color and concreteness and the rich world of imaginative praxis that, as we have seen, informs these texts.

These features continue on throughout the sixteenth century in an unparalleled series of Telugu *mahāprabandhas* such as Tenali Ramakrishna's *Pāṇḍuraṅgamāhātmyamu* (Praises of Panduranga), Pingali Suranna's *Kaḷāpūrṇodayamu* (The Sound of the Kiss) and *Prabhāvatīpradyumnamu* (The Demon's Daughter), and Ramarajabhushana's *Vasucaritramu* (The Story of Vasu). The latter work, one of the masterpieces of premodern Telugu, is intertextually attuned to, perhaps modeled after, the first three chapters of Peddana's book. The sheer volume of outstanding, sustained, heavily intertextual literary output in Telugu over a few decades compares, one might say, with the nineteenth-century Russian novel. Poets and readers clearly found the new genre compelling. We note in passing that some of these works have been conventionally classified by modern Telugu critics as "erotic books," *śṛṅgārakāvyas*, written for the pleasure and amusement of their patrons. This notion is certainly both impoverished and misguided, as is any attempt to read these works in the light of Kashmiri *rasa* theory (à la Abhinavagupta). A deeper critical understanding of works of this period has yet to be achieved.

Nonetheless, we can say that, taken as a whole, the sixteenth-century Telugu literary explosion, with Peddana at its forefront, speaks to a new awareness and a bold definition of the human being. This human being is radically autonomous and conscious of his or her inner life. Both men and women are fascinated by the other's body, perceived with a burning intensity that finds its way into words. (Look, for example, at Peddana's description of Varuthini as seen by the supposedly detached Pravara in 2.27 and the following verses; and compare Varuthini's overt description of Pravara's beauty, 2.36, and her memory of it in his absence, 3.6). Along with this sheer physicality we find, again and again, rich imaginative projections from one mind into another and an abiding interest in these mental mechanisms. The sixteenth-century poets have psychologized their characters in a way that goes beyond any earlier works; they focus on the interiority of the person as revealed by words, action, and detailed observation of the contours of emotion. This awareness of the new human individual is complemented by an innovative attention to the natural world around him or her. We see the world with new eyes. Nature itself is conceptualized, perhaps for the first time in South Asia, as a self-driven domain distinct, in crucial ways, from the human world that impinges on it.[20]

Let us look at one striking example from our text of scientific description of natural processes in slow motion, detail by precise detail:

Wherever a dry leaf falls, in the little hollow
it leaves behind, a drop of sap appears,
hardens, and then falls off. Then,
a tiny bud emerges, light green like a baby
parrot's wing. Slowly it opens just a little,

reddish like the buds of the *karavīra* tree.
Soon there are many of them, like garlands
woven from the red down of the bulbul,
and as they grow and widen, veins develop,
and the stems turn green and stand up.
Gradually the shades of green thicken
and a sheen appears, brighter day by day,
until there are leaves hanging down—
a whole crowd, beautiful to the eyes.
It happened then, on every tree and vine.

We find similar attentiveness to the life of birds and forest
animals and to landscape, carefully observed and recorded.
Note the dynamic quality of the following moment in the
hunting scene:

One wild boar, hearing the hunters' voices, raised its
snout and, taking charge of the herd, sniffed the wind.
As the dogs came near to attack, he turned his neck aside
and, grunting, warded them off with his tusks, but they
came at him again, and now he bit off chunks of flesh
from one or two of them. The dogs caught his testicles
and shook him, but fiercely he dragged them into the
thicket, worrying them, turning them round until he
was pierced by spears and, with his intestines hanging
out, trying to run away but unable to, tortured by thirst,
exhausted, settled on his haunches, still burning the
hunters with his eyes.

The poet is interested in every detail of this gory scene, presented to the reader without any attempt to ameliorate its impact; he must have witnessed such things himself and taken exhaustive notes. Once again, we wish to stress that such descriptions are unprecedented in South Asian literature; they also required the invention of a new kind of Telugu capable of precision at this level of minute observation.

Theoretical exploration of the natural world went hand in hand with a systematic interest in the inner workings of language.[21] One way to formalize what has happened is as follows: the axiomatic inseparability of sound and meaning breaks apart, and a new space is opened up for playful experimentation. Thus in all these works, but most prominently in Ramarajabhushana's *Vasucaritramu* and Pingali Suranna's *Rāghavapāṇḍavīyamu* (Ramayana and Mahabharata Combined) and *Kaḷāpūrṇodayamu,* sustained *śleṣa* (paronomasia) dehabituates linguistic routine and reveals a hidden world of potential, effectual sounds and meanings, compounded in unfamiliar ways. In the *Kaḷāpūrṇodayamu,* this paronomastic space eventually materializes as perceived reality; the superimposition or interweaving of two linguistic levels necessarily issues into existential excess. The poetic analysis of this process begins in Peddana. Concomitant with this penetrating linguistic ontology is the consolidation of a strong notion of literary fiction, which first emerges in Srinatha but now achieves a full-fledged, self-conscious, reflexive prominence.[22] Literary fiction implies a notion of true and effective illusion—Peddana's central theme.

Note that this concept of true illusion is already present as the content of the opening, benedictory verses to the

Manucaritramu. For example:

> "So you hunters can show some kindness too."
> That's what the daughter of the stony mountain
> says, making fun of him, and Shiva smiles,
> guised as a hunter, as he blesses Arjuna
> with the mightiest of weapons.
> We pray that he gives Krishnaraya, our king,
> all the good things he wants.

Parvati is, paradoxically, the daughter of a stony mountain. Shiva, by his magic (*śāmbarī*), has taken the form of a hunter, and in this form he has given his worshiper, Arjuna, the unconquerable *pāśupata* weapon so he can protect himself from his enemies. Parvati, of course, sees through the magical form—she knows who the fierce hunter is—but she still takes the guise seriously as the basis for an intimate joke. The projected illusion is at once totally real and transparently unreal to those who know it for what it is. The illusion creates its own reality and, at the same time, allows you to see beyond it. It is this same true illusion—with its surprising element of compassion—that may ensure that Krishndevaraya will get "all the good things he wants."[23]

5

Let us take a closer look at the nature of the illusion that permeates the fabric of the narrative.[24] One stable feature of literary fiction is a perspectivism built into the way the story is told; the poet allows us to see the world through the eyes of his various characters. In this sense, no description is monovalent. Observe how Varuthini is described when the real Pravara first sees her (2.24–27). In fact, even before he sees her, he smells her; the poet elaborately characterizes the femininity of this fragrance, but Pravara's apparent conclusion is only that he has found a human presence to help him. Verse 27, however, offers an overwhelmingly erotic description of Varuthini as Pravara sees her. Does this extraordinary vision have any impact on him? Seemingly not. Why, then, has the poet taken the trouble to present Varuthini in such exquisite detail?

Now consider Varuthini's perception of the Pseudo-Pravara, again offered to us in elaborate and explicit detail:

And there he was—lifting his arms high
over and over, above the bushes, exposing
golden bracelets, chanting Veda in the braided style
in a voice sweet as the vina, his red lips quivering,
while his eyes, looking this way and that,
wove fiery garlands in the sky,
and his glistening body, like molten gold,
lit up the whole garden, and his long hair,
which could have reached his thighs,
tied into a knot, was dark as a snake, so dark
the bees could borrow its hue
on interest. He was picking flowers for the god,
false Brahman that he was,
and she saw him.

The reader clearly sees the pseudo-ness of this new Maya-Pravara. We are told that Varuthini, however, takes him at face value, totally accepting the illusion as real. The poet is telling us something here through the words he has chosen. The innocent conclusions his characters come to, in both cases, after the rich expressivity of his diction, may conceal something. So once again we want to ask: why is this vast effort invested in depicting a perception internal to the text and thus made accessible to the reader outside the text?

Here we need to revert to the question we asked earlier. What enables Varuthini's pregnancy, ostensibly from the seed of the Pseudo-Pravara gandharva? The critical verse (4.3) is not free from problems of interpretation:

> You know that the gandharva, making love to
>   Varuthini
> in the body of a Brahman, asked,
> out of fear, that she keep her eyes closed.
> And that young woman, being in love,
> readily agreed. Then, in the depth of her desire,
> that promise fulfilled itself. In that moment
> of intense happiness, the image of the gandharva who,
> by his magic, had captured the flame
> from Pravara's body, was fixed
> in her mind. She became pregnant with it.
> Nine months passed.

It is clear that the flame from Pravara's body (*tat-pravara-deha-samiddha-śikhi-dīpti*) is the main agent. If we read this "flame" as an accusative, as the modern commentators do, then the gandharva has acquired it through his magical power (*śāmbarīmahima*). It is, however, both possible and tempting to read the "flame" in this clause as a nominative, that is, as the subject that was fixed in Varuthini's mind—in which case we have to assume that this same flame serves as an elided object for what the gandharva has acquired (*sangrahiñcinaṭṭi gandharvamūrti*).[25] In any case, the basic elements remain stable: we have Pravara's body as assumed by the gandharva, we have Pravara's burning image active in Varuthini's mind (reinforced by the false image she sees in the gandharva, though not while making love), and we have the flame that constitutes the fertile seed. Each of these components is necessary, and they act together. As a result, as Viswanatha says, the baby that is born, Svarochi, is Pravara's child, not the gandharva's.[26]

But, perhaps strangely, Peddana stresses the gandharva's image (*gandharvamūrti*) along with the flame, and he also pointedly uses the phrase *śāmbarī*-[*mahima*], the gandharva's magic—the same word that appears in the benedictory verse discussed above (1.2), where Parvati observes Shiva's magical guise (*śāmbarībhilluḍu*). Both these words lead us to suspect that at some nonarticulated level Varuthini knows that the man she is sleeping with is not the real Pravara but a useful illusion that she does not want to know. Just as Pravara's initial vision of Varuthini suggests the complexity of his own mental and emotional state, so Varuthini's perception of the Pseudo-Pravara implies a complexity that the text never spells out. Varuthini, in this case, is like the Parvati of the introduction, who takes the Pseudo-Hunter for real at the same time she is teasing him. In each case there is a half-conscious acceptance of illusion for a purpose.

This kind of subtle suggestion and complexity in the building of character makes this book into a piece of innovative literary fiction embodying an imaginative richness with its own distinctive truth-value. The *purāṇic* proto-text gives us flat characters who act for a largely moralistic purpose. Peddana has made complex human beings out of them and given them a deep interiority and levels of knowledge of which, paradoxically, they themselves may not be fully aware. In this dramatic move, building upon the precedent established by Srinatha a century earlier, Peddana opened up a path that later sixteenth-century Telugu poets happily followed.

6

In the Telugu literary tradition, Peddana is imagined as one of the *aṣṭadiggajālu,* the Eight Poet-Elephants who hold up the earth. They are said to have been seated, each in a cardinal direction of space, around Krishnadevaraya in a pavilion called *Bhuvanavijaya,* "Victory over the World." Among these poets, Peddana is imagined as the true master, whom Krishnadevaraya himself honored by tying with his own hands an anklet of victory (*gaṇḍapěṇḍěramu*) on his left foot. The anklet proudly displayed carved images of all the poets whom Peddana had conquered and outdone. This set of images seems to have crystallized retrospectively in the seventeenth century, over a century after Peddana's death. However, it has made a lasting impression on the Telugu mind, including even scholars and historians who have taken it to be historical.

In short, Peddana became for the later tradition the archetype of the true poet, like Kalidasa for Sanskrit and Kampan for Tamil. In a wider, comparative perspective, we might think of Peddana, like Dante, as the epitome of an entire civilizational moment. Peddana's work has the deceptive stylistic accessibility together with a depth of thought and meaning, which is anything but accessible, that we find in Kalidasa, Kampan, and Dante, among others; perhaps this is a rule that could be generalized for the greatest poets anywhere.

The extreme lyricism of the *Manucaritramu* fascinated the modern Romantic poets in Telugu (the *bhāvakavitvamu* poets of the early twentieth century) and at least one great modern painter, Mokkapati Krishnamurti, active at the same time. Krishnamurti painted a remarkable image of Varuthini playing the vina as Pravara saw her. Poor Pravara, in the imagination of the Romantic poets, also had an afterlife: Samavedamu Janakiramasarma wrote a long poem, issued as a separate booklet, in which he describes Pravara's inner thoughts—in particular, his undying regret—after he had rejected Varuthini and gone home. As usual for the Romantic poets, failure in love is what really counts, and here Peddana has supplied a perfect prototype.

Modern Telugu critics, with the outstanding exception of Viswanatha Satyanarayana, have tended to focus exclusively on the first three chapters of the book. Our own reading of Peddana's great work, by contrast, depends on seeing it as a whole. We argue that the last three chapters are no less integral to the book, and to its expressive themes and coherent meaning, than are the first three alone. By effectively truncating the book to the first three chapters, the tradition has lost a major key to understanding it. The hyperrealism of chapter 4, the fast-paced narrative of chapter 5 followed by an elaborate description of Svarochi's wedding (akin to Kalidasa's *Kumārasambhava* 7), and the moving conclusion in chapter 6, including the lyrical description of the ten avatars of Vishnu—all these are masterfully crafted and strongly linked to the issues broached in the first half of the book. Pervading *all* the chapters is the new texture of detailed *varṇana* description, which is not located in or limited to any of the characters per se but operates as an overriding aesthetic technique replete with its own meta-poetic meaning, strongly allied to the central themes we have outlined in this introduction. Let us, in closing, ask ourselves why the poet has chosen this new mode of profound attentiveness to vivid, singular, naturalistic detail, at work both inside and outside the mind.

It seems to reflect his vision of the kind of world he thinks human beings can, indeed must, inhabit. Indeed, such is the implicit definition of the new *prabandha* form Peddana created: he offers a complete world, intensified to a point where the reader comes fully alive to shimmering colors, fierce tastes, distinctive smells, the various species of living beings in their uniqueness, the movement of heavenly bodies, the seasons and shifting textures of night and day, the complex play of crisscrossing perceptions, and the vast gamut of emotional and cognitive experience that opens up at every moment in such richly appointed landscapes. Of course, each of the classic Sanskrit *prabandhakāvyas* also

produced a world of its own; indeed, this very goal was theo-
rized by Dandin, the pioneer of Sanskrit poetic theory. The
difference lies in how the reader feels the world that he or
she is being offered and in the quality of seeing that makes
this world so vibrant. Peddana's poetic arena is exclusively
this-worldly (*laukika*)—in a sense, a "secular" set of over-
lapping domains. Even his gandharvas and other nominally
immortal beings are fully humanized, endowed with minds
and bodies like ours.

What is more, the book, read as a coherent whole,
completes a circle. It opens with a description of Pravara's
city, Arunaspada, seen as an idealized social and natural land-
scape. It ends with a strong image of the no less ideal world
over which Svarochisha Manu is meant to preside. Pravara,
the awkward innocent, goes home at an early point, and we,
too, follow him there in the necessarily devious route that
his son and grandson must take. Read in this way, the book
becomes fully integrated and achieves closure. One could say
that there is, in fact, a single, sequentially composite hero:
Pravaras 1, 2, and 3, that is, the Brahman from Arunaspada,
the slowly evolving man-to-be Svarochi, and the whole
person born at the end, Svarochisha-Manu. (If you want,
you can add a fourth, the illusory Pravara who briefly takes
the place of Pravara 1.) All three of them are united by an
intense—indeed continually intensifying—relation to the
concrete physical world that surrounds them, which is, in
fact, the true subject of this book, both as the vivid reality
the characters perceive and as it is refracted in their minds,
and in ours.

In this light the *Manucaritramu* tells us about the making

of a good king, in a good world, from the disparate pieces of experience that conduce toward this goal over three generations. It also shows us, not in some theoretical or abstract manner but in practice and felt experience and language commensurate with such feeling, what it takes for anyone to become fully human.

Acknowledgments

We wish to thank Vadapalli Sesha Talpa Sayee and Kalepu Nagabhushana Rao for their meticulous and efficient production and proofreading of the Telugu text, carried out as a professional courtesy. David Shulman is profoundly grateful to Dr. M. V. Kanakaiah of Rajahmundry for teaching the *Manucaritramu* over the course of seven months and many subsequent shorter visits; the lucidity and precision of his explication of the text are without parallel. Velcheru Narayana Rao taught the text to a particularly congenial group of colleagues and students at the University of Chicago: Gary Tubb, Yigal Bronner, Ilanit Loewy Shacham, Jamal Jones, and Gautham Reddy; their responses were very helpful. For bibliographic help we, as always, are deeply grateful to Parucuri Sreenivas.

Dedication

This translation is dedicated to the memory of Viswanatha Satyanarayana, who made the *Manucaritramu* come to life.

NOTES

1   The epithet appears in the colophons to each of the chapters and in the patron's address to Peddana in the book's preface: 1.15.

2   See Narayana Rao and Shulman 2002: 9–14.

3   In fact, at least two poets before Peddana were called *āndhrakavitāpitāmaha* by their contemporaries: Shivadevayya (thirteenth century) and Koravi Sattenarana (c. 1400).

4   *Mārkaṇḍeyapurāṇa,* chapters 53, 61–80, 93–100; discussion in Shulman 2001.

5   See Pollock 1995.

6   Apparently distinct from Bilhana, the reputed author of the *Fifty Poems of the Love-Thief.*

7   See Annamayya, copper plate 196; 2:333 *(verrulāla)*; Narayana Rao and Shulman 2005: 93–94.

8   See Narayana Rao and Shulman 2012.

9   See, e.g., Vemparala Suryanarayana Sastri, introduction to his edition, p. 5.

10   For a full discussion, see Narayana Rao and Shulman 2012: 30–34.

11   *Śṛṅgāranaiṣadhamu* 1.35; Narayana Rao and Shulman 2012: 31–33.

12   The term is Satyanarayana's, perhaps from a lecture. See Narayana Rao 2008: 49.

13   Translation from Narayana Rao and Heifetz 1987: 153. Original in Laksmikanta Sastri n.d.: 296.

14   A king should not praise himself; he needs the court poet to do this for him.

15   Bear in mind that the narrative itself, including the homily toward the end, is already present in the *Mārkaṇḍeyapurāṇa.*

16   See Sewell 1900: 314–315; Narayana Rao, Shulman, and Subrahmanyam 2011.

17   *Āmuktamālyada* 1.50; Manucaritramu 1.17.

18   *Kāvyādarśa* 1.14–19.

19   Narayana Rao and Shulman 2002: 40–43.

20   See Shulman 2013.

21   See Afterword to Narayana Rao and Shulman 2002.

22   See Narayana Rao and Shulman 2012 and also Shulman 2012: 204–231.

23   The figure, as Satyanarayana noted, is *viṣamālaṅkāra,* "Incongruity." Viswanatha Satyanarayana (1967) has emphasized the theme of illusion as adumbrated by the *avatārika* verses.

24   Viswanatha Satyanarayana 1967 noted the prominence of the theme of illusion and misperception in the opening verses of the text, which adumbrate the way the story develops.

25   This seems to be the reading of Viswanatha Satyanarayana 1967: 11.

26   Ibid., 12. Not by chance, throughout the later chapters of the *Manucaritramu,* Svarochi is often tellingly referred to as "Varuthini's son."

NOTE ON THE TEXT

We have based our text on the careful second edition of Tanjanagaramu Tevapperumalayya (1919). The printed texts of the *Manucaritramu* are remarkably stable, though we have noted nontrivial variants. The *editio princeps,* by Juluri Appayya, working for C. P. Brown, was published in Madras in 1851, though with Brown's idiosyncratic orthography (lacking silent nasals, the *arasunna,* and the so-called *baṇḍi-ra* liquid). Perhaps for this reason, subsequent editions did not follow Appayya and Brown but based themselves on the palm-leaf manuscripts. Many of these subsequent editions have excellent commentaries, among which Komanduru Anantacarya (the Tanjanagaramu commentator) is particularly helpful (it was closely followed in parts by Vemparala Suryanarayana Sastri, 1968).

The relative paucity of textual variation may mean that existing manuscripts go back to a single archetype, or, what amounts to much the same thing, reflect a stage of careful scholarly editing and standardization at a very early point, perhaps already in the seventeenth century at the time when the classical Telugu canon was established. In the end there is no way to tell. We have refrained from documenting insignificant variation attested in some of the printed editions, including the first edition by Tanjanagaramu.

The Story of Manu

ప్రథమాశ్వాసము

అవతారిక

౧

శా. శ్రీవక్షోజ కురంగనాభ మెదపై
జెన్నొంద విశ్వంభరా
దేవిం దత్కమలాసమీపమున౯ బ్రీ
తి౯ నిల్చినా౦డే యనం
గా వందారు సనందనాది నిజభ
క్త్రేణికిం దో౦చు రా
జీవాక్షుండు గృతార్థు౦ జేయు శుభదృ
ష్టి౦ గృష్ణరాయాధిపున్.

౨

ఉ. ఉల్లమునందు నక్కటిక
మూనుట మీకులమందు౦ గంటి మం
చల్లన మేలమాడు నచ
లాత్మజ మాటకు లే౦తనవ్వు సం
ధిల్ల౦ గిరీటి౦ బాశుపత
దివ్యశరాఢ్యుని౦ జేయు శాంబరీ
భిల్లు౦డు గృష్ణరాయల క
భీష్టశుభప్రతిపాది గావుతన్.

2

Chapter 1

1

His chest shows the musk
from Lakshmi's breasts, so his worshipers,
Sanandana and the rest,[1] wonder
if he's brought his other wife, the Earth,
to live there beside her.[2]
May this god with eyes luminous
as the lotus look kindly on our king.

2

"So you hunters can show some kindness too."
That's what the daughter of the stony mountain
says, making fun of him, and Shiva smiles,
guised as a hunter, as he blesses Arjuna
with the mightiest of weapons.[3]
We pray that he gives Krishnaraya, our king,
all the good things he wants.

౩

ఉ నాలుగు మోములన్ నిగమ
నాదము లుప్పతిలం బ్రచండవా
తూలహతిం జనించు రొద
తోడి గుహావళి నొప్పు మేరువుం
బోలెఁ బయోజపీఠి ముని
ముఖ్యులు గొల్వఁగ వాణిఁ గూడి పే
రోలగ మున్న ధాత విభ
వోజ్జ్వలుఁ జేయుతఁ గృష్ణరాయనిన్.

౪

ఉ అంకముఁ జేరి శైలతన
యాస్తన దుగ్ధము లానువేళ బా
ల్యాంక విచేష్టఁ దొండమున
నవ్వలి చన్గబళింపఁబోయి యా
వంకఁ గుచంబు గాన కహి
వల్లభహారముఁ గాంచి వే మృణా
ళాంకురశంక నంటెడు గ
జాస్యునిఁ గొల్తు నభీష్టసిద్ధికిన్.

3

From his four mouths, the sounds of four Vedas emerge,
and thus he looks like the mountain of gold,*
its caverns echoing as a great wind rushes through.
He sits in state on his lotus throne
together with Speech, his wife. All sages
worship him. May Brahma, lord of creation,
make Krishnaraya radiant with power.

4

Seated on his mother's lap,
sucking at her breast, playing
as a child plays, he moves his trunk
to grab the other breast.
And there is no breast there.
Instead, he finds a snake
hanging from the neck—or is it
a succulent lotus stem? May this god
with the elephant's head give me
what's good for me.[4]

---

* Mount Meru.

౫

సీ. చేర్చుక్కగా నిడ్డ చిన్నిజాబిల్లిచే
సిందూరతిలకంబు చెమ్మగిల్ల
నవతంసకుసుమంబు నందున్న యెలదేఁటి
రుతి కించిదంచితశ్రుతుల నీన
ఘనమైన రారాపు చనుదోయి రాయిడిఁ
దుంబీఫలంబు తుందుదుకుఁ జెందఁ
దరుణాంగుళిచ్చాయ దంతపుసరకట్టు
లింగిలీకపు వింతరంగు లీన

తే. నుపనిషత్తులు బోటులై యొలగింపఁ
బుండరీకాసనమునఁ గూర్చుండి మదికి
నించువేడుక వీణ వాయించు చెలువ
నలువరాణి మదాత్మలో వెలయుఁగాత.

౬

క. కొలుతున్ మధురు విద్యా
నిలయుం గరుణాకటాక్ష నిబిడజ్యోత్స్ని
దళితాశ్రితజన దురిత
చ్చుల గాఢధ్వాంతసమితి శరకోపయతిన్.

6

5

On her forehead a red dot shimmers
in the light of the moon in her hair.
Bees hovering over the flower in her ear
make gentle music.
The gourd on her vina that rubs against her full breasts
resonates with her breathing.
The delicate color of her fingers reflected on the ivory frets
casts a strange reddish glow.
The Upanishads are her companions
as she sits on her lotus throne,
playing the vina
with joy. I want her,
Brahma's wife,* to appear
in my mind.

6

I pay respects to my teacher, Shathakopa Yati, the true abode
of learning.
For all who approach him, the moonlight flooding from his
kind eyes
dispels the darkness of bad deeds.

---

* Sarasvati, goddess of the arts.

౭

మ   వనజాక్షోపము వామలూరుతనయున్
దైవ్యాయనున్ భట్టబా
ణుని భాసున్ భవభూతి భారవి సుబం
ధున్ బిల్లణంం గాళిదా
సుని మాఘున్ శివభద్ర మల్లణకవిం
జోరున్ మురారిన్ మయూ
రుని సోమిల్లిని దండి బ్రస్తుతులం బే
ర్కొందున్ వచశ్శుద్ధికిన్.

౮

ఆ   వ్యాసరచిత భారతామ్నాయ మాంధ్ర భా
షగ నొనర్చి జగతిం బొగడు గనిన
నన్నపార్యు దిక్కనను గృతక్రతు శంభు
దాసు నెఱ్ఱసుకవిం దలంతు భక్తి.

౯

మ   భరమై తోచు కుటుంబరక్షణకుగాం
బ్రాల్మరి చింతన్ నిరం
తర తాళీదళసంపుటప్రకర కాం
తారంబునం దర్భపుం
దెరువాటుల్దెగి కొట్టి తద్జ్ఞ పరిష
ద్విజ్ఞాత చౌర్యక్రియా
విరసుండై కొఱంతం బడుం గకవి పృ
థ్వీభృత్సమీపక్షితిన్.

7

To purify my speech, let me say the names of the great poets—
Valmiki, born from an anthill, who was like Vishnu himself,
Dvaipayana, the island-born, Bhatta Bana, Bhasa,
*   Bhavabhuti, Bharavi,*
Subandhu, Bilhana, Kalidasa, Magha, Shivabhadra,
*   Malhana, Cora, Murari,*
Mayura, Saumilli, and Dandin.

8

Nannaya[5] made Vyasa's Mahabharata, as good as the Veda,
*   into Telugu.*
He's praised for this all over the world.
I think of him along with Tikkana,
who performed a sacrifice,[6] and Errana, Shiva's servant.

9

A rogue poet, for want of any other means to feed his family,
steals, in desperation, from the vast forest of palm-leaf
*   manuscripts.*
But scholars catch him at it, his poetry loses its charm,
and he's put in the stocks under the gaze of the king.[7]

౧౦

క అని యిష్టదేవతా వం
దన సుకవిస్తుతులు౦ గుకవితతినికృతియు౦ జే
సి నవీనకావ్య రచనకు
ననుకూల కథల్దలంచు నా సమయమునన్.

౧౧

సీ ఉదయాచలేంద్రంబు మొదల నెవ్వని కుమా
రతకు౦ గ్రొంచాచల రాజమయ్యె
నావాడపతి శకంధర సింధురాధ్యక్షు
లరిగా౦పు లెవ్వాని ఖరతరాసి
కాపంచగౌడ ధాత్రీపదం బెవ్వాని
కసివాఞుగా నే౦గునట్టి బయలు
సకల యాచకజనాశాపూర్తి కెవ్వాని
ఘనభుజాదండంబు కల్పశాఖి

తే ప్రబల రాజాధిరాజ వీరప్రతాప
రాజపరమేశ బిరుదవిబ్రాజి యొవ్వ౦
డట్టి శ్రీకృష్ణదేవరాయాగ్రగణ్య౦
డెక్కనా౦డు కుతూహలం బుప్పతిల్ల.

10

After praying to the gods, praising good poets
and denouncing bad ones, I was thinking of a good story
for the new kind of poem I want to write. At that time

11

Shri Krishnadevaraya was holding court.
By conquering Udayagiri, he had become like Kumara,
commander of the gods,
who split open the Kraunca Mountain.
The kings of Navada, Sakandhara, and the Gajapati[8]
paid tribute to his sharp sword.
He made the kingdoms of the five Gaudas[9]
a space for a stroll.
His strong arm was a wishing tree showering gifts
on everyone who came to him to ask.
He is called King of Kings, Mightier than the Mighty,
God among Kings,
Supreme.

౧౨

సీ ఇందీవరంబులనీను క్రాల్గన్నుల
శరదిందుముఖులు చామరము లిడఁగఁ
బణినసూను కణాద బాదరాయణ సూత్ర
ఫక్కి విద్వాంసు లుపన్యసింపఁ
బార్ష్యభూమి నభీరుభటకదంబకరాళ
హేతిచ్చుటాచ్చాయ నిరులు కొనఁగ
సామంతమండనోద్దామ మాణిక్యాంశు
మండలం బొలసి యూరెండ గాయ

తే మూరురాయరగండపెండార మణిమ
రీచిరించోళీఁ గలయ నావృతము లగుచు
నంకపాళి నటద్దుకూలాంచలములు
చిత్రమాంజిష్ఠ విభ్రమశ్రీ వహింప.

౧౩

క భువనవిజయాఖ్య సంస
ద్భువనస్థిత సింహపీఠిఁ బ్రాజ్ఞులగోష్ఠిం
గవితామధురిమ దెందము
దవులం గొలువుండి సదయతన్ ననుఁ బల్కెన్.

12

On either side, women with eyes like blue sapphires
and faces radiant as the moon
were fanning him with yak-tail fans.
Scholars were discussing the fine points of Paninian
        grammar,
Kanada's atomistic philosophy, and Badarayana's
        metaphysics.
Swords held by fearless warriors cast a dark glow.
Jewels on the crowns of defeated kings were spreading a cool
        sunlight.
He was wearing the anklet that proved he was
the Best of the Three Warriors, and the jewels that studded it*
reflected rich hues on the white cloth he was wearing,
covering his crossed legs.

13

Seated enthroned in the hall known as "Conquest of the
        World,"
in the company of learned people,
he was struck by the joy of poetry, so he turned to me
and gently said:

---

* The Ashvapati (Sultan), Gajapati (king of Orissa), and Narapati,
   "lord of men" = Krishnaraya.

౧౪

తే సప్తసంతానములలో౦ బ్రశస్తి౦ గాంచి
ఖిలము గాకుండునది ధాత్రి౦ గృతియ కాన
కృతి రచింపుము మాకు శిరీషకుసుమ
పేశల సుధామయోక్తుల౦ బెద్దనార్య.

౧౫

క హితు౦డవు చతురవచోనిధి
వతుల పురాణాగమేతిహాస కథార్థ
స్మృతియుతు౦డ వాంధ్రకవితా
పితామహు౦డ వెవ్వ రీడు పేర్కొన నీకున్.

౧౬

క మనువులలో స్వారోచిష
మనుసంభవ మరయ రససమంచిత కథలన్
విన నింపు కలిధ్వంసక
మనఘ భవచ్చతురరచన కనుకూలంబున్.

14

14

"They say that out of the seven kinds of children a person
    might have,*
the only one that lasts is a poem.
Make a poem for me, Peddanarya,
with words soft as the softest of flowers, the śirīṣa,
and sweet.

15

You're a friend. You're good at words.
You carry in your mind all the stories of the purāṇas,
āgamas, *and* itihāsas. *You're the creator*[10]
of Telugu poetry. No one
is equal to you.

16

Among the stories about the first kings of men
the 'Birth of Svarochisha' is particularly good
to listen to. It has many gripping episodes,
and it cures the evils of time. It's well suited
to your talent.

---

* A well, a temple, a tank, a garden, an actual son, an endowment,
  and a book.

౧౭

వ. కావున మార్కండేయ పురాణోక్తప్రకారంబునం జెప్పు
మని కర్పూరతాంబూలంబు వెట్టినం బట్టి మహాప్రసాదం
బని మొదంబున నమ్మహాప్రబంధ నిబంధనంబునకుం
బ్రారంభించితి నేతత్కథానాయకరత్నం బగు
నమ్మహీనాథు వంశావతారం బెట్టి దనిన.

౧౮

సీ. కలశపాథోరాశి గర్భవీచిమతల్లి
కడుపార నెవ్వానిం గన్నతల్లి
యనలాక్షు ఘనజటావనవాటి కెవ్వాడు
వన్నెవెట్టు ననార్తవంపుబువ్వ
సకలదైవత బుభుక్షాపూర్తి కెవ్వాడు
పుట్టుగానని మేని మెట్టపంట
కటికిచ్చెకటితిండి కరముల గిలిగింత
నెవ్వాడు తోగకన్నెనవ్వంజేయు

తే. నతడు వొగడెందు మధుకైటభారి మఱందిఁ
కళల నెలవగువాడు చుక్కలకు తేడు
మిసిమి పరసీమ వలరాజు మేనమామ
వేవెలుంగులదొరజోడు రేవెలుంగు.

17

Compose it, following the Mārkaṇḍeyapurāṇa.*" That's what
he said as he gave me fragrant camphor and betel.*[11] *I took them
and thanked him for choosing me. Then I started work on this
great book. Now let me tell you the family history of this king
who is the first listener to this story.*

18

*First there was the moon—born from the deepest wave
in the ocean of milk.
He's a flower for all seasons, imparting beauty
to the wild hair of the fire-eyed god.**
He's a constantly growing crop, not dependent on rain
to feed the ever-hungry gods.
With delicate rays that dispel thick darkness, he tickles
the Blue Water Lily and makes her laugh.*[12]
*He's Vishnu's brother-in-law, king of the stars.
He's the light of the heavens, and the uncle of Desire.
He's a friend of the sun who illumines the day, while he
shines at night in his shifting shapes.*

---

* Shiva.

౧౯

తే   ఆ సుధాధాము విభవమహాంబురాశి
కుబ్బుమీఱింగ నందనుఁ దుదయమయ్యె
వేదవేదాంగ శాస్త్రార్థ విశదవాస
నాత్త ధిషణాధురంధరుం డైన బుధుఁడు.

౨౦

క   వానికిఁ బురూరవుఁడు ప్ర
జ్ఞానిధి యుదయించె సింహసదృశుఁడు తద్భా
జానికి నాయువు తనయుం
డై నెగడె నతండు గనె యయాతినరేంద్రున్.

౨౧

క   అతనికి యదుతుర్వసు లను
సుతు లుద్భవమొంది రహిత సూదనులు కళా
న్వితమతులు వారిలో వి
ప్రుతకీర్తి వహించెఁ దుర్వసుఁడు గుణనిధియ్యె.

19

To that ocean of life, the moon,
a son was born—Budha by name,
his mind replete with precise memories
of the Veda, the Vedic sciences, and all
the first texts.

20

His son was Pururavas, a treasure of wisdom,
courageous as a lion. His son was Ayus,
and Ayus's son was King Yayati.

21

He had two sons: Yadu and Turvasu.
Both were killers of their enemies,
artistic in temperament. Of them,
Turvasu became the more famous.
He was very good.

౨౨

తే   వానివంశంబు తుళువాన్వాయ మయ్యె
నందుఁ బెక్కండ్రు నృపు లుదయంబు నొంది
నిఖిలభువనప్రపూర్ణ నిర్ణిద్రకీర్తి
నధికులైరి తదీయాన్వయమునఁ బుట్టి.

౨3

మహాస్రగ్ధర.

ఘనుఁడై తిమ్మక్షితీశాగ్రణి శతకమర
గ్రావసంఘాత వాతా
శనరా దాశాంతదంతిస్థవిర కిరుల జం
జాటముల్మాన్పి యిమ్మే
దిని దోర్దండైకపీఠిం దిరము పటిచి కీ
ర్తిద్యుతుల్రోదసిం బ
ర్వ నరాతుల్సమ్రులై పార్శ్వములఁ గొలువఁ దీ
వ్రప్రతాపంబు సూపెన్.

౨౪

క   వితరణఖని యాతిమ్మ
క్షితిపగ్రామణికి దేవకీదేవికి నం
చితమూర్తి యాశ్వరప్రభుఁ
డతిపుణ్యుఁడు పుట్టె సజ్జనావనపరుఁడై.

22

His family turned into the Tulu line.
Many kings were born in it.
Their fame, which filled the whole earth,
never slept. In that family

23

Timma was born—a powerful man
who gave some rest to all those who bear
the burden of the earth: the as-if turtle,
the row of mountains, the king of snakes
that feast on air, the ancient boar, and the elephants
that hold up space.[13] *He held the earth steady*
in his strong arms. He showed his burning strength.
His fame spread up to the sky and his enemies
served him, on either side,
with bent heads.

24

To this generous man, Timma,
and his wife, Devaki Devi,
Ishvara was born. He was a handsome man,
full of virtues. He took care of all good people.

౨౫

చ బలమదమత్త దుష్టపుర
భంజనుండై పరిపాలితార్యుండై
యిలపయిc దొంటి యీశ్వరుండై
యీశ్వరుండై జనియింప రూపాఠిన్
జలరుహనేత్రలం దొఅగి
శైలవనంబుల భీతచిత్తులై
మెలంగెడు శత్రుభూపతుల
మేనులంc దాల్చిన మన్మథాంకముల్.

౨౬

సీ నిజభుజాశ్రిత ధారుణీ వజ్రకవచంబు
దుష్టభుజంగాహితుండికుండు
వనజేక్షణామనోధన పశ్యతోహరం
దరిహంస సంసదభ్రాగమంబు
మార్గణగణపికమధుమాసదివసంబు
గుణరత్నరోహణక్షోణిధరము
బాంధవసందోహపద్మవనీ హేళి
కారుణ్యరసనిమ్నగాకళత్రంc

తే డన జగంబుల మిగులంc బ్రఖ్యాతిc గాంచె
ధరణీధవదత్త వివిధోపదావిధా స
మార్జితశ్రీ వినిర్జిత నిర్జరాల
యేశ్వరుండు తిమ్మభూపతి యీశ్వరుండు.

25

He destroyed the cities of his arrogant foes
and protected noble people, like Shiva himself.
On the bodies of enemy kings,
all marks of love were erased
when they had to leave their wives behind
and take to hills and forests, their minds
clouded by fear.

26

He was like impenetrable armor for those who took refuge
*   with him.*
A snake-catcher of the snakes that were his enemies.
A charmer who steals the hearts of beautiful women
*   at first sight.*
A monsoon cloud drenching the geese that were his foes.
A joy to his supplicants, as when spring comes for cuckoos.
A mine of good qualities, like a mountain rich
*   in precious stones.*
A radiant joy to his relatives, like the sun to a lotus pond.
An ocean deep with affection.

That's how he was known throughout the world—
as a man who conquered the king of heaven
with the wealth that came to him as gifts
from other kings.

౨౭

క ఆ యీశ్వరనృపతికిఁ బు
న్యాయతమతియైన బుక్కమాంబకుఁ దేజ
స్తోయజహితు లుదయించిరి
ధీయుతు లగు నారసింహ తిమ్మనరేంద్రుల్.

౨౮

క అందు నరసప్రభుఁడు హరి
చందన మందారకుంద చంద్రాంశు నిభా
స్పంద యశస్తుందిల ది
క్కందరుఁ డై ధాత్రి యేలెఁ గలుషము లడఁగన్.

౨౯

ఉ శ్రీరుచిరత్వ భూతిమతి
జిత్వరతాకృతి శక్తికాంతులన్
ధీరత సారభోగముల
ధీనిధి యీశ్వర నారసింహుఁ డా
వారిజనాభ శంకరుల
వారి కుమారుల వారితమ్ములన్
వారి యనుంగుమామలను
వారి విరోధులఁ బోలు నిమ్మహిన్.

27

To him and to his wife Bukkamamba,
a woman of good thoughts, two sons were born:
Narasimha and Timma.
They were brilliant.

28

The first of them, Narasa, became king
and ruled the world. His fame was white as
sandal paste, the wishing trees in bloom,
white jasmine, and moonlight. All bad things
went away.

29

Let us list his qualities in order:
radiance, wealth, intelligence,
ambition, beauty, energy, brilliance,
courage, strength, and joyfulness.
Each one of them brings to mind a god,
in the same order: Vishnu, Shiva,
their respective sons, Brahma and Kumara;
their brothers, Manmatha and Virabhadra;
their uncles, the Moon and Mainaka;
and the uncles' enemies, Rahu and Indra.
It was all in the family.

30

సీ అంభోధివసన విశ్వంభరావలయంబుఁ
దనబాహుపురి మరకతముఁ జేసె
నశ్రాంతవిశ్రాణ నాసారలక్ష్మికిఁ
గవికదంబముఁ జాతకములఁ జేసెఁ
గకుబంతనిఖిలరాణ్ణికరంబుఁ జరణమం
జీరంబు సాలభంజికలఁ జేసె
మహనీయ నిజవినిర్మలయశస్సురసికి
గగనంబుఁ గలహంసకంబుఁ జేసె

తే నతిశిత కృపాణకృత్త మత్తారివీర
మండలేశ సకుండల మకుట నూత్న
మస్తమాల్యపరంపరా మండనార్చి
తేశ్వరుండగు నారసింహేశ్వరుండు.

31

తే ఆ న్నృసింహప్రభుండు దిప్పాంబవలన
నాగమాంబికవలన నందనులఁ గాంచె
వీరనరసింహరాయ భూవిభుని నచ్యు
తాంశసంభవుఁ గృష్ణరాయక్షితీంద్ర.

30

He turned the earth, clothed by the oceans,
into an emerald worn on his armlet.
By the constant shower of his giving,
he made poets into cātaka *birds that feed on raindrops.*
He converted all kings ruling to the end of space
into figurines to decorate his anklets.
He transformed the sky itself into a goose
playing in the pond of his limpid fame.
With his sharp sword he offered Shiva a garland
made of the severed heads, complete with crowns
and earrings, of all his enemies.
That was Narasimha.

31

Narasimha had two sons, one from each of his wives,
Tippamba and Nagamba—Viranarasimharaya and
    Krishnaraya,
who was an aspect of Vishnu himself.

౩౨

క   వీరనృసింహుఁడు నిజభుజ
దారుణకరవాల పరుషధారాహత వీ
రారి యగుచు నేకాతప
వారణముగ నేలె ధర నవారణమహిమన్.

౩౩

క   ఆవిభు ననంతరంబ ధ
రావలయముఁ దాల్చె గృష్ణరాయఁడు చిన్నా
దేవియు శుభమతి తిరుమల
దేవియునుం దనకుఁ గూర్పు దేవేరులు గాన్.

౩౪

సీ   తొలఁగెను ధూమకేతుక్షోభ జనులకు
నతివృష్టిదోషభయంబు వాసెఁ
గంటకాగమభీతి గడచె నుద్ధతభూమి
భృత్కటకం బెల్ల నెత్తువడియె
మాసె నఘస్ఫూర్తి మరుభూములందును
నెల మూఁడువానలు నిండఁ గురిసె
నాబాలగోపాల మఖిల సద్వ్రజమును
నానందమున మన్కి నతిశయిల్లెఁ

తే   బ్రజల కెల్లను గడు రామరాజ్య మయ్యెఁ
జారుసత్త్వాఢ్యుఁ డీశ్వర నారసింహ
ఘూవిభుని కృష్ణరాయఁ డభ్యుదయ మొంది
పెంపు మీఱంగ ధాత్రిఁ బాలింపుచుండ.

32

Viranarasimha killed all his mighty enemies
with the harsh blade of his terrible sword.
He gave shade to the whole world.
His splendor was unstoppable.

33

After him Krishnaraya took control of the world
with his two loving wives, Cinna Devi
and Tirumala Devi, who had good thoughts.

34

People were free from calamities that comets foretell.
They had no more fear of severe rains.
The danger of armed invasions passed.
The capital cities of haughty hostile kings fell into ruin.
The power of sin waned.
Every month it rained thrice, even on arid lands.
All good people, from children to cowherds, lived in joy.
It was like the kingdom of Rama everywhere
when Krishnaraya, rich in vital power, son of Narasimha
and grandson of Ishvara, ruled the earth,
going from strength to strength.

౩౫

మ   అల పోత్రిప్రభుదంష్ట్ర భోగివరభో
     గ్గ్రాళిరా లుద్భుటా
     చలకూటోపలకోటి రూపుచెడ ని
     చ్చుల్రాయఁగా నైన మొ
     క్కలు భూకాంతకు నున్ననయ్యె నరస
     క్షాపాలు శ్రీకృష్ణరా
     యల బాహ్మృగనాభిసంకుమదసాం
     ద్రాలేపపంకంబునన్.

౩౬

ఉ   క్రూరవనేభదంతహత
     కుడ్య పరిచ్యుతవజ్రపంక్తిఁ బో
     ల్పారు మిడుంగుఋంబురువు
     లంచు వెసం గొనిపోయి పొంత శ్యం
     గారవనద్రుమాళి గిజి
     గాఁడులు గూఁడులఁ జేర్చు దీపికల్
     గా రహిఁ గృష్ణరాయమహి
     కాంతుని శాత్రవపట్టణంబులన్.

35

First there were the tusks of the great boar.
Then came the hard stones embedded in the snake's many
      hoods,
and finally the jagged rocks on the mountain peaks.
All of them rubbed against her body and left her wounded.
Now the earth was healed and her skin became soft
from the musk and civet on Krishnaraya, son of Narasimha,
as he gently held her in his arms. [14]

36

Rampaging elephants charge at the walls with their tusks
and the diamonds that are dislodged look like fireflies
to the weaver birds, [15] *who collect them to use as lamps*
to light their nests in trees that once lined gardens
in cities that were hostile to our king.

౩౨

సీ   తొలుదొల్త నుదయాద్రి శిలఁ దాకి తీండ్రించు
       నసిలోహమున వెచ్చనయి జనించె
       మటి కొండవీ డెక్కి మార్కొని నలియొైన
       యల కసవాపాత్రు నంటి రాజె
       నట సాఁగి జమ్మిలోయఁ బడి వేఁగ దహించెఁ
       గోస బిబ్బెర్చెఁ గొట్టానఁ దగిలెఁ
       గనకగిరిస్ఫూర్తిఁ గరఁచె గౌతమిం గ్రాఁచె
       నవుల నాపొట్నూర రవులుకొనియె

తే   మాడెములు ప్రేల్చె నొడ్డది మసి యొనర్చెఁ
       గటకపురిఁ గాల్చె గజరాజు గలఁగి పఱవఁ
       దేఁకచి చ్చున నొర యుద్ధురతఁ గృష్ణ
       రాయబాహుప్రతాపజాగ్రన్మహాగ్ని.

౩౦

మ   ధర కెందూళులు కృష్ణరాయల చమూ
       ధాటీగతిన్ విన్ధ్యగ
       హ్వరములఁదూఁగఁగ జూచి తా రచటఁ గాఁ
       పై యుండుటం జాల న
       చ్చెరువై యొఱ్ఱిని విన్తచీఁకటులు వ
       చ్చెం జూడరే యంచు వే
       సారిదిం జూతురు వీరరుద్రగజరా
       ట్టుద్ధాన్తముద్ధాంగనల్.

37

This fierce blaze was first sparked off when his steel sword
  struck
the flint fort at Udayagiri. Next it climbed Kondavidu[16]
and consumed King Kasavapatra, as if he were a haystack.
It went on to Jammi Valley and burnt it up.
Then it hit Kona and Kottam. It melted down the Golden
  Mountain
and brought the Godavari to a boil.
It set Potnuru aflame. It scorched Mademulu and reduced
  Oddadi
to ashes. Finally it was the turn of Katakapuri,* where the
  Gajapati king
ran for his life. Krishnaraya's power
was a chain of fires, one igniting the next.

38

"Look at this amazing
red darkness that's coming at us,"
say the women of King Virarudra Gajapati,
hiding in caves in the Vindhya Mountains
and watching with innocent wonder
as the red dust kicked up by Krishnaraya's army
penetrates their safe havens.

---

* Modern Cuttack.

౩౯

చ అభిరతిం గృష్ణరాయండు జ
యాంకములన్ లిఖియించి తాళస
న్నిభముగం బొట్టునూరికడ
నిల్చిన కంబము సింహభూధర
ప్రభ తిరునాళ్ళకుం దిగు సు
రప్రకరంబు కళింగమేదినీ
విభు నపకీర్తి కజ్జలము
వేమఱుం బెట్టి పఱించు నిచ్చలున్.

౪౦

మహాస్రగ్ధర.

ఎకరాలన్ మందువా సాహిణములం గల
భద్రేభ సందేహవాహ
ప్రకరంబుం గొంచుం దత్తత్త్ప్రభువులు వనుపన్
రాయబారుల్విలోకో
త్సుకులై నిత్యంబు శ్రీకృష్ణనియవసరముల్
చూతు రందంద కొల్వం
దక యాప్రత్యూష మాసంధ్యము పనివడి త
న్మందిరాళింద భూమిన్.

39

Gods who come down from heaven to celebrate the festival
of the Lord at Simhachalam are eager to read the inscription
that Krishnaraya set up near Potnuru, on a pillar tall as a
       palm tree,
to announce his victories, so they blacken it over and over
with the dark disgrace of the Kalinga king, so the letters
stand out.[17]

40

Ambassadors from many kings
bearing gifts of elephants and horses,
housed in stables nearby, are always anxiously waiting
for a chance to see the king. You can find them
at the entrance to the palace every day, from sunrise
to sunset, hoping against hope.

౪౧

చ మదకలకుంభికుంభ నవ
మౌక్తికముల్గనుపట్టు దట్టమై
వదలక కృష్ణరాయ కర
వాలమునం దగు ధారనీట న
భ్యుదయమునొంది శాత్రవుల
పుట్టి మునుంగఁగ ఫేనపంక్తితోఁ
బొదిగిని పైపయిన్ వెడలు
బుద్బుదపంక్తులు వోలెఁ బోరులన్.

౪౨

సీ వేదండభయద శుండాదండనిర్వాంత
వమధువుల్పైఁజిలుక్క వారి గాఁగ
దత్కర్ణవిస్తీర్ణ తాళవృంతోద్ధూత
ధూళి చేటలఁ జల్లు దుమ్ము గాఁగ
శ్రమబుర్పురత్తురంగమ నాసికాగళ
త్పంకంబు వైచు కర్దమము గాఁగఁ
గుపిత యోధాక్షిప్త కుంతకాంతారభే
లనములు దండఘట్టనలు గాఁగఁ

తే జెనఁటి పగఆ ప్రతాపంబు చిచ్చు లార్చు
కరణి గడిదేశములు చొచ్చి కలఁచి యలఁచు
మూరురాయరగండాంక వీరకృష్ణ
రాయ భూభ్యుదయంకర ప్రబలధాటి.

36

41

Thick rows of pearls
cling to the sharp edge of Krishnaraya's sword
as he wields it in battle, fast as a racing stream,
cutting through the temples of elephants in rut.
Are they bubbles surfacing in rows
as enemy boats capsize and sink, and all that's left
is a wake of foam?

42

His elephants provide streams of water from their trunks.
The wind from their massive ears stirs up heaps of dust.
Foam from the nostrils of war horses stretched to their limit
descends like a blanket of mud.
Spears cast in thousands by furious warriors
finish off the flames
when the vast army of Krishnaraya,
"Mightiest of the Three Kings,"
moves to put out the fires
lit by his enemy kings.

షష్ట్యంతములు

౪3

క ఏవంవిధ గుణవంతున
కావల్గత్తురగ బహువిధారోహ కళా
రేవంతున కతిశాంతున
కావిష్మృతకీర్తి ధవళితాశాంతునకున్.

౪౪

క పుంభానుపుంఖ సైంధవ
రింఖాసంఘాతజాత రేణ్వగ్ర తమో
రింఖద్రిపున్యపదహర
ప్రేంఖ దసుగ్రసనజఠరభృత్యసిఘణికిన్.

౪౫

క అవిరళ వితరణ విద్యా
నవరాధేయునకు సజ్జనవిధేయునకుం
గవితాస్త్రీలోలునకున్
ఖవిటంక నటద్యశోభికల్లోలునకున్.

43–47

For one rich in such qualities,
for an expert rider adept at handling any sort of horse,
for one who is quiet at heart,
whose brilliant fame turned all space white,
whose sword is a snake filling its belly with the life breaths
of enemies trembling in the darkness caused by dust
kicked up by his horses' hooves in one continuous charge,
for Karna reborn, a paragon of the art of giving,
for one who is loyal to good people,
for the lover of Lady Poetry,
for one whose fame rolls like waves to the end of space,
whose blazing prowess, unbearable to the lords of space,
makes the sun redundant,
who captured the eldest son of the Kalinga king
in less than half a minute,
whose mind, with all its thoughts and words, rests at the feet
of Lord Venkatesvara, the ultimate source of kindness,

for Krishnaraya, son of Narasimha and the grandson
    of Ishvara,

౪౬

క దిగధీశాసహ్య ధగ
ద్ధగితేద్ధరుచిప్రతాప తపనస్ఫురణ
స్థగిత ద్యుమణికి నిమిషా
ర్ధగృహీత కళింగరాజతనయాగ్రణికిన్.

౪౭

క కరుణాకర వేంకటవిభు
చరణస్మరణప్రసంగ సంగతమతి కీ
శ్వరనరసింహ మహీభ్ఘు
ద్వరనందన కృష్ణరాయ ధరణీపతికిన్.

కథా ప్రారంభము

౪౮

వ అభ్యుదయపరంపరాభివృద్ధిగా నాయొనర్పం బూనిన
స్వారోచిష మనుసంభవం బను మహాప్రబంధంబునకుం
గథాక్రమం బెట్టి దనిన జైమినిముని స్వాయంభువమను
కథా శ్రవణానంతరంబున మీఁద నెవ్వండు మను వయ్యె
నెటీంగింపు మనవుఁడు బక్తులు మార్కండేయుండు
క్రోష్టికిం జెప్పినప్రకారంబున నిట్లని చెప్పం దొడంగె.

48
wishing him an always escalating happiness,
I am composing this book called
"The Birth of Svarochisha Manu."

If you'd like to know how the story unfolds, listen.
After hearing the story of Svayambhuva Manu, Jaimini
    asked the wise birds,
"After him, who was the next Manu?[18] Tell me, please."
    The birds began to speak,
just as Markandeya had once told the story to Kroshti.

౪౯

మ   వరణాద్వీపవతీ తటాంచలమునన్
        వప్రస్థలీచుంబితాం
        బరమై సౌధసుధాప్రభాధవళిత
        ప్రాలేయరుజ్మండలీ
        హరిణంబై యరుణాస్పదం బనఁగ నా
        ర్యావర్తదేశంబునం
        బుర మొప్పున్ మహికంఠహార తరళ
        స్ఫూర్తిన్ విడంబించుచున్.

౫౦

సీ   అచటి విప్రులు మెచ్చ రఖిలవిద్యాప్రౌఢి
        ముది మది దప్పిన మొదటివేల్పు
        నచటి రాజులు బంటు నంపి భార్గవు నైన
        బింకానఁ బిలిపింతు రంకమునకు
        నచటి మేటి కిరాటు లలకాధిపతి నైన
        మును సంచిమొద లిచ్చి మనుప దక్షు
        లచటి నాలవజాతి హలముఖత్తవిభూతి
        నాదిభిక్షువు భైక్షమైన మాన్చు

తే   నచటి వెలయాంద్రు రంభాదులైన నొరయఁ
        గాసెకొంగున వారించి కడపఁగలరు
        నాట్యరేఖాకళాధురంధరనిరూఢి
        నచటఁ బుట్టిన చిగురుఁ గొమ్మైనఁ జీవ.

49

There was a city called Arunaspada in the country where
    good people live,
on the banks of the Varana River. Its citadel kissed the sky,
and its houses were painted so white that they washed
    away
the dark spot on the moon. It shone like a pendant
on the neck of Lady Earth.

50

The Brahmans there were so proud of their learning in
    all fields
that they disdained even Brahma, the first god, for
    growing senile.
The warriors were so tough they could send a servant
to summon even Rama of the ax to their presence.
The merchants were rich enough to put Kubera back in
    business
with a start-up loan if ever he went bankrupt.
The farmers prospered from their plows. They could give
    so much to Shiva,
the first beggar, that he'd never need to beg again.
The courtesans were so expert in dancing
that they could dismiss the most beautiful women from
    heaven
with a single flourish of their saris.
There even a budding branch was harder than iron.[19]

౫౧

ఉ ఆ పురిఁ బాయకుండు మక
రాంకశశాంక మనోజ్ఞమూర్తి భా
షాపరశేషభోగి వివి
ధాధ్వర నిర్మల ధర్మకర్మదీ
క్షాపరతంత్రుఁ డంబురుహ
గర్భకులాభరణం బనారతా
ధ్యాపన తత్పరుండు ప్రవ
రాఖ్యుఁ డలేఖ్యతనూవిలాసుఁడై.

౫౨

ఆ వానిచక్కఁదనము వైరాగ్యమునఁ జేసి
కాంక్షసేయు జారకామినులకు
భోగబాహ్య మయ్యెఁ బూచిన సంపెంగ
పొలుపు మధుకరాంగనలకుఁ బోలె.

౫౩

ఉ యౌవనమందు యజ్వయు ధ
నాఢ్యుఁడునై కమనీయకౌతుక
శ్రీవిధిఁ గూఁకటుల్‌గొలిచి
చేసిన కూరిమి సోమిదమ్మ సౌ
ఖ్యావహయై భజింప సుఖు
లై తలిదండ్రులు గూడి దేవియున్
దేవరవోలె నుండి యిలు
దీర్పఁగఁ గాఁపుర మొప్పు వానికిన్.

51

A man called Pravara lived in that city, never leaving it.
No painter could do justice to his beauty.
He was like the love god reborn. Handsome as the moon.
A great linguist. Intent on all kinds of rites
and duties. A jewel of a Brahman.
His one great love was to teach.

52

He was free from desire, so his beauty was totally
beyond the reach of any and all women
who wanted him, like the fragrance
of the champak flower for all hovering bees.[20]

53

Though young, he had already completed a Vedic rite.
He was rich too. He loved his wife.
The elders had measured the length of their hair
to be sure they were well matched.
She was the source of all his happiness.
His old parents, like Shiva and Parvati,
looked after the house.

౫౪

సీ వరణాతరంగిణీ దరవికస్వర నూత్న
కమల కషాయగంధము వహించి
ప్రత్యూషపవనాంకురములు పైకొనువేళ
వామనస్తుతిపరత్వమున లేచి
సచ్చాత్రుఁ డగుచు నిచ్చలు నేఁగి యయ్యేట
నఘమర్షణస్నాన మాచరించి
సాంధ్యకృత్యముఁ దీర్చి సావిత్రి జపియించి
సైకతస్థలిఁ గర్మసాక్షి కెఱఁగి

తే ఫల సమిత్కుశకుసుమాది బహుపదార్థ
తతియు నుదికిన మడుఁగుదేవతలుఁ గొంచు
బ్రహ్మచారులు వెంటరా బ్రాహ్మణుండు
వచ్చు నింటికిఁ బ్రజ తన్ను మెచ్చి చూడ.

౫౫

శా శీలంబుం గులమున్ శమంబు దమముం
జెల్వంబు లేఁబ్రాయముం
బోలం జూచి యితండు పాత్రుఁ డని యే
భూపాలుఁ డీ వచ్చినన్
సాలగ్రామము మున్నుగాఁ గొనఁడు మా
న్యక్షేత్రముల్ పెక్కు చం
దాలం బండు నొకప్పుడుం దఱుఁగ దిం
టం బాఁడియుం బంటయున్.

54

You could see him every day walking from the river
with his students in tow carrying fruits, firewood,
darbha grass, flowers, and clean-washed clothes.
He'd get up at dawn, when the breeze from the Varana
carrying the sharp fragrance of half-open lotus flowers
caressed his body. He would chant the morning prayer
to Vishnu[21] upon waking, then bathe in the river
to cleanse himself of sins, perform
the dawn ritual, meditate on the Savitri mantra
and, standing on the riverbank, greet the rising sun
who sees everything.

55

He was good, born in the right family, gentle, disciplined,
young, and handsome. Many kings wanted to give him
    gifts,
but he accepted nothing, not even a *sālagrāma* stone.[22]
He had enough. His fields yielded everything he needed.
There was always plenty of milk and rice.

೫೬

తే వండ నలయదు వేవురు వచ్చిరేని
నన్నపూర్ణకు నుద్ధియా నతనిగృహిణి
యతిథు లేతేర నడికిరేయైనc బెట్టు
వలయు భోజ్యంబు లింట నవ్వారి గాcగ.

೫೭

సీ తీర్థసంవాసు లేతెంచినారని విన్న
నెదురుగా నేcగు దవ్వెంతరయైన
నేcగి తత్పదముల కెఱcగి యింటికిc దెచ్చుc
దెచ్చి సద్భక్తి నాతిథ్యమిచ్చు
నిచ్చి యిష్టాన్నసంతృప్తులcగా జేయుc
జేసి కూర్చున్నచోc జేరవచ్చు
వచ్చి యిద్ధరc గల్గు వనధిపర్వతసరి
త్తీర్థమాహాత్మ్యముల్ దెలియ నడుగు

తే నడిగి యోజనపరిమాణ మరయు నరసి
పోవలయుc జూడ ననుచు నూర్పులు నిగుడ్చు
ననుదినము తీర్థసందర్శనాభిలాష
మాత్మ నుప్పొంగ నత్తరుణాగ్నిహోత్రి.

೫೮

క ఈ విధమున నభ్యాగత
సేవాపరతంత్ర సకల జీవనుcడై భూ
దేవకుమారకుc డుండం
గా విను మొకనాcడు కుతప కాలమునందున్.

56

His wife never tired of cooking. She was like the goddess
of food, Annapurna. Even if a thousand guests turned up
late at night, she would feed them all they wanted.

57

But—he had always wanted to travel.
Anytime he heard that pilgrims had come from far away,
he'd rush to receive them, even at some distance,
and wash their feet and take them home,
and honor them as his guests and feed them
fine food and make them happy. Then, when they were
     seated
comfortably, he'd draw near and ask them all about
oceans, mountains, rivers, and places of power,
and exactly how far they were from his place.
Then he would sigh heavily: "Someday I should go
and see them." That young Brahman had fire
to tend at home.[23]

58

His whole life was given to serving unannounced guests.
One day, late in the afternoon,

౫౯

సీ ముడిచిన యొంటి కెంజడ మూయ ముప్వన్నె
మొగము కిరీటముగ ధరించి
కకపాల కేదార కటక ముద్రితపాణిం
గుఱుచ లాతాముతోఁ గూర్చి పట్టి
ఱైనేయమైన యొడ్డాణంబు లవణిచే
నక్కళించిన పొట్ట మక్కళించి
యారకూటచ్చాయ నవఘళింపఁగఁ జాలు
బడుగుదేహంబున భస్మ మలఁది

తే మిట్టయూరమున నిడుయోగపట్టె మెఱియఁ
జెవుల రుద్రాక్షపోఁగులు చవుకళింపఁ
గావికుబుసంబు జలకుండికయును బూని
చేరెఁ దద్దేహ మౌషధసిద్ధుఁడొకఁడు.

౬౦

తే ఇట్లు చనుదెంచు పరమయోగీంద్రుఁ గాంచి
భక్తిసంయుక్తి నెదురేఁగి ప్రణతుఁ డగుచు
నర్ఘ్యపాద్యాది పూజనం బాచరించి
యిష్టమృష్టాన్నకలన సంతుష్టుఁ జేసి.

౬౧

క ఎందుండి యొందుఁ బోవుచు
నిందుల కేతెంచినార లిప్పుడు విద్వ
ద్వందిత నేఁడు గదా మ
న్మందిరము పవిత్రమయ్యె మాన్యుఁడ నైతిన్.

50

59

a certain siddha, a specialist in herbs, arrived.
He wore a tiger's skin on his head, covering his red
    matted hair.
In his hand, circled by a five-metal bracelet, he carried
a bag and a yogi's stick to rest his arms.
A doeskin belt was tightly bound around his waist,
making his belly bulge. His thin body, shimmering like
    polished brass,
was covered with ash. A strap useful in yogic postures
was hanging from his broad chest, and *rudrākṣa* beads
dangled from his ears. He was dressed
in ochre, with a water pot
in one hand.

60

Pravara saw the great yogi
arriving and went toward him, bowed to him in reverence,
honored him with water to sip and to wash his feet,
and made him happy with delicious food.

61

Then he said: "Where are you coming from
and where are you headed? You are honored
by learned people, and I am honored
by your presence in my house today.

౬౨

క మీమాటలు మంత్రంబులు
మీమొట్టినయొడ ప్రయాగ మీపాద పవి
త్రామలతోయము లలఘు
ద్యేమార్గఝురాంబుపానరుక్త్యము లుర్విన్.

౬౩

ఉ వానిది భాగ్యవైభవము
వానిది పుణ్యవిశేష మెమ్మెయిన్
వాని దవంధ్యజీవనము
వానిది జన్మము వేఱు సేయ కె
వ్వాని గృహాంతరంబున భ
వాద్యశయోగిజనంబు పావన
స్నానవిధాన్నపానముల
సంతస మందుచు బోవు నిచ్చలున్.

౬౪

తే మౌనినాథ కుటుంబజంబాలపటల
మగ్న మాద్యశ గృహమేధి మండలంబు
నుద్ధరింపంగ నౌషధ మొందు గలదె
యుష్మదంఘ్రిరజోలేశ మొకటి దక్క.

52

62

Whatever you say is a mantra.
Wherever you go is Prayaga.[24]
The water that washes your feet
duplicates on earth
the river from heaven.

63

When yogis like you come to visit,
bathe, eat, drink, and rest, and leave
in joy, the man of that house finds himself
lucky. He is really blessed, and truly fulfilled
in all ways. His life
is a life.

64

Householders like me,
mired in the cares of family life—
what can make us free other than the specks of dust
on the soles of your feet?"

౬౫

క నా విని ముని యిట్లను వ
త్తా విను మావంటి తైర్థికావళి కెల్లన్
మీవంటి గృహస్థుల సుఖ
జీవనమునఁ గాదె తీర్థసేవయుఁ దలఁపన్.

౬౬

సీ కెలఁకుల నున్న తంగెటిజున్ను గృహమేధి
యజమానుఁ దంకస్థితార్థపేటి
పండిన పెరటి కల్పకము వాస్తవ్యండు
దొడ్డిఁ బెట్టిన వేల్పుగిడ్డి కాఁపు
కడలేని యమృతంపు నడబావి సంసారి
సవిధమేరునగంబు భవనభర్త
మరుదేశపథ మధ్యమప్రప కులపతి
యాఁకటి కొదవు సస్యము కుటుంబి

తే బధిరపంగ్వంధ భిక్షుక బ్రహ్మచారి
జటి పరివ్రాజ కాతిథి క్షపణ కావ
ధూత కాపాలికా ద్యనాథులకుఁ గాన
ఘాసురోత్తమ గార్హస్థ్యమునకు సరియె.

54

65

The yogi answered him.
"Son, listen to me.
Your good life at home
is what sets pilgrims like us
free to move from place to place.

66

Honey from *tangedu* flowers nearby,
cash in your pocket,
the wish-giving tree, ripe with fruit, in your backyard,
the wish-giving cow in your pen,
a well you can walk into that never dries up,
a mountain of gold within reach,
a drink of cool water on a hot day,
a square meal when you're hungry—
a family man is all these to the deaf, lame, blind,
beggars and bachelors, renouncers, vagrants,
unannounced guests, monks, naked itinerants,
skull holders, and all other homeless people.
There's nothing like family life."

౬౽

క నావుఁడు బ్రవరుం డిట్లను
దేవా దేవర సమస్త తీర్థాటనమ్ము
గావింపుదు రిలపై నటు
గావున విభజించి యడుగఁ గౌతుక మయ్యెన్.

౬౭

శా ఏయే దేశములన్ వసించితిరి మీ
రేయే గిరుల్చూచినా
రేయే తీర్థములందుఁ గ్రుంకిడితి రే
యే ద్వీపముల్మెట్టినా
రేయే పుణ్యవనాళిఁ ద్రిమ్మరితి రే
యే తోయధుల్డాసినా
రాయా చేటులలఁ గల్లు వింతలు మహా
త్మా నా కెటింగింపరే.

౬౯

తే పోయి సేవింపలేకున్నఁ బుణ్యతీర్థ
మహిమ వినుటయ నఖిలకల్మషహరంబ
కాన వేఁడెద ననిన న మ్మౌనివర్యుఁ
దాదరాయత్తచిత్తుఁడై యతని కనియె.

67

Now Pravara said: "Honored sir,
you've seen all the holy places.
Tell me something about each of them.

68

What are the countries you have visited? The mountains
you have climbed? The rivers you've bathed in?
The islands you've explored? The godly forests
you've entered? The oceans you have come to?
Tell me about all of them, in all their new
and wonderful details.

69

If I can't go there myself, the next best thing
is to hear about their power.
That will make me pure. That's why I'm asking you."
The siddha replied from his kind heart.

౭౦

ఉ ఓ చతురాస్యవంశ కల
శోదధిపూర్ణశశాంక తీర్థయా
త్రాచణశీలినై జనప
దంబులుఁ బుణ్యనదీనదంబులుం
జూచితి నందు నందుఁ గల
చోద్యములుం గనుఁగొంటి నాపటీ
రాచల పశ్చిమాచల హి
మాచల పూర్వదిశాచలంబులన్.

౭౧

శా కేదారేశు భజించితిన్ శిరమునం
గీలించితిన్ హింగుళా
పాదాంభోరుహముల్ప్రయాగనిలయుం
బద్మాక్షు సేవించితిన్
యాదోనాథసుతాకళత్రు బదరీ
నారాయణుం గంటి నీ
యా దేశం బన నేల చూచితి సమ
స్తాశావకాశంబులన్.

70

"You are like a full moon rising over the milky ocean
of Brahman families. Driven by the desire to visit
holy places, I've gone everywhere.
Seen everything—countries, rivers flowing
east and west, marvels of all kinds—in the space
between Sandal Mountain,[25] the Western Mountain,
Snow Mountain, and the Mountain of the East.

71

I worshiped the lord of Kedara. I put my head to the feet
of the goddess Hingula. I served Vishnu of the beautiful
    eyes
who lives in Prayaga. I saw Narayana at Badari,
married to the Ocean's daughter. Why mention this place
or that? I've seen everything under the sky.[26]

౬౩

వ అది యట్లుండె వినుము గృహస్థరత్నంబ లంబమాన
రవిరథతురంగ శృంగార చారు చామరచ్చుటా
ప్రేక్షణక్షణోద్దీప చమరసముదయంబగు నుదయంబునం
గల విశేషంబులు శేషఫణికి నైన లెక్కింప శక్యంబె
యంధకరిపు కంధరావాస వాసుకి వియోగభవ
దుర్వ్యథాభోగ భోగినిభోగభాగపరివేష్ఠిత పటీర విటపి
వాటికావేల్ల దేలాలతావలయంబగు మలయంబునం
గల చలువకు విలువ యొయ్యది యకటకట
వికటకూటకోటివిటంక శృంగాటకాడొకమాన
జరదిందు బింబగళదమృతబిందు దుర్దినార్ద్రీకృత
సల్లకీపల్లవప్రభంజనపరాంజన హస్తిహస్తంబగు
నస్తంబునం గల మణిప్రస్తరంబుల విశ్రాంతిం జింతించిన
మేనం బులక లిప్పుడుం బొడమెడు స్వస్వప్రవర్ధిత
వర్ధిష్ణు ధరణీరుహసందేహ దేహదప్రధానసమానఖీల
దైలబిలవిలాసినీవిలాస వాచాల తులాకోటి
కలకలాహూయయమానమానస మదాలస
మరాళంబగు రజతశైలంబు నేలంబులం గాల గళు
విహారప్రదేశంబులం గన్న సంస్కృతిక్లేశంబులు వాయువే
సతతమదజలస్రవణ పరాయణైరావణవిషాణకోటి
సముట్టంకిత కటకపరిస్ఫురత్కురువింద
కందళవ్రాతజాతాలాత శంకాపసర్పదభ్రము
భ్రమీవిభ్రమధురంధరంబగు మేరుధరాధరంబు
శిఖరంబుల సోయగంబులు గలయం గనుంగొనుట
బహుజన్మకృతసుకృత పరిపాకంబునం గాక
యేల చేకూఆ నేర్చు నే నిట్టి మహాద్భుతంబు
లీశ్వరానుగ్రహంబున నల్పకాలంబునం గనుంగొంటి
ననుటయ నీషదంకురిత హసన గ్రసిష్ణు గండయుగళుం
డగుచుఁ బ్రవరుం డతని కిట్లనియె.

72

Let that be. Listen, my householder friend. On the sunrise mountain, yaks crane their necks to catch a glimpse of the splendid yak-tail banners that adorn the horses yoked to the chariot of the rising sun. Could even the thousand-tongued snake* count all the wonders of that place?

Then there's Malaya Mountain to the south. It's a cool place, priceless. That's where all the female snakes coil themselves around the sandalwood trees, enveloped by vines of cardamom, to cool their fiery yearning for their husband, who has taken up residence on Shiva's neck, far away.

On the sunset mountain, the great elephant of the west breaks off the buds of the *sallaki* branches that are soaked with a continuous drizzle of elixir dripping from the waning moon that lingers in the mountain passes and the crevices tucked among the tall peaks. If I think about how I used to rest there, seated on pedestals of precious stone, I break out in goose-bumps even now.

And you've no doubt heard of Silver Mountain, where elegant yaksha women come to hasten the blossoming of the trees they have nurtured, and the chiming of their anklets invites languid royal geese to join them. There are secret places there where black-neck Shiva enjoys his time with Parvati. Once you see those places, all the sorrows of existence will vanish.

The elephant Airavana,[27] continually in rut, strikes the mountain slopes with his tusks and digs up the bright red *kuravinda* flowers, and his mate, certain that she's seeing

---

* Adishesha.

౭౩

చ వెఅవక మీ కొనర్తు నోక
విన్నప మిట్టివి యెల్లఁ జూచి రా
నెఅకలు గట్టుకొన్న మఱీ
యేంద్లును బూండ్లును బట్టుఁ బ్రాయపుం
జిఅుతతనంబు మీ మొగము
సెప్పక చెప్పెడు నద్దిరయ్య మా
కెఱుఁగఁ దరంబె మీ మహిమ
లీర యొఱుంగుదు రేమి చెప్పుదున్.

౭౪

క అనినఁ బరదేశి గృహపతి
కనియెన్ సందియముఁ దెలియ నడుగుట తప్పా
వినవయ్య జరయు రుజయును
జెనకంగా వెఅచు మమ్ము సిద్ధుల మగుటన్.

firebrands, retreats in fear. Such remarkable sights occur all the time on Mount Meru. Only a fortunate man whose karma has ripened over many births will be able to see them. I myself have seen all this in a very short span of time thanks to god's blessings." Pravara, with a little smile that swallowed up his cheeks, said to him:

73

"Forgive my boldness in asking. It would take years
and years to see all this, even if one had wings.
But I can tell just by looking at your face
that you're very young. How can someone like me
know your powers? Only you can know them.
What can I say?"

74

The stranger replied, "What's wrong in asking? Neither age nor sickness dares to touch us. We're siddhas.

೭౫

మ పరమంబైన రహస్య మౌ నయిన డాఁ
పం జెప్పెదన్ భూమిని
ర్జరవంశోత్తమ పాదలేప మను పే
రం గల్గు దివ్యౌషధం
పు రసం బీశ్వరసత్కృపం గలిగెఁ ద
ద్ద్వారిప్రభావంబునం
జరియింతుం బవమాన మానస తిర
స్కారిత్వరాహంకృతిన్.

౭౬

క దివి బిసరుహబాంధవ సైం
ధవ సంఘం బెంత దవ్వు దగ లే కరుగున్
ఘువి నంత దవ్వు నేమును
రవరవ లే కరుగుదుము హుటాహుటి నడలన్.

౭౭

మ అనినన్ విప్రవరుండు కౌతుకభర
వ్యగ్రాంతరంగుండు భ
క్తినిబద్ధాంజలిబంధురుండు నయి మీ
దివ్యప్రభావం బెఱుం
గని నా ప్రల్లదముల్సహించి మునిలో
కగ్రామణీ సత్కృపన్
నను మీ శిష్యుని దీర్ఘయాత్రవలనన్
ధన్యాత్ముఁగాఁ జేయరే.

75

It's a secret, but I'll tell you. I won't hide it. You're a
Brahman, like god on earth. The sap of a certain magical
plant was given to me by the kindness of god. It's an ointment
for one's feet. Through its power, I move around, confident,
faster than wind or mind.

76

We move as fast and as far
as the horses that pull the sun,
and we're never weary."

77

The Brahman, restless and eager,
folded his hands and said: "You're a great man.
Pardon my impudent words. How could I have known
your power? Be kind to me. I'm your pupil.
I wish to travel to the holy places.
Make it happen."

౬౮

క అనుటయు రసలింగము నిడు
తన వత్రువ ప్రేఁపసజ్జ దంతపుబరణిన్
నినిచిన యొకపస రిది యది
యని చెప్పక పూసెఁ దత్పదాంబుజయుగళిన్.

౬౯

క ఆ మం దిడి యతఁ డరిగిన
భూమీసురుఁ డరిగెఁ దుహిన భూధర శృంగ
శ్యామల కోమల కానన
హేమాద్యాదరీర్ఝరీ నిరీక్షాపేక్షన్.

౭౦

వ అనిన విని యమ్మహీసురవరుఁ డట్లరిగి యొట్లు
ప్రవర్తించె నతని పుణ్యవర్తన శ్రవణంబు మనంబునకు
హర్షోత్కర్షంబు గల్పించెఁ దర్వాతి వృత్తాంతంబు
గృపాయత్త చిత్తంబున నానతీయ వలయు నని
యడుగుటయును.

78

The siddha opened his basket of cane where he kept
his mercury *liṅga*[28] and took out
an ivory casket. He smeared a certain juice
on Pravara's feet without saying
a word.

79

The siddha left, and the Brahman
instantly took off, burning
with the wish to see the snow-capped peaks
of the Himalayas, the dark beckoning forests,
caves glittering with gold, and rushing rivers.

80

Hearing the birds say this, Jaimini asked: "What happened
next? This story of great piety is very exciting. Please have
the goodness to go on."

౧౧

శా   గంగా స్వచ్ఛతరంగ భంగిక యశో
గాఢచ్చవిచ్చన్న సా
రంగాంకాంక నిరంకుశప్రతికళా
ప్రౌఢిప్రియంభావుకా
గాంగేయాచలచాప నూపుర వచో
గాంభీర్యలీలాస్పదా
బంగాళాంగకళింగ భూప సుభటా
బ్రశ్రేణి ఝుంఝూనిలా.

౧౨

క   మండలికతపన శోభిత
కుండలిపతిశయన కర్ణకుండలిత రసా
ఖండకవికావ్య దిగ్వే
దండప్రతిదళన కలహ తాడిత పటహో.

81

My king! Your fame, white as the spotless waves
of the Ganges, has washed away the blot on the moon.
You have unchallenged authority in every art.
You speak with the depth of the thousand-tongued first snake
that adorns Shiva's foot. You are the whirlwind
that swept away the powerful armies of Bengal and Orissa.

82

You scorch rival kings like the sun.
The exquisite poems made by your poets
hang like earrings on the ears of God.
Your battle drums split the eardrums
of the elephants who hold up the earth
on every side.

౭3

ఉత్సాహ.

కుకురు కాశ కురు కరూశ
కోసలాంధ్ర సింధు బా
హ్లీక శకాంగ వంగ సింహ
ళేశ కన్యకామణి
ప్రకర పాణిఘటిత రత్న
పాదుకా కలాచికా
ముకుర వీటికాకరండ
ముఖ్య రాజలాంఛనా.

గద్యము.

ఇది శ్రీమదాంధ్ర కవితాపితామహ సర్వతోముఖాంక
పంకజాక్ష పాదాంబుజాధీన మానసేందిందిర
నందవరపుర వంశోత్తంస శతకోపతాపస ప్రసాదాసాదిత
చతుర్విధ కవితామతల్లి కాల్లసాని చొక్కయామాత్యపుత్త
పెద్దనార్య ప్రణీతంబైన స్వారోచిషమనుసంభవం బను
మహాప్రబంధంబునందుఁ బ్రథమాశ్వాసము.

83

Princesses from the lands of Kukuru, Kasha, Kuru, Karusha,
*   Kosala,*
Andhra, Sindhu, Bahlika, Shaka, Anga, Vanga, and
*   Simhala*
bring to you your jeweled sandals, spittoon,
mirror, and your box of betel nuts and leaves—
all signs of your royalty.

The great poem called "The Birth of Svarochisha Manu" was
written by Allasani Cokkayamatya's son Peddanarya, known
to all as the "Creator God of Telugu Poetry," who comes from
a family of Nandavara Brahmans, whose mind hovers like a
bee around the lotuslike feet of lotus-eyed Vishnu, and who was
blessed by his guru Shathakopa with the ability to compose all
four kinds of fine poetry.[29] *Chapter 1 ends here.*

ద్వితీయాశ్వాసము

౧

క	శ్రీఖండ శీతనగ మ
	ధ్యాఖండక్షోణిమండలాఖండల వి
	ద్యాఖేలనభోజ సుధీ
	లేఖద్రుమ కృష్ణరాయ లీలామదనా.

౨

వ	అవధరింపుము. జైమినిమునీంద్రునకుం
	బ్రజ్ఞాసాంద్రంబులగు పక్షీంద్రంబు లవ్వలికథ యిట్లని
	చెప్పం దొడంగె.

3

చ	అటం జని కాంచె భూమిసురుం
	డంబరచుంబి శిరస్సరజ్ఝరీ
	పటల ముహుర్ముహుర్లుతద
	భంగ తరంగ మృదంగ నిస్వన
	స్ఫుట నటనానురూప పరి
	ఫుల్ల కలాప కలాపిజాలముం
	గటక చరత్కరేణు కర
	కంపిత సాలము శీతశైలమున్.

72

Chapter 2

1

Listen, Krishnaraya, love god in human form,
ruling like Indra over the entire earth between
Sandal Mountain and Snow Mountain.
You're like Bhoja[1] when you play with your poets,
like a tree that grants all wishes
to the wise.

2

Those eminently intelligent birds went on telling the story
to Jaimini, as follows.

3

The Brahman went and saw Snow Mountain, its tall peaks
kissing the expanse of sky, with many rivers rushing
downward, rumbling like the beating of a drum,
on and on, while peacocks danced in time,
spreading their splendid tails,
and elephants roaming the slopes
shook the *sal* trees with their trunks.

౪

వ కాంచి యంతరంగంబున దరంగితం బగు
హర్షోత్కర్షంబున.

౫

క నరనారాయణ చరణాం
బురుహద్వయ భద్రచిహ్న ముద్రిత బదరీ
తరుషండ మండలాంతర
సరణిన్ ధరణీసురుండు సన జన నెడుటన్.

౬

క ఉల్లల దలకాజలకణ
పల్లవిత కదంబముకుళ పరిమళ లహరీ
హల్లోహల మద బంభర
మల్లధ్వను లెసంగ విసరె మరుదంకురముల్.

4

He saw it, and waves of joy rushed through his mind.

5

The Brahman walked along a path
lined by jujube trees,
where Nara and Narayana[2] had left their footprints,
and as he walked, in front of him

6

bees were buzzing, drunk on waves of fragrance
from *kadamba* buds blossoming through the spray
of the Alaka River in spate,
and a gentle breeze carried
that sweet sound.

౨

సీ   తొండము ల్సాచి యందుగుఁ జిగుళ్ళకు నిక్కు
      కరుల దంతచ్ఛాయ గడలుకొనఁగ
      సెలవుల వనదంశములు మూఁగి నెఱవెట్టఁ
      గ్రోల్పులుల్పాదరింద్ల గుఱకలిడఁగ
      సెలయేటి యిసుకలంకల వరాహంబులు
      మొత్తంబులై త్రవ్వి ముస్తెలెత్త
      నడ్డంబు నిడుపు నాపడ్డలగతి మనుఁ
      బిళ్ళు డొంకలనుండి క్రేళ్ళుదాఁటఁ

తే   బ్రబల భల్లుక నఖభల్ల భయదమథన
      శిథిల మధుకోశ విసర విశీర్ణ మక్షి
      కాంతరాంతర దంతురితాతపమునఁ
      బుడమి తిలతండులన్యాయమున వెలుంగ.

౩

క   పరికించుచు డెందంబునఁ
      బురికొను కౌతుకముతోడ భూమీసురుఁ డ
      గ్గిరికటక తట నిరంతర
      తరుగహన గుహావిహార తత్పరమతియై.

7

Elephants stretched their trunks to catch hold of tender
    leaf buds
on the *andugu* trees, and their tusks gleamed in the sun.
Tigers were snoring in the bushes while forest flies
pricked the edges of their lips.
Wild boars were digging up roots on the sand islands
in the mountain rivers.
Gayal, like big cattle, came jumping out of the wild shrubs.
Bears tore open honeycombs with their fearsome claws
and bees pouring out, flying through the air,
cast spots of shadow on the earth,
bathed in sunlight, here and there,
like white rice mingled with black sesame seeds.

8

The Brahman was looking,
his excitement rising. He was eager
to see it all—every cave hidden
in the forests that covered the slopes
of that mountain, leaving no gap.

౯

సీ. నిడుదపెన్నెటీగుంపు జడగట్ట సగరు ము
మ్మనుమండు తపము గైకొనినచోటు
జరఠ కచ్చప కులేశ్వరు వెన్ను గానరా
జగతికి మిన్నేఱు దిగినచోటు
పుచ్చడీకతనంబు పోఁబెట్టి గిరికన్య
పతిఁ గొల్వ నాయాస పడినచోటు
వలరాచరాచవాఁ డలికాక్షు కనువెచ్చఁ
గరఁగిన యల కనికరపుఁజోటు

తే. తపసి యిల్లాంద్ర చెలువంబుఁ దలఁచి తలఁచి
మున్ను ముచ్చిచ్చును విరాళిఁ గొన్నచోటు
కనుపప్పులు వేల్పుఁబడవాలుఁ గన్నచోటు
హర్షమునఁ జూచి ప్రవరాఖ్యుఁ డాత్మలోన.

9

The place where Sagara's great-grandson,
Bhagiratha, sat in penance until his thick long hair
turned to dreadlocks—
and where the river from the sky
came crashing down to earth, exposing the spine
of the ancient tortoise—
and where Parvati, the mountain's daughter,
setting aside her shyness, served her future husband
and suffered hardship—
the sad place where the prince of passion
was burnt to cinders by the fire
from Shiva's third eye—
and where even blameless fire
was consumed by desire for the beauty
of the Brahmans' wives,
where the reeds and grasses
gave birth to Kumara, general of the gods[3]—

the Brahman was overjoyed
to see it all.

౧౦

చ విలయకృశానుకీలముల
   వేడిమిc బోడిమి మాలి వెల్కిడిం
   గలసిన భూతధాత్రి మటి
   క్రమ్మఅ రూపయి నిల్చి యొషధుల్
   మొలవంగc జేయునట్టి నయ
   ముం బ్రతికల్పము నెట్లు గాంచు నీ
   చలిమలవల్ల నుల్లసిలు
   చల్లదనంబును నూనకుండినన్.

౧౧

సీ పసుపునిగ్గులు దేఱు పాంపజన్నిద మొప్పc
    బ్రమథాధిపతి యింటిపఱ్ఖైఅతింగె
    శచి కీంఅ గఆపుచుc జడలేట సురరాజు
    జలకేళి సవరించు చెలు వెఱింగె
    నదనుతో జేఱి చన్నవిసి యొషధుల మ
    న్మొఱదపు కొండల కెల్లc బిదుక నెఱింగె
    వేల్పుఅింతులలోన విఱ్ఝివీంగుచు మేన
    నవరత్న రచనల రవణ మెఱింగెc

తే బరిపరివిధంపు జన్నంపుc బరికరంపు
    సొంపుసంపద నిఖిల నిలింపసభయు
    నప్పటప్పటికిని జిహ్వ త్రుప్పు డుల్ల
    నామెత లెఱింగె నీతుషారాద్రికతన.

80

10

"In every cycle, at the end of the world,
this earth is burnt to ash
and then again takes shape,
as beautiful as ever,
and everything grows back.
None of this would ever happen
without this mountain
to cool things down.

11

Here Shiva, lord of ghosts,
a snake stained yellow across his chest,
found a wife.[4] Here, in Sky River,
Indra discovered the joy of water games
while teaching his wife how to swim.
Here earth took the form of a cow, heavy with milk,
and nursed the hills, which burst into green.
Here Mena, swelling with pride among all the women
of the gods, learned how to wear the nine precious jewels.
Here all the gods found delicious taste and did away
with the boring blandness on their tongues
because this mountain provided whatever was needed
for their rites.

౧౨

మ తలమే బ్రహ్మకు నైన నీనగ మహా
త్త్యం బెన్న నే నియ్యెడం
గల చోద్యంబులు తేపు గన్గొనియెదం
గాకేమి నేఁ డేఁగెదన్
నలినీబాంధవభానుతప్త రవికాం
తస్యంది నీహారకం
దళ చూత్కారపరంపరల్పయిపయిన్
మధ్యాహ్నమ్ము దెల్పెడిన్.

౧౩

తే అనుచుఁ గ్రమ్ముఱువేళ నీహారవారి
బెరసి తత్పాదలేపంబు గరఁగిపోయెఁ
గరఁగిపోవుట యెఱుంగఁగ దద్ధరణిసురుఁడు
దైవకృతమున కిల నసాధ్యంబు కలదె.

౧౪

మ అతఁడట్లౌషధహీనుఁడై నిజపురీ
యాత్రామిళత్కాఁతుకో
ద్ధతిఁ బోవన్ సపదిస్ఫుటార్తిఁ జరణ
ద్వంద్వంబు రా కుండినన్
మతిఁ జింతించుచు నవ్విధం బెటీఁగి హో
నన్నిట్లు దైవంబ తె
చ్చితె యీ ఘోరవనప్రదేశమునకున్
సిద్ధాపదేశంబునన్.

82

12

Not even God the creator
could do justice to the greatness
of this mountain! I'll come back tomorrow
to see more. Today
I have to go home. I can hear the sound
of snow melting on the sun-baked rocks, and that means
it's high noon."

13

He tried to turn back, but the water from melting snow
had washed the juice off his feet. The poor Brahman didn't
notice. Who can outdo fate?

14

Without that magical juice, his feet
couldn't move. He wanted to go home
in the worst way. A sudden grief
took hold. He thought to himself:
"God, you used that siddha
to bring me to this godforsaken place!

౧౭

క ఎక్కడి యరుణాస్పదపుర
మెక్కడి తుహినాద్రి క్రొవ్వి యే రా౯ దగునే
యక్కట మును సనుదెంచిన
దిక్కిది యని యొఱుంగ వెడలు తెరు వెయ్యదియో.

౧౮

మ అకలంకౌషధసత్త్వముం దెలియ మా
యా ద్వార కావంతి కా
 శి కురుక్షేత్ర గయా ప్రయాగములు నే
సేవింప కుద్దండగం
డక వేదండ వరాహ వాహరిపు ఖ
ధ్లవ్యాఘ్ర మిమ్మంచు౯గొం
డకు రా౯ జెల్లునె బుద్ధిజాడ్య జనితో
న్మాదుల్గదా శ్రోత్రియుల్.

15

Where is my Arunaspada
and where is this Snow Mountain?
Why did I come here? Was I out of my mind?
I don't even know the way I took
to get here. How will I get back?

16

If I wanted to test the power
of that damned juice, I could have gone
to holy places like Maya,* Dvaraka,
Avanti, Kashi, Kurukshetra, Gaya,
or Prayaga. Why did I have to choose
a place infested by rhinoceroses, elephants,
wild boars, wild buffaloes, and tigers?
But then we're crazy. That's how Brahmans
who chant the Veda are made.

---

* Haridwar.

౧౭

సీ॥ నను నిముసంబు గానక యున్న నూ రెల్ల
నరయు మజ్జనకుఁ దెంతడలునొక్కొ
యెప్పుడు సంధ్యలయందు నిలువెళ్ళునీక న
న్నోమెడుతల్లి యొంతొఱలునొక్కొ
యనుకూలవతి నాడు మనసులో వర్తించు
కులకాంత మది నెంత కుందునొక్కొ
కెడఁ దోడునీడలై క్రీడించు సచ్చాత్ర
లింతకు నెంత చింతింతురొక్కొ

తే॥ యతిథి సంతర్పణంబు లేమయ్యెనొక్కొ
యగ్ను లే మయ్యెనొక్కొ నిత్యంబు లైన
కృత్యములఁ బాపి దైవంబ కినుక నిట్లు
పాఱివైచితె మిన్నులు పడ్డచోట.

౧౮

క॥ నను నిలు సేరు నుపాయం
బొనరింపఁగఁ జాలు సుకృతి యొకఁ డిదవఁడొకో
యనుచుం జింతాసాగర
మున మునిఁగి భయంబు గదురఁ బోవుచు నెదురన్.

17

If my father doesn't see me
for even a minute, he hunts all over the village.
My mother won't even let me leave the house
after dark.
My loving wife, who is always in my heart—
she must be in agony.
And what about my students, always as close to me
as my shadow?
All of them must be worried.
Who's there to look after guests
or tend the fires?
Cruel fate—you've taken me away
from my daily rites and duties and cast me off
in this place at the end of the world where the sky
falls to earth.

18

Is there no kind soul somewhere nearby
who could take me home?"
He was drowning in a sea of sorrow
and terrified. He kept on walking
and saw before him

౧౯

సీ. కులిశధారాహతి పొలుపునఁ బైనుండి
యడుగు మోవఁగ జేగుఱైన తటులఁ
గనుపట్టు లోయ గంగానిర్ఝరము వాఱఁ
జలువయో నయ్యేటి కెలఁకులందు
నిసుకవెట్టిన నేల నేచి యర్కాంశులఁ
జొఱనీక దట్టమై యిరులు గవియు
క్రముక పున్నాగ నారంగ రంభా నాళి
కేరాది విటపి కాంతారవీథిఁ

తే. గెఱలు పిక శారికా కీర కేకి భృంగ
సారసధ్వని దనలోని చంద్రకాంత
దరులు ప్రతిశబ్ద మీన గంధర్వ యక్ష
గానఘూర్ణిత మగు నొక్క కోనఁ గనియె.

౨౦

క. కనుఁగొని యిది మునియాశ్రమ
మను తహతహ వొడమి యిచటి కరిగిన నాకుం
గననగు నొక తెఱకువ యని
మనమునఁ గల దిగులు కొంత మట్టువడంగన్.

19

a wooded corner of a valley lined with red rock
as if the mountain had been cut straight from the top
all the way down by Indra's diamond weapon.
The Ganges was flowing there, and on the cool, sandy
    banks
of the river the forest was so thick that the rays of the sun
couldn't enter, and in that darkness areca and *ponna,*
orange, banana, and coconut trees were growing.
The calls of cuckoos, mynahs, parrots, peacocks,
bees, and herons were echoing off the moonstones,
and the whole valley was ringing with the music
of singers from heaven.[5]

20

Seeing all this, he thought, eager,
"Sages must be living here.
If I go there, they'll show me a way."
He calmed down just a little.

౨౧

చ నికట మహీధరాగ్రతట
నిర్గత నిర్ఝరధారఁ బాసి లో
యకుఁ దల క్రిందుగా మలఁక
లై దిగు కాలువ వెంటఁ బూచు మ
ల్లిక లవలంబనంబుగ న
లిప్రకరధ్వని చిమ్మి రేఁగ లో
నికి మణిపట్టభంగసర
ణిన్ ధరణీసురుఁ డేఁగి చెంగటన్.

౨౨

శా తావుల్క్రేవలఁ జల్లు చెంగలువ కే
దారంబు తీరంబునన్
మావుల్క్రోవులు నల్లిబిల్లిగొను కాం
తారంబునం దైందవ
గ్రావాకల్పిత కాయమాన జటిల
ద్రాక్షా గుళుచ్చంబులం
బూవుందీవెల నొప్పు నొక్క భవనం
బున్ గారుడేత్క్రీర్ణమున్.

౨౩

క కాంచి తదీయ విచిత్రో
దంచిత సౌభాగ్యగరిమ కచ్చెరువడి య
క్కాంచనగర్భాన్వయమణి
యించుక దఱియంగ నచటి కేఁగెడు వేళన్.

21

From the waterfall at the peak,
a stream was trickling down into a valley, twisting
and turning, with jasmine flowering on either side
and bees buzzing intensely. Holding on
to the jasmine bushes, the Brahman walked down a
    staircase
made of precious stones.

22

He saw a building studded green with emeralds,
near a paddy field filled with fragrant
red lilies. *Goraṇṭa* vines were winding around
mango trees, and grapes were hanging in thick bunches
from latticework made of moonstones, richly covered
with more vines and flowers.

23

Amazed at the extravagant beauty
of the place, the young Brahman
went closer.

౨౪

క మృగమదసౌరభవిభవ
ద్విగుణీత ఘనసార సాంద్ర వీటీగంధ
స్థగితేతర పరిమళమై
మగువ పొలుపుౙ దెలుపు నొక్క మారుత మొలసెన్.

౨౫

మ అతౙ డా వాతపరంపరా పరిమళ
వ్యాపారలీలన్ జనా
న్వీత మిచ్చోటని చేరౙ బోయి కనియెన్
విద్యుల్లతావిగ్రహన్
శతపత్రేక్షణౙ జంచరీకచికురం
జంద్రాస్యౙ జక్రస్తనిన్
నతనాభిన్ నవలా నొకానొక మరు
న్నారీశిరోరత్నమున్.

౨౬

తే అమల మణిమయ నిజమందిరాంగణస్థ
తరుణ సహకారమూల విత్తర్ధిమీౙద
శీతలానిల మొలయ నాసీన యైన
యన్నిలింపాబ్జముఖియు నయ్యవసరమున.

24

One part musk enhanced by two parts camphor:
densely packed betel sent its fragrance,
masking all others, announcing
the presence of a woman.

25

He followed the fragrance
carried by the breeze, wave after wave,
thinking, "There are people here."
Then he saw her—

a body gleaming like lightning,
eyes unfolding like flowers,
hair black as bees,
a face lit up with beauty,
proudly curved breasts,
a deep navel—
a woman, but from another world.

26

She was sitting on a raised platform
at the foot of a young mango tree
in the courtyard of her house, which was built
of precious gems. And, as a cool wind
gently blew against her face,

౨౬

సీ	తత నితంబాభోగ ధవళాంశుకములోని
	యంగదట్టపుఁ గావిరంగువలన
	శశికాంతమణిపీఠి జాజువాఅఁగఁ గాయ
	లుత్తుంగకుచపాళి నత్తమిల్లఁ
	దరుణాంగుళీధూతతంత్రీస్వనంబుతో
	జిలిబిలిపాట ముద్దులు నటింప
	నాలాపగతిఁ జొక్కి యరమొడ్పుఁ గనుదోయి
	రతిపారవశ్య విభ్రమము దెలుపఁ

తే	బ్రౌడిఁ బలికించు గీత ప్రబంధములకుఁ
	గమ్రకరపంకరుహ రత్నకటక ఝణరఝు
	ణధ్వనిస్ఫూర్తి తాళమానములు గొలుప
	నింపు దళుకొత్త వీణ వాయింపుచుండి.

27

the red skirt inside the white half-sari
that veiled her thighs turned
the glowing moonstone beneath her
red, and the gourds of the vina rubbed against
her firm breasts as her delicate fingers seemed
to caress sweet music from the strings,
and she was languid with longing,
her eyes half-closed as if,
flowing with the song, she was lost
in making love, beyond herself
with pleasure, while the bracelets
on her hands chimed the rhythm of the song
she was singing with expert skill,
and there was joy, brilliant joy,
as she played on.

౨౮

ఉ అబ్బురపాటుతోడ నయ
నాంబుజములెవికసింపఁ గంతి పె
ల్లుబ్బి కనీనికల్వికసి
తోత్పలపంక్తులఁ గ్రమ్మరింపఁగా
గుబ్బ మెఱుంగుఁ జన్నవ గ
గుర్వైడువన్ మదిలోఁసఁ గోరికల్
గుబ్బటిలంగఁ జూచె నల
కూబరసన్నిభు నద్దరామరున్.

౨౯

ఉ చూచి ఱ్ఱులంఱ్ఱుఖత్కటక
సూచిత వేగ పదారవిందయ్యె
లేచి కుచంబులుం దుఱుము
లేనడు మల్లల నాడ నయ్యేడం
బూచిన యొక్క పోఁకనును
బోదియఁ జేరి విలోకనప్రభా
వీచికలం దదీయ పద
వీకలశాంబుధి వెల్లిగొల్పుచున్.

28

Amazed, she opened her eyes wide
and light poured out,
the pupils blossomed
like flowers, and her breasts
came alive as she thrilled to the sight
of that Brahman, a god on earth,
handsome as a young god,*
while thoughts went wild
in her mind.

29

She saw him. Stood up
and walked toward him, the music
of her anklets marking the rhythm,
her breasts, her hair, her delicate waist
trembling. Stood by a smooth areca tree
as waves of light from her eyes
flooded the path that he was walking.

---

* Specifically, Nalakubara, Kubera's son.

౩౦

మ   మునుమున్ పుట్టెడుకొంకు లొల్యము నిడన్
మొదంబు విస్తీర్ణతం
జొనుపం గోర్కులు గ్రేళు ద్రిప్ప మదిమై
చ్చుల్ఠెప్ప లల్లార్ప న
త్యనుషంగస్థితి ఠీచ్చుపా టొసఁగ నొ
య్యారంబునం జంద్రికల్
దనుకం జూచె లతాంగి ఘూసురుఁ బ్రపు
ల్లన్నేత్ర పద్మంబులన్.

౩౧

క   పంకజముఖి కప్పుడు మై
నంకురితము లయ్యెఁ బులక లావిష్మృత మీ
నాంకానలసూచక ధూ
మాంకురములుఁ బోలె మఱియు నతనిం జూడన్.

30

First there was doubt,
a certain hesitation,
then a widening joy as
desires raced within her:
her mind was crying "Yes!"
her eyelids blinking,
for she was close to him now,
unable to move,
as her eyes, wide as the open lotus,
enfolded him in brilliant moonbeams.

31

She stared at him.
Like tiny bursts of smoke
that proved she was burning
with love, the hairs on her body
stood on end.

౩౨

ఉ తొంగలితెప్పలం దొలంగం
ద్రోయుచుం బైపయి విస్తరిల్లు క
న్నుంగవ యాక్రమించుకొను
నో ముఖచంద్ర నటంచుం బోవనీ
కంగజుం డానవెట్టి కది
యన్ గుటి వ్రాసె ననంగ జాటి సా
రంగమదంబు లేజెమటం
గ్రమ్మె లలాటము డిగ్గి చెక్కులన్.

౩౩

మ అనిమేషస్థితి మాన్పె బిత్తరపుంజూ
పస్వేదతావృత్తి మా
న్పె నవస్వేదసమృద్ధి బోధకళ మా
న్పైన్ మోహవిభ్రాంతి తో
డనె గీర్వాణవధూటికిన్ భ్రమరకీ
టన్యాయ మొప్పన్ మను
ష్యుని భావించుట మానుషత్వము మెయిం
జూపట్టె నానత్తటీన్.

౩౪

వ ఇట్లతని రూపరేఖావిలాసంబులకుం జొక్కి
యక్కమలపత్రేక్షణ యాత్మగతంబున.

100

32
Musk trickled in thin lines of sweat
from her forehead to her cheeks,
as if the god of desire were marking a limit
for her still-widening eyes,
lest they shake off their lids entirely
and take over
her face.

33
Fluttering glances healed
her inability to blink, and for the first time
she was sweating.[6] Even her surpassing
understanding was healed by the new
confusion of desire. Like the beetle that,
from concentrating on the bee, *becomes*
a bee,[7] by taking in that human being
she achieved humanity
with her own body.

34
Drunk on his beauty and movements, she was thinking:

౩౫

ఉ ఎక్కడివాఁడె యక్రుతన
యెందు జయంత వసంత కంతులన్
జక్కఁదనంబునం గెలువఁ
జాలెడువాఁడు మహీసురాన్వయం
బెక్కడ యీతనువిభవ
మెక్కడ యేలని బంటుగా మరం
డక్కఁగొనంగరాదె యక
టా నను వీఁడు పరిగ్రహించినన్.

౩౬

సీ వదనప్రభూతలావణ్యాంబుసంభూత
కమలంబు లన వీని కన్ను లమరు
నిక్కి వీనులతోడ నెక్కసక్కెములాడు
కరణి నున్నవి వీని ఘనభుజములు
సంకల్పసంభవాస్థానపీఠిక వోలె
వెడఁదరొయ్యె కనుపట్టు వీని యురము
ప్రతిఘటించు చిగుళ్ళపై నెట్టువాఁటిన
రీతి నున్నవి వీని మృదుపదములు

తే నేరటేటియసల్తెచ్చి నీరజాప్తు
సానఁ బట్టిన రాపాడి చల్లి మెదిపి
పదను సుధ నిడి చేసెనో పద్మభవుఁడు
వీనఁ గాకున్న గలదె యీ మేని కాంతి.

102

35

"Where did he come from, this man
more lovely than Kubera's son or Spring
or the moon or Love himself?[8] There's no one
to compare to him.
Can a Brahman be so handsome? If only
he would take me, Love
would be my slave.

36

His face is an ocean of beauty, and his eyes
the lotus blossoms moving on the waves.
His shoulders are high enough
to rub against his ears.
His wide chest is the throne
where the love god holds court.
His tender feet are red with anger
at the leaf buds that dare to rival them.
Brahma the creator must have brought mud
from the Jambu River, mixed it with motes
of sunlight, and kneaded in the elixir of life
to produce a perfect texture
when he made him.

౩౽

క సుర గరు డోరగ నర ఖే
చర కిన్నర సిద్ధ సాధ్య చారణ విద్యా
ధర గంధర్వ కుమారుల
నిరతము గనుగొనమె పోల నేర్తురె వీనిన్.

౩౮

మ అని చింతించుచు మీనకేతనధను
ర్ఝ్యాముక్త నారాచ దు
ర్ధిన సమ్మోర్చిత మానసాంబురుహయై
దీపించు పెందత్తఆం
బునఁ బేఠెత్తిన లజ్జ నంఫ్రికటకం
బుల్మ్రోయ నడ్డంబు ని
ల్చిన నయ్యచ్చరఁ జూచి చేరఁ జని ప
ల్కెన్ వాఁడు విబ్రాంతుఁడై.

37

We've seen them all.
Gods, *garuḍas, nāgas,*
those who move through the sky like *kinnaras,* siddhas,
    sādhyas,
cāraṇas, vidyādharas, and gandharvas, and then humans—
we've seen young males from all these classes.
None of them can compare with him."

38

Her heart was shaken by
overpowering passion, like a lotus
caught in a storm. In haste,
breaking out of her shyness, her anklets ringing,
she stood directly in his path. He saw her,
very close, and said, in some confusion:

౩౯

ఉ ఎవ్వతె వీవు భీతహరి
ణేక్షణ యొంటిc జరించె దోట లే
కివ్వనభూమి భూసురుcడ
నేc బ్రవరాఖ్యుcడc ద్రోవ తప్పితిం
గ్రొవ్వున నిన్నగాగ్రమున
కుం జనుదెంచి పురంబుc జేర నిం
కెవ్వెధిc గాంతుc దెల్పcగద
వే తెరు వెద్ది శుభంబు నీ కగున్.

౪౦

క అని తనకథ నెఱీంగించినc
దన కనుcగవ మొఱుంగు లుబ్బుc దాటంకములుం
జనుcగవయు నడుము వడcకcగ
వనిత సెలవివాఆ నవ్వె వానికి ననియెన్.

౪౧

ఉ ఇంతలు కన్నులుండc దెరు
వెవ్వరి వేcడెదు భూసురేంద్ర యే
కాంతమునందు నున్న జవ
రాంద్ర నెపంబిడి పల్కరించులా
గింతియ కాక నీ వెఱుంగ
వే మును వచ్చిన త్రోవచొప్పు నీ
కింత భయంబు లే కడుగ
నెల్లిద మైతిమి మాట లేటికిన్.

39

"Who are you, young woman
with darting eyes like a frightened doe, moving alone
in this wild land? I'm a Brahman.
My name is Pravara.
I've lost my way. Like a fool,
I chose to come to this mountain peak.
I want to go home. What's the way
out? Show me, and god will bless you."

40

As he told her his story, her eyes
grew bright. Her earrings, breasts, and waist
were quivering now, as she parted her lips
and smiled:

41

"You have such beautiful eyes yourself—can't you see
your way? You just want to strike up
a conversation with a woman you found
alone. Surely you know
the way you came. You ask so boldly.
Maybe you just want to play."

౪౨

వ   అని నర్మగర్భంబుగాc బలికి క్రమ్మఱి నమ్ముగువ
యమ్మహీసురున కిట్లనియె.

౪౩

సీ   చిన్ని వెన్నెలకందు వెన్నుదన్ని సుధాబ్ధిc
      బొడమిన చెలువ తోcబుట్టు మాకు
      రహి వుట్ట జంత్రగాత్రముల నూల్గరంగించు
      విమలగాంధర్వంబు విద్య మాకు
      ననవిల్తు శాస్త్రంపు మినుకు లావర్తించు
      పని వెన్నతోడc బెట్టినది మాకు
      హాయమేధ రాజసూయము లనc బేర్పడ్డ
      సవనతంత్రంబు లుంకువలు మాకుc

తే   గనకనగసీమc గల్పవృక్షముల నీడc
      బచ్చరాచట్టుగమి రచ్చపట్టు మాకుc
      పద్మసంభవ వైకుంఠ భర్గ సభలు
      సాముగరిడీలు మాకు గోత్రమరేంద్ర.

42

So she said, teasing him, playfully hiding her meaning,
    and went on:

43

"The goddess born from the ocean of milk*
in the wake of the crescent moon
is our sister. Our gift is in making
music to fan desire, with voice and lute,
so pure it can melt a stone.
The arts and sciences of making love
come naturally to us, with our mother's milk.
Men go through huge sacrifices—offering up
horses, crowning kings[9]—just
to win our hand. We perform
on stages set with emeralds, in the shade
of wishing trees on Golden Mountain,
and the courts of the great gods
are where we hone our skills.

———

* Lakshmi.

౪౪

క పేరు వరూధిని విప్రకు
మార ఘృతాచీ తిలోత్తమా హరిణీ హే
మా రంభా శశిరేఖ లు
దారగుణాఢ్యలు మదీయలగు ప్రాణసఖుల్.

౪౫

మ బహురత్నద్యుతి మేదురోదర దరీ
భాగంబులం బొల్చు ని
మ్మిహికాహర్మ్యమునం జరింతు మెపుడుం
ప్రేమన్ నభోవాహినీ
లహరీ శీతలగంధవాహపరిఖే
లన్మంజరీసౌరభ
గ్రహణేందిందిర తుందిలంబు లివి మ
త్కాంతార సంతానముల్.

౪౬

క భూసుర కైతవకుసుమశ
రాసన మాయింటి విందవైతివి గైకో
మ్మా సముదంచన్మణిభవ
నాసీనత సేద దేటి యాతిథ్యంబున్.

44

My name, young man,
is Varuthini. You must have heard
of Ghritaci, Tilottama, Harini,
Hema, Rambha, and Sasirekha.[10]
They're my friends.

45

We spend our days in love,
wandering through caves lit by jewels
on Snow Mountain. Cool winds
rinsed by the spray of the heavenly Ganges
play upon blossoms alive with bees
on the wishing trees in my private gardens.

46

You say you're a Brahman, but really
you're the king of love. You have come to me
as a guest; allow me to welcome you
to my jeweled home, where you can rest.

౪౭

తే కుందనమువంటి మేను మధ్యందినాత
పోష్మహతిఁ గందె వడ దాఁకె నొప్పులొలుకు
వదన మస్మద్ద్యహంబు పావనము సేసి
బడలికలు వాసి చను మన్న బ్రాహ్మణుండు.

౪౮

ఉ అండజయాన నీ వొసఁగు
నట్టి సపర్యలు మాకు వచ్చె నిం
దుండఁగ రాదు పోవలయు
నూరికి నింటికి నిప్పు డేను రా
కుండ నొకండు వచ్చి మటీ
యొందునె భక్తియ చాలు సత్క్రియా
కాండముఁ దీర్ప వేగ చనఁ
గా వలయుం గరుణింపు నాపయిన్.

౪౯

ఉ ఏ నిఁక నిల్లు సేరుటకు
నెద్ది యుపాయము మీ మహత్త్యముల్
మానిని దివ్యముల్మదిఁ ద
లంచిన నెందును మీ కసాధ్యముల్
గానము గానఁ దల్లి ప్రజ
లన్ ననుఁ గూర్పు మటన్న లేఁత న
వ్యాననసీమఁ దోఁప ధవ
ళాయతలోచన వాని కిట్లనున్.

47

The noon sun has burned your body, tender as gold;
the wind has wilted your handsome face.
Honor my house by your presence,
refresh yourself here for a while."

48

The Brahman answered:
"Your offer, young lady, is very kind,
but I have to go.
Home. To my village. Now.
Consider I have come.
What counts is your affection.
I have rituals to perform.
I have to go. Fast.
Forgive me, please.

49

There must be some way
I can reach my home. You have
the power. You're a woman of the gods.
There is nothing you cannot do.
Mother, bring me to my people."

A little smile played on her lips, reflected in her eyes.

೫౦

ఉ ఎక్కడియూరు కాల్ నిలువ
కింటికిఁ బోయెద నంచుఁ బల్కె దీ
వక్కట మీకుటీరనిల
యంబులకున్ సరిరాక పోయెనే
యిక్కడి రత్నకందరము
లిక్కడి నందనచందనోత్కరం
బిక్కడి గాంగసైకతము
లిక్కడి యా లవలీనికుంజముల్.

೫౧

ఉ నిక్కము దాఁప నేల ధర
ణీసురనందన యింక నీపయిం
జిక్కె మనంబు నాకు ననుఁ
జిత్తజుబారికి నప్పగించెదో
చొక్కి మరందమద్యముల
చూఆలఁ బాటలువాడు తేంట్ల సొం
పెక్కినయట్టి పూవుఁబొద
రిండ్లను గోఁగిట గారవించెదో.

೫౨

క అనుటయుఁ బ్రవరుం డిట్లను
వనజేక్షణ యిట్లు వలుక వరుసయె వ్రతులై
దినములు గడపెడు విప్రులఁ
జనునే కామింప మది విచారము వలదే.

50

"Where is that village of yours?
You won't even rest your feet, you only want
to go home. What a loss!
Are your village huts better than
what is here, our jewel-lit caves,
sandalwood gardens, sandbanks on the river,
these beds of moonlight vines?

51

"To tell you the truth,
my mind is stuck on you. Do you want to leave me
to the torments of love, or hold me
on ravishing beds of flowers where the bees sing,
drunk on honey?"

52

So she had said it—and Pravara replied,
"Young woman, how can you say that
to me, a Brahman committed
to the rites day after day? This love
is not proper. Don't you know that?

౯3

ఉ వేలిమియున్ సురార్చనయు
విప్రసపర్యయుఁ జిక్కె భుక్తికిన్
వేళ యతిక్రమించె జన
నీజనకుల్కడు వృద్ధు లాఁకటన్
సొలుచుఁ జింతతో నెదురు
సూచుచునుండుదు రాహితాగ్ని నేఁ
దూలు సమస్తధర్మములుఁ
దెయ్యలి నేఁడిలు సేరకుండినన్.

౯౪

ఉ నావుడు విన్నఁబాటు వద
నంబున నించుక దేఁపఁ బల్కె నో
భావజరూప యిట్టి యెల
ప్రాయము వైదికకర్మనిష్ఠలం
బోవఁగ నింక భోగములఁ
బొందుట యొన్నఁడు యజ్ఞకోటులం
బావను లొటకున్ ఫలము
మా కవుఁగిళ్ళ సుఖించుటే కదా.

53

I have to feed the fires, worship the gods,
and serve the Brahmans.
It's long past meal time.
My mother and father are very old; they must be waiting
for me, no doubt uneasy, and faint with hunger.
As for me, I am responsible
for all the fires: if I don't reach home
today, my whole world
will crumble."

54

Now her face fell, as she said,
"Handsome man,
if you let your youth go by
in these dreadful rites,
when will you enjoy your life?
Isn't the point of all these rituals
to go to heaven
to make love to us?

౫౫

సీ సద్యోవినిర్చిన్న సారంగనాభికా
హృతమై పిసాళించు మృగమదంబు
కసటువో బీఱెండ౸ గర౸గి కట్టల నంటి
గమగమ వలచు చొక్కపు జవాజి
పొరలెత్తి ఘనసార తరువుల౸ దనుౡదాన
తొర౸గిన పచ్చకప్పురపు సిరము
గొజ్జంగి పూౡ బొదల్ గురియంగౡ బటికంపు
దొనల నిండినయట్టి తుహినజలము

తే వివిధకుసుమ కదంబంబు దివిజతరుజ
మృదులవసన ఫలాసవామేయ రత్న
భూషణంబులు గల విందు భోగపరుౡడ
వయి రమింపుము నను౸గూడి యనుదినంబు.

౫౬

క అంధనకు౸ గొఅయె వెన్నెల
గంధర్వాంగనల పొందు గా దని సంసా
రాంధువున౸ బడియె దకట ది
వాంధము వెలుౡగు గని గొంది నడ౸గిన భంగిన్.

118

55

Musk freshly taken from the navel of the musk deer—
fragrant civet stuck on branches and melted in the sun
to burn away its caustic taste—
powdered camphor that flaked and fell of itself
from camphor trees—
cool water dripping from *gojjangi* bushes
into crystal cups—to say nothing
of the endless supply of flowers, of many sorts,
soft silken clothes, fruit liqueurs, as many jewels
as you want—they're all here
for you. Enjoy yourself, and make love to me
every day.

56

Would a blind man miss the moonlight?
You're rejecting the company of a godly woman.
You prefer to fall back into the dark well
of family life. You're like an owl who sees daylight
and rushes to hide in its dark corner.

౯౨

ఉ ఎన్నిభవంబులం గలుగు
నిక్రశరాసన సాయకవ్యథా
ఖిన్నత వాడి వత్తలయి
కేలం గపోలము లూంది చూపులన్
విన్నదనంబు దేంపం గను
వేందుఱునం బయిగాలి సోంకినన్
వెన్నవలెం గరంగు నలి
వేణులం గౌంగిటం జేర్చుభాగ్యముల్.

౯౩

క కుశలతయే వ్రతముల నగు
నశనాయాసమున నింద్రియ నిరోధమునం
గృశుండ వయి యాత్మ నలంచుట
సశరీరస్వర్గ సుఖము సమకొని యుండన్.

౯౪

తే అనినం బ్రవరుండు నీ వన్న యర్థ మెల్ల
నిజము కామికుండైనవానికి నకామం
డిది గణించునె జలజాక్షి యొటీంగితేని
నగరమార్గంబుం జూపి పుణ్యమునం బొమ్ము.

120

57

How many lives must you live
to embrace a woman who melts like butter
the moment a breeze that has touched your body
touches her—and who grows thin and sad, dying to see
    you,
her cheeks resting on her palms? How many lives
must you live for that lucky moment?

58

Does it make sense to torture your body
by fasting and killing your senses, wearing yourself down,
while the heaven of happiness
is right in front of you?"

59

"Whatever you say makes good sense," replied Pravara,
"to a man who wants a woman. One who doesn't feel
    desire—
why should he care? If you know the way to my town,
lady with lovely eyes, show it to me now, and god
will bless you.

౬౦

క బ్రాహ్మణుౕ డిండ్రియవశగతి
జిహ్మచరణైక నిపుణ చిత్తజనిశితా
జిహ్మగముల పాలై చెడు
బ్రహ్మానందాధిరాజ్య పదవీచ్యుతుౕడై.

౬౧

వ అనిన నత్తెఆవ యక్కఆకరి పలుకుల కులికి గఆిగఆీం
గఆవౕ గరకరిం జెఆకువిలుకాౕడు పరౕగించు విరిదమ్మి
గొరకలు నెఆౕకులౕ జూఆుకుచుఆుక్కనం గాౕడినౕ
గడుం గెరలి పరిణత వివిధ విబుధతరుజనిత
మధురమధురసం బానుమదంబు నడటునం
జిదిమిన నెఆుంగక మదనహరునైనౕ జదురునం
గదియ గమకించు తిమురునం గొమిరెప్రాయంపు
మదంబునను ననన్యకన్యాసామాన్య
లావణ్యరేఖామదంబుననను నొంటిపాటునం గంటికిం
బ్రియుండై తంగేటిజుంటిచందంబునం గొంటుౕదనం
బెఆుంగకకుఆింగటనున్న యమ్మఆహీసురవరకుమారు
తారుణ్యమొఆ్గ్యంబులం జేసి తన వైదగ్ధ్యంబు
మెఆయౕ గలిగె నని పల్లవించు నుల్లంబు
నుల్లాసంబునం గదురు మదంబున నోసరించక
చంచలద్యుగంచలప్రభ లతని ముఖాంబుజంబునం
బొలయ వలయమణిగణచ్ఛాయాకలాపంబు లుప్పరం
బెగయౕ గొప్పు చక్కంజెక్కుచు జక్కవగిబ్బులం
బోని గబ్బిగుబ్బలం జొబ్బిల్లు కుంకుమరసంబునం
బంకిలంబులగు హారముక్తాతారకంబుల నఖ
కోరకంబులం గీఆి తీరువడం జేయుచుౕ బతిత
వనతరుకుసుమకేసరంబులు రాల్చు నెపంబునం

60

A Brahman lost in his senses is prey to the sharp arrows
of the love god, who is skilled at leading one astray.
Such a man will be ruined, falling from the path
that leads to the kingdom of pure joy."

61

When he said that, the woman was shaken by his cruel words.
The love god was shooting an unbroken stream of arrows
that cut into her tendermost places. She was enraged. She
was so drunk on the honey of those heavenly trees that
even if you pinched her, she wouldn't notice. She was proud
enough to face even the killer of desire himself in hand-to-
hand combat, and she had the full pride of youth and incom-
parable beauty, unknown among women. She'd found an
innocent, handsome young man, as easy to take in as the
honey of the *taṅgeḍu* flower, and because of him she could
show off all her graces. Her mind was dancing with joy. She
was completely confident, unhesitating. She cast flashes
from the corners of her tremulous eyes straight on to his
face. She raised her hands high, so that the light from her
bangles lit up the sky as she straightened her hair. With her
fingernails she scraped off spots of saffron that dotted the
necklace of pearls on her breasts, big and round as *cakravāka*
birds. As if to shake off filaments of flowers fallen from the
trees in the forest, she slipped the end of her sari off her
breasts. She was looking sternly in every direction in order to

బయ్యెద విదల్చి చక్క సవరించుచు నంతంతం బొలయు
చెలులం దలచూపక యుండఁ దత్తఅంబునంజేసి
బొమ్మముడిపాటుతో మగిడిమగిడి చూచుచుఁ
జిడిముడిపాటు చూపుల నంకురించు జంకెనల
వారించుచుం జేరి యిట్లనియె.

౬౨

శా ఎందే డెందము గందళించు రహిచే
నేకాగ్రతన్ నిర్వృతిం
జెందుం గుంభగతప్రదీపకళికా
శ్రీదీప నెందెందుఁ బో
కెందే నింద్రియముల్సుఖంబుఁ గను నా
యింపే పరబ్రహ్మ 'మా
నందో బ్రహ్మ' యటన్న ప్రాఁజదువు నం
తర్బుద్ధి నూహింపుమా.

౬3

తే అనుచుఁ దన్నొడఁబఱుచు నయ్యమరకాంత
తత్తఅముఁ జూచి యాత్మ నతండు దనకు
సిగ్గు వెగటును బొడమ నిస్స్పృహతఁ దెలుపు
నొక్కచిఅునవ్వు నవ్వి యయ్యువిద కనియె.

scare off her girlfriends, who might show up at any moment.
Now she approached him and said:

62

"When the heart unfolds in love, when it finds release
from within in undivided oneness, like a steady flame
glowing in a pot, when the senses attain
unwavering delight—that joy
is really real. Think about the ancient words:
ānando brahma, joy
is ultimate."

63

He saw her eagerness to get him,
and in his heart he felt embarrassed
and disgusted. He smiled a dry smile
to show his lack of interest
and said to her:

౬౪

శా ఈ పాండిత్యము నీకు(దక్క మటి యెం
దే(గంటిమే కామశా
స్త్రోపాధ్యాయివి నా వచించెదవు మే
లోహో త్రయీధర్మముల్
పాపంబుల్రతి పుణ్య మంచు నీ(క నే
లా తర్కముల్మొక్కల
క్మీపథ్యాగమసూత్ర పంక్తికివె పో
మీ సంప్రదాయార్థముల్.

౬౨

మ తరుణీ రేపును మాపు హవ్యములచే
తం దృప్తు(డో వహ్నిస
త్కరుణాదృష్టి నొసంగు సౌఖ్యము లెఱుం
గన్ శక్యమే నీకు నా
కరణుల్దర్భలు నగ్నులుం ప్రియములై
నట్లన్యముల్గా వొడల్
తిరమే చెప్పకు మిట్టి తుచ్చసుఖముల్
మీసాలపై(దేనియల్.

64

"You talk like a scholar. We've never seen one
like you before. You seem to be an expert in the science
of love. You say the path of the Vedas
is wrong, and making love is right. Why argue
with you? This is how your tradition interprets
the texts about the path to final freedom.

65

Young lady, how could you possibly know
that happiness that comes from the god of fire
when he is satisfied by offerings made to him day
after day, morning and evening? Nothing is dearer to me
than the firesticks, *darbha* grass, and the three fires
themselves. Will the body last? Don't speak to me
about these fleeting pleasures, like honey
on a mustache."

౬౬

చ అనుటయు మాట లేక హృద
యాబ్జము జల్లన మోము వెల్లనై
కనలుచు నీరుదేఱు తెలి
గన్నుల నాతనిఁ బుల్కు పుల్కనం
గనుఁగొని మాటలం బోదువు
గద్గదికం దలయూఁచి యక్కటా
వనిత తనంతఁ దా వలచి
వచ్చినఁ జుల్కన కాదె యేరికిన్.

౬౭

మ వెతలం బెట్టకు మింక నన్ననుచు నీ
వీబంధ మూడన్ రయో
ద్ధతి నూర్పుల్నిగుడన్ వడిన్ విరులు చిం
దం గొప్ప వీడం దనూ
లత తోడ్తోఁ బులకింపగా ననునయా
లాపాతిదీనాస్యయై
రతిసంరంభము మీఱి నిర్ఝరవధూ
రత్నంబు పైపాటునన్.

128

66

So he said. She had no words. Her heart
sank, and her face went pale. Inside
she was on fire. With tears in her eyes
she looked at him, showing him
she was displeased. She shook her head
and said, her voice quivering:
"That's how it is. When a woman comes
asking for love on her own, men think
she's cheap.

67

Don't torture me anymore." She rushed at him,
the knot of her sari coming undone, her breath
coming faster, hair falling loose and scattering flowers,
her body tingling. Her face was begging him.
She—immortal beauty that she was—was desperate
to make love.

౬౭

శా॥ ప్రాంచద్భూషణ బాహుమూల రుచితోఁ
బాలిండ్లు పొంగారఁ బై
యంచుల్మోవఁగఁ గౌఁగిలించి యధరం
బాసింప 'హా శ్రీహరీ'
యంచున్ బ్రహ్మణుఁ డీర మోమిడి తదీ
యాంసద్వయం బంటి పొ
మ్మంచుం ద్రోచెఁ గలంచునే సతుల మా
యల్ధీరచిత్తంబులన్.

౬౯

క॥ త్రోపుపడి నిలిచి ఘనల
జ్జా పరవశ యగుచుఁ గొప్పు సవరించి యొడల్
దీపింప నతనిఁ జూచుచఁ
గోపమునం జూచి క్రేఁటుకొనుచుం బలికెన్.

౭౦

ఉ॥ పాటున కింతు లోర్తురె కృ
పారహితాత్మక నీవు త్రోవ ని
చ్చోట భవన్నఖాంకురము
సోఁకెఁ గనుంగొనుమంచుఁ జూపి య
ప్పాటలగంధి వేదననె
పం బడి యేడ్చెఁ గలస్వనంబుతో
మీటిన విచ్చు గుబ్బచను
మిట్టల నశ్రులు చిందువందఁగన్.

68

She fell on him, pressed against him with her swelling
breasts, lit up by the jewels on her upper arms.
She pursed her lips, expecting him to kiss her.
"God help me!" cried the Brahman,
turning his face away. Then he put his hands
on her shoulders and pushed her hard.
Strong minds aren't disturbed by the games
women play.

69

She almost fell, but stood her ground.
She was deeply ashamed.
She fixed her hair. Her body was radiant.
With burning anger she looked at him,
cleared her throat, and said:

70

"You stone-hearted man! Can you push a woman
just like that? Look what you did. You've hurt me here
with your nails." She showed him. Then she started
to cry, sweetly sobbing as if she were in pain, her tears
rolling down her round, full breasts.

౬౧

క ఈ విధమున నతికరుణము
గా వనరుహనేత్ర కన్నుగవ ధవళరుచుల్
గావిగిన నేఁచ్చి వెండియు
నా విప్రకుమారుఁ జూచి యలమటఁ బల్కెన్.

౬౨

ఉ చేసితి జన్మముల్దపము
చేసితి నంటి దయావిహీనతం
జేసిన పుణ్యముల్ఫలము
సెందునె పుణ్యము లెన్నియేనియుం
జేసినవాని సద్గతియె
చేకుఆ భూతదయార్ద్ర బుద్ధి కో
భూసురవర్య యింత దల
పోయవు నీ చదు వేల చెప్పుమా.

71

She wept plaintively, her white eyes, lovely as the lotus,
turning red. Looking sadly at the Brahman, she said:

72

"You said you've made offerings to the fire
and prayed. Did any good come from all those things
you've done with no kindness in your heart?
All you need is kindness—and the rest
will follow. What use is your learning if you don't know
this simple truth?

౨౩

సీ వెలివెట్టిరే బాడబులు పరాశరుఁ బట్టి
దాశకన్యాకేళిఁ దప్పుఁజేసి
కులములో వన్నె తక్కువయ్యైనే గాధి
పట్టికి మేనక చుట్టటికము
ననుపుకాఁడై వేల్పు నాగవాసముఁ గూడి
మహిమ గొల్పడియొనే మాందకర్ణి
స్వారాజ్య మేలంగ నీరైరె సుర లహ
ల్యాజారుఁ డైన జంభాసురారి

తే వారికంటెను నీ మహత్త్వంబు ఘనమె
పవనపర్ణాంబుభక్షులై నవసి యినుప
కచ్చడాల్గట్టుకొను మునిమ్రుచ్చు లెల్లఁ
దామరసనేత్ర లిండ్ల బందాలు గారె.

౨౪

తే అనిన నేమియు ననక యవ్వనజగంధి
మేని జవ్వాదిపస గదంబించు నొడలు
గడిగికొని వార్చి ప్రవరుండు గర్భపత్య
వహ్నిని ట్లని పొగడె భావమునఁ దలంచి.

73

Did Brahmans expel Parashara from his caste because of
what he did with that fisher girl?
Did Vishvamitra lose status in his clan
because he took Menaka?
Did the sage Mandakarni lose his powers
when he lived with godly women?
Did the gods dismiss Indra from his throne
just because he was Ahalya's lover?[11]
Are you greater than all of them?
All those pseudo-sages who pretend to live
on wind, water, and leaves, who wear chastity belts made
   of iron—
aren't they prisoners in the arms of ravishing women?"

74

Pravara didn't say anything. He washed off the fragrance
of her body, still lingering on his skin. He took a cleansing
sip of water. He praised
the household fire, forming it in his mind.

౨౫

మ దివిషద్వర్గము నీ ముఖంబునన తృ
ప్తిం గాంచు నిన్నీశుఁగా
స్తవముల్సేయు శ్రుతుల్సమస్త జగదం
తర్యామివిన్ నీవ యా
హవనీయంబును దక్షిణాగ్నియును నీ
యం దుద్భవించుం గ్రతూ
త్సవసంధాయక నన్నుఁ గావఁగదవే
స్వాహావధూవల్లభా.

౨౬

ఉ దానజపాగ్నిహోత్రపర
తంత్రుఁడనేని భవత్పజాంబుజ
ధ్యానరతుండనేనిఁ బర
దారధనాదులఁ గోరనేని స
న్మానముతోడ నన్నుసద
నంబున నిల్పు మినుండు పశ్చిమాం
భోనిధిలోనఁ గ్రుంకకయ
మున్న రయంబున హవ్యవాహనా.

75

"God of fire, all the gods are fed
through your mouth. The texts praise you
as the Lord. You live inside all worlds.
The offering fire and the southern fire
are born from you. You make all rites
a celebration. Loving husband of Svaha:
Help me now!

76

If I've truly been devoted to giving, praying,
and keeping the fires alive—if my mind is always
focused on your feet—if I have never wanted
another man's wife or money—
put me in my house, this minute, in dignity,
before the sun sinks into the western sea."

౬౨

 వ   అని సంస్తుతించిన నగ్నిదేవుం డమ్మహీదేవు దేహంబున
సన్నిహితం డగుటయు నమ్మహో భాగుండు గండు మీఁటి
పొడుపుఁగొండ
నఖండసంధ్యారాగప్రభామండలాంతర్గతుండగు
పుండరీకవనబంధుండునుంబోలె
నుత్తప్రకనకద్రవధారాగౌరంబగు తనుచ్ఛాయాపూరంబున
నక్కాన వెలింగించుచు నిజగమననిరోధిని యగు
నవ్వరూథిని హృదయకంజమున రంజిల్లు
నమందానురాగరసమకరందంబు
నందంద పొంగంజేయుచుఁ బావకప్రసాదలబ్ధంబగు
పవనజవంబున నిజమందిరంబున కరిగి
నిత్యకృత్యసత్కర్మకలాపంబులు నిర్వర్తించె నని
మార్కండేయుండు క్రోష్టికిం జెప్పెనని చెప్పిన.

౬౩

క   జైమిని యా దివ్యఖగ
గ్రామణులంజూచి వేడ్క గదలుకొనంగా
నామీఁద వరూథిని విధ
మే మయ్యె నెఱుంగఁ జెప్పరే నా కనుడున్.

77

As he praised him like this, Fire came into his body. Pravara
became stronger. Like the sun in the midst of the red
morning sky, his body was shining like a flood of molten
gold, turning the forest yellow and intensifying the passion
for him in the heart of that woman who was holding him
back from going. With the speed of wind, a gift of the
god of fire, he reached his home and performed his daily
rituals. That's what Markandeya told Kroshti.

78

Jaimini looked at the birds, his curiosity aflame,
and said: "What happened after that to Varuthini?
Tell me."

౯౯

శా॥ నిస్తంద్రప్రతిభా సుధీనుత దిశో
న్మీలద్యశశ్శ్రీవధూ
హస్తాగ్రామలకాయమాన మహనీ
యాంభోజగర్భాండ సై
న్యస్త్రోమొత్తరజో వ్రజస్థగిత కృ
ష్ణాగోతమీమధ్యభూ
మ్యస్త్రోకోత్కలరాట్పురీహరణలీ
లావార్య శౌర్యోదయా.

౭౦

క॥ బిసరుహనయనా నవవిధ
కుసుమాయుధ యవధికుధరకూటాంచల భూ
విస్ఫుమర తేజశ్చుంపక
భసల దసత్కీర్తిమలిన పరిపంథిన్నృపా.

79

King, your mind is always awake.
Intelligent people praise you.
Your fame, spreading in all directions,
holds the world in its hand, like a life-giving fruit.
The dust raised by your marching army
cloaks the country between the Krishna and Godavari rivers.
Your unstoppable courage casually conquered
the capital of the Utkala* kings!

80

In the eyes of women in this world, you're a new god of love.
Your power, reaching to the mountain at the end of all space,
is like the champak flower, untouched by black bees, which are
the bad names of your foes. [12]

---

* Modern Orissa.

౬౩

కవిరాజవిరాజితము.

నల నృగ రంతి భగీరథ భారత
నందన కల్ప యనల్పయశ
శ్చులుకితలోక విలోకివధూజన
సూనశరాసన మానఖనీ
ప్రళయఘనాఘన ఘోష జయానక
భాంకృతి భీమచపేట లుఠ
త్కులబరిగీకటకక్షితిరక్షక
కన్నడరాజ్య రమారమణా.

గద్యము.

ఇది శ్రీమదాంధ్ర కవితాపితామహ సర్వతోముఖాంక
పంకజాక్ష పాదాంబుజాధీన మానసేందిందిర
నందవరపుర వంశోత్తంస శఠకోపతాపస ప్రసాదాసాదిత
చతుర్విధ కవితామతల్లి కాల్లసాని చొక్కయామాత్యపుత్ర
పెద్దనార్య ప్రణీతంబైన స్వారోచిషమనుసంభవం బను
మహాప్రబంధంబునందు ద్వితీయాశ్వాసము.

81

You're like the legendary emperors of the past,
Nala, Nriga, Ranti, Bhagiratha, and Yudhishthira.
Your endless fame swallows up the world.
You drive any woman who sees you
mad with love. You're deep
in dignity. The heartbreaking pounding
of your battle drums broke the king of Kataka
in his capital Kalabarigi, so he fell to the earth.
Great king of the Kannada land!

The great poem called "The Birth of Svarochisha Manu" was
written by Allasani Cokkayamatya's son Peddanarya, known
to all as the "Creator God of Telugu Poetry," who comes from
a family of Nandavara Brahmans, whose mind hovers like a
bee around the lotuslike feet of lotus-eyed Vishnu, and who was
blessed by his guru Shathakopa with the ability to compose all
four kinds of fine poetry. Chapter 2 ends here.

తృతీయాశ్వాసము

౧

క శ్రీవేంకటేశ పదప
    ద్మావేశిత సదయహృదయ హరనిటల నట
    త్నావక పరిభావి మహః
    ప్రావృతనిఖిలాశ కృష్ణరాయమహీశా.

౨

వ అవధరింపు మమ్మహోత్తునకుం బక్తు లిట్లనియె.

౩

శా ఆ భూదేవకుమారుఁ డేఁగినఁ దదీ
    యానూన రమ్యాకృతిం
    దా భావంబున నిల్పి యంగభవకో
    దండోగ్రమార్వేరవ
    క్షోభాకంపిత ధైర్యయై యలఁత న
    చ్చే నిల్వ కచ్చెల్వ త
    ద్బాభృన్మేఖల వెంటఁ గానలబడిన్
    దుఃఖాబ్ధినిర్మగ్నయై.

144

Chapter 3

1

Your heart is always reaching out to
the feet of the Lord of the Venkata Hills.
Your splendor, brighter than the fire
in Shiva's third eye, fills all space.
Listen, King Krishnaraya!

2

This is what the birds said to that great man:

3

When the young Brahman left her,
his captivating image still fixed in her mind,
Varuthini was badly shaken by the incessant twanging
of the love god's bow. She couldn't stay there
anymore. She started walking, lost
in sorrow, on the forest paths curving round the mountain.

145

౪

క తిరుగుచు ధరణీసురవరుc
దరిగిన చొప్పరసి యరసి యటc(గానక యా
హరిణాంకముఖి సఖీజన
పరివృతయై మగిడిం వచ్చి భావములోనన్.

౫

ఉ అక్కట వాc(డు నాతగుల
మాటిడిసేసి దయావిహీనుc(డై
చిక్కక త్రోచి పోయె దరిc
జేరc(గరాని వియోగసాగరం
బెక్కడ నీc(దుదాన నీc(క
నీకొఱినోములు నోc(చినట్టి నే
నెక్కడ వాని కౌంగి లది
యెక్కడ హా విధి యేమి సేయుదున్.

౬

ఉ కమ్మనికుందనంబు కసు
గందనిమే నెలదేcటి దాcటులన్
బమ్మెరవోవ దీలుc దెగ
బారెడు వెండ్రుక లిందుబింబముం
గిమ్మననీదు మోము గిరి
క్రేపులు మూcపులు కొను గానరా
దమ్మకచెల్ల వాని విక
చాంబకములశతపత్రజైత్రములౌ.

4

She walked and walked, looking at all the paths
he might have taken, and couldn't find him.
She came back, followed by her girlfriends,
and she was thinking:

5

"Damn it, that heartless man
walked away from my love.
He pushed me into an endless ocean
of longing. How can I keep myself
from drowning? My prayers
were too few, and his embrace
is too far. God, what can I do?

6

His body is fragrant gold.
His long hair defies the darkest of dark bees.
His face outshines any moon.
His shoulders are tall as mountains.
His waist is so thin you can't see it.
And as for his gleaming eyes—they're far beyond
the beauty of a lotus in full bloom.

౭

ఉ చొక్కపుఁ బ్రాయమున్ మిగుల
సోయగముం గల ప్రాణనాయకుం
డెక్కుడు వశ్యతన్ రతుల
నేఁకటఁ దీర్చి సమేళ మొప్పఁగా
నక్కున గారవించి ప్రియ
మందఁగ నోఁచని యింతిదైన యా
చక్కఁదనం బదేమిటికి
జవ్వన మేటికిఁ బ్రాణ మేటికిన్.

౮

ఉ ఎంత తపంబు సేసి జని
యించిన వారొకో మర్త్యభామినుల్
కాంతుఁడవజ్ఞ చేసినను
గాయము వాయుదు రే నమర్త్యనై
చింతల వంతలం జివికి
సిగ్గటితిన్మృతి లేని నాదుచె
ల్వింతయు శూన్యగేహమున
కెత్తిన దీపిక యయ్యె నక్కటా.

౯

వ అని వితర్కించుచుఁ గ్రించుఁదనంబునం
బునఃపునః పరిభవకారియై కాతీయంబెట్టు సిరిపట్టి
బెట్టెయం గాఁడి చను నలరంపకట్టియల గుట్టుచెడి
వెచ్చవెచ్చనై హెచ్చి విచ్చలవిడిం గాయు నుద్దామ
విరహ దవదహనదాహంబున దేహంబు తల్లడిల్ల

7

If a woman doesn't have the good luck
of having a lover who is young and handsome
and who makes love to her whenever she wants,
who really loves her, what good is her beauty
and her youth? Why be alive?

8

Human women are lucky.
If their lover rejects them, they die.
But me—I'm immortal! I have to suffer
this shameless sorrow. My beauty
that cannot die is a lamp lit
in an empty house."

9

All this was in her mind, and meanwhile the mean-spirited
love god was shooting arrows of flowers at her, humiliat-
ing her over and over. Because of them, her defenses were
breached, and her body started to shake, scorched by the
wildfire of longing. She sighed long and hard, so that a

మల్లడిగొని పెల్లడరు నిట్టూర్పుగాడ్పు విసరులం గస
రెత్తి యంతకంత కంతరంగంబున నింతంతనరాక
పొంగి చింతాసాగరంబు వేగిరంబ వెల్లివోడిచె ననం
దుడిచిన నడంగక సారెకుం దారకల నీరిక లెత్తు
పాగరన నిగనిగ లినుమడిగ నిగుడ మిగులు వగల
బుగులుబుగులున నెగసి యొగసి యొప్పులకుప్ప
లగు తెప్పలం జిప్పిలు కాటుక లప్పళించి కరంచి
దరదళదరుణకమలదళ శోణంబులగు దృక్కోణంబులం
దిగువాఱు కన్నీరు చెన్నారు కర్ణద్వయీగోళంబులు నిండి
తనుతాపతప్తంబగు హాటకతాటంకయుగళంబునం
బడి క్రొంబోగ లెగయింప బిసకిసలయ సగంధంబగు
మణిబంధంబునఁ జికురబంధంబుఁ జేర్చుకొని పొరలం
దుటిమిన విరు లురుల నరవిరిసి కవిసి యిరులుకొను
గరగరని నెఱికురులు గుఱిగడవఁ బెరఁగినవగుటం
జేసి రాశివడి మొయిమూసికొని గ్రహగణంబులం జెన్నగు
మిన్ను విఱిగి పయింబడిన వడువున బెడంగువడఁ
గలయం దలకొను పులక మొలకపయిరునకుం
బాఱు దుర్వారవారిపూరంబనం గ్రమక్రమంబున
నంగంబులం గ్రమ్ము చెమ్మటల మిన్నేటి పెన్నీటివఱ్ఱున
మునుంగకుండ సవరించిన మించు కుంభప్లవంబనం
బరిభ్రష్టోత్తరీయంబై బయలువడి యబ్బురంపు
గుబ్బచనుదోయి నిబ్బరంపు మెఱుంగులీనం గుపిత
హరనయనశిఖిశిఖాభస్మీకృత స్మరవిరహాశోకంబునం
బడి చందురునిం బట్టుకొని యడలు రతిరమణీ
చందంబునం గుసుమితలతాంతనిశాంత
శశికాంతవేదికాంతరంబున మేను సేర్చి వివిధ
దశాంతరంబుల వేఁగుచుండె నంత.

burning wind stirred the ocean of grief to high tide. The brilliant pupils of her eyes, now red as lotus petals, seemed to be emitting dark smoke, for tears, which kept on coming even when she tried to wipe them away, melted her mascara and flowed down her cheeks onto her earrings—and they, hot from the touch of her body, steamed and sizzled. She rested her thick hair on her wrists, fragrant as lotus stems, and flowers were scattered everywhere as the hair came loose and, since it had grown so long, darkened her whole body as if the sky with its planets had fallen over her and made her still more beautiful. Like a flood rushing through a field of growing sprouts, sweat swept over her skin, bristling with goose-bumps; her lovely breasts, uncovered, looked like a raft made of two large pots to keep her from drowning in that overflow. She lay down on a moonstone covered with flowering vines, like Rati, the love god's wife, holding on to his friend the moon as she grieved for her husband, burnt to ash by Shiva's eye. She was going through the various agonies of love.

౧౦

చ తరుణీ ననన్యకాంత
నతిదారుణ పుష్పశిలీముఖవ్యథా
భర వివశాంగి నంగభవు
బారికి నగ్గముసేసి క్రూరుండై
యరిగె మహీసురాధముం డ
హంకృతితో నని రోషభీషణ
స్ఫురణ వహించెనో యన న
భోమణి దాల్చెం గషాయదీధితిన్.

౧౧

సీ ఉరుదరీకుహర సుస్తోత్థ శార్దూలముల్
ఝురవారి శోణిత శంకం ద్రావ
వనకుంజమధ్య శాద్వలచరన్మృగపంక్తి
దావపావక భీతిం దల్లడిల్ల
నాశ్రమాంతర భూరుహగ్రముల్మునికోటి
బద్ధకాషాయ విభ్రాంతిం జూడ
ఘనసానుశృంగ శృంగాటకంబులం గాంచి
యమరులు హేమాద్రి యనుచు వ్రాలం

తే గాసెం బేశలరుచిం గింశుకప్రవాళ
ఘుస్పణ కిసలయ కంకేళి కుసుమగుచ్ఛ
బంధుజీవ జపారాగ బాంధవంబు
లన్నగంబున జరతారుణాతపములు.

10

"That idiot of a Brahman, full of himself,
has cruelly left this young woman, who was totally
in love with him, to be tortured, helplessly,
by the fierce arrows of desire." As if on fire with anger
at this thought, the sun turned red.

11

Tigers, waking from sleep in mountain caves,
came to drink from the stream, thinking it was blood.
Deer roaming on the grassy slopes, among the trees,
were frightened, thinking the forest was on fire.
Sages in their hermitages looked up at the treetops to see
if their ochre robes were hung there to dry.
Gods descended on the peaks, mistaking them
for Meru, the Golden Mountain.
Scarlet as saffron, coral, or heaps of crimson flowers,
the soft, dense light of the setting sun
painted the forest red.

౧౨

శా శ్రేణుల్గట్టి నభోంతరాళమునంబాం
ఆం బక్షు లుష్ణాంశుపా
షాణవ్రాతము కోష్ణ మయ్యె మృగతృ
ష్ణావార్ధు లింకెన్ జపా
శోణం బయ్యెం బతంగబింబము దిశా
స్తోమంబు శోభాదరి
ద్రాణం బయ్యె సరోజషండములు ని
ద్రాణంబు లయ్యెం గడున్.

౧3

క తరణీ యిదె గ్రుంకుచున్నాం
డరుదెమ్మని చంద్రుం బిల్వ నరిగెడు రజనీ
తరుణీమణిదూతిక లన
నరిగెం దూర్పునకు నీడ లతిదీర్ఘములై.

౧౪

క క్రుంకె నపరాంబురాశిం
బంకజబంధుండు దదీయ బడబాముఖ వీ
క్లాంకురితకుతుకరథ్య ని
రంకుశవేగాపహృత శతాంగుండుం బోలెన్.

12

Birds flew in formation through the sky.
The hot sun stones cooled down.
Mirages of water dried up.
The orb of the sun turned red as the hibiscus rose.
Space was drained of color,
and the lotus went to sleep.

13

Shadows stretched toward the east, as if they were
messengers of love sent by night[1]
to tell the moon: "The sun is setting.
Come now."

14

The sun sank rapidly into the western ocean
as if the horses that pull the sun's chariot,
aroused by a glimpse of the mare's face[2]
under the water, had broken
into a gallop.

౧౫

వ   ఆ సమయంబున.

౧౬

సీ   ఏ విహంగముఁ గన్న నెలుఁగింఛుచును సారె
          కును సైకతంబులఁ గూడఁ దారుఁ
      దారి కన్గొని యది తనజోడు గాకున్న
          మెడ యెత్తి కలయంగ మింట నరయు
      నరసి కన్నీటితో మరలి తామర యెక్కి
          వదన మెండఁగ సరోవారి నద్దు
      నద్ది త్రావఁగ సైఁప కట్టెట్టు గన్గొని
          ప్రతిబింబ మీక్షించి బ్రమసి యుఱుకు

తే   నుఱికి యొఱకలు దడియ వేఁటొక్కతమ్మి
      కరుగు నరిగి రవంబుతోఁ దిరుగుతేంట్లఁ
      బోఁడుచు ముక్కున మఱియును బోపు వెదక
      సంజఁ బ్రియుఁ బాసి వగ నొక్క చక్రవాకి.

156

15

At that moment,

16

the *cakravākī* honks
whenever she sees a male and follows him
to the sandy shore. Following him, she sees
that he is not her mate, and now she stretches her neck
and scans the sky. Scanning, with tears in her eyes,
she returns to rest on a lotus leaf. Her mouth dry,
she sips a drop of water. Sipping it, not wanting more,
she looks this way and that, sees her own reflection
in the water, and jumps on it, thinking it might be
her beloved. Jumping in, her wings wet, she moves on
to another lotus. Moving on, forlorn, she pecks at the bees
humming there, then continues her search
as evening falls, to her grief.[3]

౧౭

సీ	రవిబింబపతనదీర్ఘ పయోధిగర్భని
	ర్గత శేషఫణీఫణారత్న రుచియొ
	దివసావసాన సంధీప్తాస్తగిరి శిఖా
	జ్యోతిర్లతా ప్రతానాతపంబొ
	తపనధూర్దండ నిర్దళితదిక్కటదృశ్య
	కమలజాండ కటాహ కనకఘృణియొ
	చండీశ తాండవోత్సవ సంభృతత్రకపా
	హస్తాగ్రదీపగభస్తి చయమొ

తే	ద్రాగ్విదాహచ్చిదావినిద్రాణ మదవ
	దంజనాలాన మూలశయ్యా విధాన
	వారుణాధోరణాకల్పితోరు శోణ
	మృత్తికా రాశియో యన మెఱసె సంధ్య.

౧౮

క	బహుళజలప్లవమాన
	ద్రుహిణాండము చెమ్మ యుడికి రూక్షార్కవిభా
	రహితతఁ గాటుకపట్టెను
	రహి చెడి యన నంధతమస రాసులు బెరసెన్.

17

The sky burned red.
Was it the ruby from the hood of the first snake
showing through the depths of the ocean that broke open
when the setting sun fell into it?
Was it the glow on Western Mountain
from phosphorescent vines that light up
at the end of every day?
Was it a golden light pouring from the vast pot
that is the universe, cracked open
when the sun's chariot smashed against it
with its front pole?
Was it light from the lamp held high by Night
when Shiva dances in fury?
Or was it the expanse of red earth spread by
the elephant driver of the western sky so that Anjana,
the huge elephant of the west, can lie down
at the base of his post and thus quench
his thirst?[4]

18

In the absence of sunlight to keep it dry,
the egg-shaped universe, which floats on water,
turned black with mold and lost its beauty—or so it
    seemed
as darkness spread through the sky.

౧౯

సీ. మృగనాభిపంకంబు మెయినిండ నలఁదిన
మాయాకిరాతి మైచాయఁ దిగడి
నవపింఛమయభూష లవధరించి నటించు
పంకజాక్షునిచెల్వు సుంక మడిగి
కాదంబ నికురంబ కలితమ్మై ప్రవహించు
కాళిందిగర్వంబుఁ గాకుసేసి
తాపించవిటపి కాంతార సంవృతమైన
యంజనాచలరేఖ నవఘళించి

తే. కవిసె మఱియును గాకోల కాలకంఠ
కంఠ కలకంఠ కరిఘటా ఖంజరీట
ఘనఘనాఘనసంఘాత గాఢకాంతిఁ
గటికిచీఁకటి రేదసీ గహ్వరమున.

౨౦

క. అంతటఁ బ్రాచి నిశాపతి
యంతికగతుఁ డౌట విని ముఖాలంబి తమః
కుంతలములు దీర్పఁగఁ గొను
దంతపుదువ్వెన యనంగ ధవళిమ దేఁచెన్.

160

19

It was darker than the skin of Parvati, who smeared musk
all over her body in order to turn herself
into a huntress.[5]
Darker than the dancing Krishna, adorned
with peacock feathers.
Darker than the Black River, Yamuna, with its flocks
of black-footed, black-beaked geese.
Darker than dark Anjana Mountain, covered with forests
of dark trees.
Dark like crows, the peacock's neck, the cuckoo,
herds of elephants, blackbirds, a mass of monsoon clouds.
That's how dark the darkness was that filled the earth.

20

Then a streak of white appeared in the eastern sky,
like an ivory comb that the lady of the east
picked up to comb her long, black hair
when she heard that the moon,
her lover, was on his way.

౨౧

చ	మరున కొసంగ గాలము త
మశ్చట గాటుకగా నవోదయ
స్పురదరుణప్రభాపథిక
శోణితసిక్త సితోడుభక్తమున్
హరిహాయదిజ్ఞభస్మ లము
నం బలి చల్లి వటాంకమున్ వసూ
త్కరభరితంబు నై వెలుంగ
గాంచి సుధానిధి నెత్తె నత్తటిన్.

౨౨

మ	జలజాగారపరంపరల్మఘవదా
శాభిత్తి దీంద్రించుచున్
దళమై వెన్నెలచిచ్చు లంటిన మిళ
ద్వాహ్యచ్ఛదశ్యామికా
చ్చలనం గంది ముడుంగుచో సిమసిమ
చ్ఛబ్ధంబుతో బుట్టు న
గ్గలపుం గ్రొంబొగలో యనంగ వెడలెన్
గర్భస్వనద్బృంగముల్.

162

21

Making the darkness a magical ointment for his eye, Time
mixed the redness of the rising moon, like a wayfarer's
blood, with white stars to make a dish of blood rice, which
he then offered in sacrifice in the eastern sky so he could
see the buried treasure of moonlight, marked by the
banyan in the moon. He saw it and lifted it high, a gift to
the god of love.[6]

22

As if the moonlight streaming from the east had singed
its outer petals black and thick smoke were pouring out
from inside with a sizzling sound,
the lotus closed as buzzing bees
fled in panic.

౨౩

సీ శిథిలంౖ కైరవదళశ్రేణి నొక్కులు దీరె
శశికాంతపంక్తుల జలము లూరెం
గేరి కాంతులతోం జకోరికల్రతింం గేరె
వారాశిగర్వంబు మేర మీటంం
ద్రోపడి యిరులు పటాపంచలై పాఱ
దిక్కుఖంబుల వింతతెలివి సేరెం
జక్రవాకంబు లబ్జకుడుంగములు దూఱంం
గామినీకాంతుల కలంంక దేఱె

తే మదనుం డమ్ముల నూఱి హిమంబు పేఱె
జడిసి విరహిణి వగం గూరె జారచోర
దర్పములు జాఱె రవికరతాప మాఱంం
జూడం జూడంగం దారక స్ఫురణ దాఱె.

౨౪

మ స్ఫుట సౌగంధిక రాగ రక్తరుచి మైంం
బూనెం జపాసన్నిధి
స్ఫటికంబట్లుదయాద్రి గైరిక శిర
స్నా నస్థితిం జంద్రుం డ
చ్చోటు వాయన్ శుచియయ్యె నొ(బ్రకృతి న
చ్చుండైన సన్మార్గియె
న్నటికిం గూటమివంక వచ్చువికృతి
న్మగ్నుండు గానేర్చునే.

23

Night lilies that had wilted by day were now sharp
    and fresh.
Moonstones everywhere were dripping wet.
Moonbirds, feasting on moonlight, made love
    with delight.
The pride of the ocean was at its peak.
Darkness, defeated, fled in fear.
Space smiled with a newfound clarity.
Ruddy geese hid inside the lotus patches.
Lovers stopped quarreling.
The love god honed his arrows.
Dew gathered.
A woman separated from her lover became still more sad.[7]
Adulterers and thieves took cover.
The sun's heat faded away.
Before your eyes even the stars
lost their light.

24

Rising over the peak of Eastern Mountain,
the moon took on redness from streaks of red rock,
like a crystal placed next to a red flower. As soon as he
    passed
that place, he became his natural, clean white.
That's how it is. Keeping bad
company can't turn a good man
bad forever.

౨౫

శా ఆరూఢస్థితిఁ జంద్రికాఢవళితా
జాండంబులోఁ జంద్రుఁ డీ
ప్పారెం గాలభిషగ్వరుం డవిరతం
బై కాముకశ్రేణికిన్
మారేత్స్నాహము నిల్వఁ బాదరసమున్
బంధించి గ్రాసార్థమై
క్షీరస్థాలికఁ బెట్టినట్టి గుటికా
సిద్ధౌషధంబో యనన్.

౨౬

తే రాజు తేజస్వియై గ్రహరాజుమీఁద
నలిగి దాడిగ వెంటాడ నిలువ కతఁడు
బెగడువడి పాఱుచోఁ జెఱ్ఱఁ దగిలినట్టి
ఛాయ యిది యన నీలలాంఛనము మెఱసె.

౨౭

తే కలయ జగమునఁ గలయట్టి నలుపు లెల్లఁ
దెలుపులుగఁ జేసి నీడలు దెలుపు సేయఁ
గా వశము గామిఁ బొడము దుఃఖమునఁ బోలె
సాంద్రచంద్రిక తుహినబాష్పములు గురిసె.

25

In a sky filled with moonlight, the moon itself
was a white pill that the great pharmacist who is Time
had concocted from mercury and served in a pot of milk
to men in love, to prolong their passion.

26

The moon, rife with energy, furious
at the sun, attacked him, and the sun
was frightened and ran away. His wife,
Shadow,[8] was taken prisoner. You can see
her still—the dark spot on the moon.

27

Moonlight turned everything that was dark in the world
white. Everything but shadows.
Grieving at this failure, she[9] shed
tears of dew.

౨౭

వ మఱియు వికసితకైరవంబు లగు సరోవరంబుల
నిజధవళధళధళ్యంబున నాక్రమించి యందు
నానందించు నరవిందమందిరకుం బుట్టినింటి
సొబగు చూపి, చూపఱకు నిందుబింబం బీది గ్రహంబు
లివి యను నంతరంబు లేకుండ నేకవర్ణంబు
గావించి, సేవించు చకోరకదంబంబుల పుక్కిళ్ళుకుం
వెక్కసంబై ముక్కులకు నెక్కి చిక్కంబడి యొండొండ
బొండుమల్లియల దండడిం దొరఁగు పుష్పాళ్ళ నుప్పతిల్లు
నెత్తావులకు వెకలులై యాడు మొకరి తుమ్మెదలు
రెదలు గల మెఱుంగుడంబురువులట్లు మిసమిసని
మెఆివ ససిమెఱుంగు మొత్తంబుల నుమిసి యుమిసి,
యందంద ప్రవహించు నిందూపల స్యందంబులకు
విందులగు నిందీవరమరందంబుల బెండడిం
బడి బందనగొను వలిమించుక్రొమ్మంచుటొదులీఁది
యాఁది వడిసడలి సుడివడుచు నొడలోము సోమరిగాలి
యలవీక సోఁకులం గదలెం గదల వనం గదలు
నుపవన కదళీ కేతకీ తాల హింతాల నారికేళ పూగావళీ
కోమల పలాశద్రోణికల నునుపుగల పొరల యొరల
శరధితరఁగల మీఁదనుం బోలె గిటీకొని, యెల్లవల్లికలుం
బూవక పూచిన ట్టుల్లసిల్ల తెల్లుల్లసిల్లిన చందంబునం
దెల్ల తెల్లనై, మొల్లమిగ నంతకంతకు దిగంతంబులు
దంతంబులు దీరిచిన యిదుపులుంబోలెఁ దీండ్రింప
రేయొండ దానగుటం జేసి యొండమావులం బుట్టించె
ననం బట్టుగల పటికంపురాచట్టునేలల నెట్టుకొని,
వెండియుం జిట్టకంబులకుం బెడమొగంబు వెట్టుకొని
పట్టఁబట్టం బోపు ప్రాణభర్తల వెంటంబడి నూపురంబులు
మొరయ వేనలులు విరియఁ గ్రమంబునం బుట్టు
నిట్టూర్పుపవనంబు జవంబునం బైటకొం గెడలింప
నందని కొఁగిటం బోదివి ప్రియంబు చిలుకం బలికి

28

Thick moonlight overpowered all the ponds of water lilies, blooming at night, with its shimmering whiteness, revealing to the goddess of wealth the true beauty of her place of birth—the milky ocean. It made everything into one vast whiteness, so no one could see difference anymore between the moon and the other planets. It choked the moonbirds, drinking it up with their beaks. It became thicker and thicker, settling on the wings of bees that were dancing amid jasmine pollen, so that they looked now like flickering white fireflies. It swam through rivulets of cold dew that had thickened with the flow of honey from white lotuses, like melting moonstones. As if flickering over the waves of the ocean, the moonlight filtered through thin layers of tender foliage from the trees in that pleasure grove—plantain, pandanus, palmyra, date, coconut, and betel—where a somnolent wind was losing speed, winding its way back and forth, so you couldn't tell if the leaves were moving or not moving. It made vines, still unblossomed, seem to bloom, like tassels of *rĕllu* reeds, white all over. In that thick, brilliant light, the very edges of space were glowing white, like doorways marked by elephant tusks. Settling on sparkling crystals, as if intent on creating mirages of its own, the moon acted the part of a nocturnal sun.

When men grew tired of being mocked by their women, they turned their faces and walked away, and the women, anklets chiming, their hair coming undone, rushed after them, trying to catch hold of them, and their breath, coming fast with the effort, blew the top part of their saris off their breasts, and still the lovers were out of reach, so the women,

ముద్దాడు జవరాండ్ర దంతచంద్రికల సాంద్రతం
బంతంబు మెఱసి, మంతనంపువేళల మాటతబ్బిబ్బునం
బుట్టు పొలయలుకలం దలలు వంచి రొద లేని
నాలియెడ్పు లేడ్పు ప్రియల ననునయింప నింపునం
జవవుమెఆసి చెక్కుటద్దంబులు నొక్కి మొగం బెగయ
నెత్తి ముత్తియంపుముంగఆ రంగునఁ గడలుకొను
బుడిబుడికస్నీటం బ్రతిఫలించి తుఆంగలించు
తనదు నిగనిగలు గనుంగొని నగెనగె ననుచుం
జుంబనం బిడం బోయి కెంగేల నదరంట వాటువడు
కాముకుల వెలవెలపాటుకూటువం గేటికిం బడగలెత్తి
పిండిచల్లినగతిం గాయ దాయ లజ్జించి బుజ్జవంబునం
బోదరిండ్లకుం దార్చి కాంతలం గవయు నంగనాచలగు
నంగనల యంగంబుల పస ముంగిటం బడఁ జలిత
కిసలయాంతరాళంబులం దూఱీతూఱీ యిరులు
విరియించి పతుల ప్రార్థనంబులం బుంభావ
సురతాడంబరంబునకుఁ దేఱుసూపి దూపటిలి
యంగరాగంబులు గరంగం జెమర్చిన చంచలాక్షుల
నిద్దంపు దనులతలం బుట్టి దట్టంబులగు చిఱుచెమట
బొట్టులం బొడకట్టి తెలుపారు మలయజంపు జిటులు
గంధంబుల యందంబు లొసంగి, సంజకడం
దారు నొడివిన సంకేతంబుల నుండక తెరువు గట్టి
పొరువుఁ దరువుల నీడల నడంగి నవ్వుతాలకు
వెనుకపాటునఁ గదిసి ముసుంగు లెడలింప బెగడి
కళవళంపు జూపుల వల్లభులం జూచి యల్లన
నగు నభిసారికల వెడందకన్నుల చెన్ను నమ్ముకొని,
పొదలు మదనోన్మాదంబునకుం బ్రోదిగా మోదంబునం
గాదంబరి గండూమించి విటకదంబంబునకుం నొసంగు
నంబురుహముఖుల యొప్పులకుప్పలగు నిప్పపూ
మొగ్గలం బోని బుగ్గలం దగ్గలిక సూపు కమ్మపంజల
వజ్రపుం జకచకల నకనకలు వీడుకొని కలికితనంబులం

striving for the embrace, speaking tender words, tried to kiss them, and the moonlight became still more dense as it was reflected from their white teeth.

Women became angry when their lovers, in the midst of making love, called them by wrong names (always a fatal mistake); bowing their heads, they appeared to be crying silently as their lovers tried to console them, caressing their cheeks, but in the tears falling rapidly and settling on noses like a nose-ring made of white pearl the men caught sight of their own reflections, full of light, which they mistook for their partners' smile and therefore tried to kiss them—and now the women, still angry, slapped them on their cheeks with their delicate hands, so the men, taken aback, turned pale, enriching the moonlight beyond measure. Like white flour sprinkled everywhere, the moonlight was burning white, and women, pretending to be too shy to make love in that brightness, coaxed their lovers into the shadow of the bushes, but the moonlight, penetrating through the quivering leaves, dispelled the darkness and disclosed on their bodies all the telltale signs of loving. Women, willingly acceding to their lovers' wish, made love to them on top, like a man; sweat pouring from their exhausted bodies melted the colors that were painted on them and settled as beads on their skin, and as the moonlight was reflected off these drops they took on the white beauty of dried, cracked sandal paste.

Men slipped away from the point of rendezvous that had been fixed in advance, at dusk, and, hiding in the shadow of the trees, came from behind to play a trick on the women who were making their way along that path, their heads covered, toward the secret meeting when the lovers tore away their

గలసి మెలసి రతాంతంబునం బరిశ్రాంతి యడంగ
నంగణంబుల నిలిచి యొండొరులకురులు
దువ్వుచు విహరించు సమయంబునం బల్లవులు
కేళి కల్లప్పుడన్నతమ మాటలు దలఁపించిన
నుదరిపడి మందస్మితంబు లంకురించు హుంకృతుల
జంకించి కంకణంబుల రత్నంపుఁ దఱకులు సెదర
నుంకించి వైచు చేమంతిపూఁబంతులం బుటపుటనై,
మిటమిటం గాయు దట్టంపుఁ బందువెన్నెల మెండున
బెందువడి డెందంబు గంది తాలిమి చిందువందై
కెందలిరుపాన్పునం దను వొందక లేచి కూర్చుండి కన్నీరు
గోట మీటుచు బోఁటితో వరూధిని యిట్లనియె.

172

hoods and scared them, and the women opened their eyes in alarm and then recognized the men for who they were and smiled, and the moonlight was drunk on those wide eyes.

The moonlight regained its waning strength as it bounced off the brilliant earrings, studded with diamonds, that were dancing on women's cheeks, which were puffed up and shiny like the buds of the *ippa* flower since they were filled with mouthfuls of wine to be given to their lovers, already more than drunk on desire.

After making love with all their skill, now ready for rest, men and women were standing in the open spaces and happily combing each other's hair when the men reminded their lovers of things they'd said at the height of passion. Startled, the women threatened them with a smile and threw at them the white chrysanthemums they were holding in their hands, thus enhancing the moonlight still further, while light scattered from their jeweled bracelets.

Seared by that fierce moonlight, her heart blistered, her patience in splinters, unable to bear her bed of flowers, Varuthini sat up, flicking away her tears with her fingernails, and said to her girlfriend:

౨౯

ఉ నోములు నోఁచినమ్మలు మ
నోరథముల్ దయివాఱ నిత్తటిం
దామరతంపరై ప్రియులుఁ
దారు విహారము సల్ప వీరిలో
నీమొయి దుఃఖశీల నగు
నే వసియింపఁ దరంబె పోద మా
రామముఁ జూడ నందు సుక
రం బగు సర్వము నంబుజాననా.

30

క అని పలికి పాన్పు డిగి కా
మిని చంద్రాతపము వేఁడిమికిఁ బైఁట చెఱం
గున ముసుఁ గిడి నిజకేళీ
వనిఁ జొచ్చి వియోగవహ్ని వడఁబడి తెగువన్.

29

"This is a place where lucky women
play with their lovers and fulfill all their fantasies.
What I am doing here among them? Misery
dogs my mind. Let's go visit
our garden. Things will be easier there,
my friend."

30

She came down from her bed
with the end of her sari wrapped around her head
to protect her from the fierce heat
of the moon. Moving into the garden,
she was still burning in the flame of separation.
In desperation

౩౧

సీ చనుఁగప్పు దొలఁగ వాసన గాలి కెదురేఁగుఁ
బరువొప్ప నలుఁగులఁ బాఱు కరణి
నిడుదవేనలి నూనెముడి వీడఁ జిగురాకుఁ
బొడఁ దూఱుఁ గార్చిచ్చుఁ గదియు కరణిఁ
బసిఁడిగాజులు పైకి వెసఁ ద్రోచి నునుఁదీఁగఁ
దెమలించు నురి త్రాడు నెమకు కరణి
మొలనూలు బిగియించి వెలఁది వెన్నెలఁ జొచ్చుఁ
బిఱుదీయ కేటిలో నుఱుకు కరణి

తే జడియ దళులకుఁ గురియు పుప్పొడుల మునుఁగు
మావి కడ నిల్చు విరుల నెత్తావిఁ గ్రోలు
విషమసాయకు నేఁపుల విసివి విసివి
తనువుఁ దొఱఁగంగఁ దలఁచి యవ్వనరుహాక్షి.

౩౨

క అట్టియెడ నమ్మృగేక్షణఁ
బట్టి సఖీజనము వెడఁగుఁ బట్టి తగవే
యిట్టి తెగు వనుచుఁ జెక్కులఁ
దొట్టిన కన్నీరు వోవఁ దుడుచుచుఁ బలికెన్.

31

she tore her sari from her breasts and rushed into the
    fragrant breeze
as if she were running into a battery of spears.
The knot of her long hair coming loose, she plunged into
    a thicket
of tender leaves, as if leaping into fire.
Pushing her golden bangles high up on her arms, she
    disentangled
a twisted vine, as if she were searching for a noose.
Tightening her belt, she sank into thick moonlight,
as if diving into a river without a thought.
Heedless of the bees, she walked straight into a heap of
    pollen.
She stood under a mango tree.
She breathed in the sweetness of flowers.
She was sick and tired of being hit by the arrows of Desire
and ready to give up her body.

32

Her friends grabbed her and scolded her:
"You crazy girl! What are you doing to yourself?"
They wiped the tears
from her cheeks and said,

33

ఉ పూ(తపసిండివంటి వల
పుం బచరించు కులంబు నీతికిన్
లే(త గదమ్మ యిత్తె(ఱ(గు
లేమ సురాంగన లెల్ల నిట్టి నీ
చే(తకు మెత్తురమ్మ దయ
సేయక తిన్నని మేను వెన్నెలన్
వే(తుర(టమ్మ యింత కను
వే(దుఱు సెల్లున(టమ్మ యింతికిన్.

3౪

చ ఉడుపతిబారికిన్ వె(ఱచి
యూ(అట యౌ నని పేరుటామనిన్
ముడివడు కంతుసేనలకు
ముయ్యేల గుట్టయినట్టి యిందు రా
నడ(గునె తాపవహ్నిౖమన
ౖమ హరిణేక్షణ ముల్లు వుచ్చి కొ
ఱ్ఱడిచిన చంద మయ్యె(బద
మా యెలదో(ట(జరింప కింటికిన్.

3౫

క అని యొడ(బడ(బల్కుచు(దో
డ్కొని వచ్చిన(బాన్పు(జేరి గురుకుచ దనపై(
గనకన(గనలేదు వెలు(గులఁ
గనికర మఱి మండు చంద్రు(గని కర మలుకన్.

33

"We're different. We put on love
like painted gold. What you're doing
is against our code. No woman from heaven
would approve. Such a beautiful body—
would you fry it in moonlight? One look,
and you're already mad with love!

34

Scared by the moon, we came here, where all the armies
of the love god camp together at the height of spring.
But why would it be any cooler in this garden?
It's like driving in a bolt after pulling out
a thorn. Let's get out of here
and go home."

35

They convinced her and took her home.
Lying on her bed, the young woman looked at the moon
that was burning her without pity with its piercing rays
and said, very angry:

౩౬

క ఓచెల్ల విరహిణీవధ
మే చతురత నీకు దురితమే చేయు పనుల్
రాచటికప్పు ఫలమే య
య్యో చంద్ర వివేక మెఱుఁగవొకో గురుసేవన్.

౩౭

సీ తొలుదొల్తఁ గమలమిత్రుని వంక రూపాట
దక్షాధ్వరధ్వంసి తన్ను గనుటఁ
బరివేషమిషమునఁ బాశంబు దాల్చుటఁ
గప్పు దేహమునందుఁ గానఁబడుటఁ
గాలవశంబునఁ గాని తోఁపక యుంట
సతతనిష్ఠురగదాన్వితతఁ గనుటఁ
బూని పాండుక్షేత్రమునఁ బ్రవర్తించుటఁ
బ్రకటానురాగతారకుఁ డగుటను

తే నంతరం బెద్ది యాత్మలో నరసి చూడ
రాజ నీకును నల ధర్మరాజునకును
బ్రాణిలోకంబు బాధలఁ బఱుచునపుడు
ధర్మపద మొక్కఁ డెక్కు డా ధన్యనందు.

180

36

"You bastard, your true talent lies in torturing
women left by their lovers. Is it because you're a king*
that you do such awful things?
Is this what you learned from serving your teacher?[10]

37

What difference is there between you and the killer god?[11]
You both took shape from the sun.
You were both kicked by the god who smashed Daksha's
    rite.
You have a halo around you. He has a noose.
You have a black blemish. He's all black.
Both of you show up when the time is ripe.
He carries a heavy club, you carry a heavy sickness.
He slept with the wife of Pandu, the pale hero.
You yourself are pale, moving through a white world.
Your eyes light up when you see the stars.
His eyes are alight with red fire.
So what's the difference? Both of you
torture others, though they say he does it
out of fairness.

---

* Raja—another name for the moon.

౩౮

చ ఒక పెనుఁబాఁపతేడు చల
మొప్ప రసాతలసీమకుం జకో
రకములు భూతధాత్రికి సు
రల్దివికిం బగ దీఱినట్లుగా
మెకమెకపాటుతోడ నిను
మ్రింగక పో రెపుడుం ద్రిలోకకం
టకుఁడవు గాన నీయొడలు
నజ్జగఁ జేసి కురంగలాంఛనా.

౩౯

క వాతాపివలన నెఱీఁగితో
శీతకిరణ కడుపుఁ జొచ్చి జీర్ణింపని యా
రీతి నినుఁ దినియు నాయువు
చేత సురల్చెదరుగాక చెఱుపవె వారిన్.

౪౦

తే త్రిపురసంహార మొనరించునపుడు హరుఁడు
బండికల్లుగ నీమేను గండి చేసె
నదియు సెలవాటి తెగటాఱివైతి చంద్ర
యకట రోహిణియొడ నపథ్యమునఁ జేసి.

182

38

You may be marked, moon, by an innocent deer,[12]
but you're the scourge of all three worlds.
The big snake Rahu in the nether world,
the moonbirds on earth, and the gods
in heaven—all of them devour you with a vengeance
without pause, reducing you
to a pulp.

39

Did you learn from Vatapi[13]
how to be eaten without being digested?
It's a good thing gods are immortal, otherwise you'd have
killed them in this way.

40

Shiva, at the time of the Triple City War,
made you into a wheel for his chariot.
He made a hole in your body.
You had a fever, but still you slept
with your wife.* It would have killed
anybody else, but, sadly,
you didn't die.[14]

* Rohini.

৪౧

తే పాలం బుట్టిన మాత్రాన మేలిగుణము
నేడు నీకేల గల్గునో నీరజారి
నీటం బుట్టిన వాండు గాండేటు వహ్ని
గాల్చుచున్నాండు జగమెల్లం గరుణలేక.

౪౨

క గోవధము సేయు తురకల
దైవంబవు నీవు మొదలం దక్కక పాంథ
స్త్రీవధము సేయ రేయుదె
నీవర్తన మేమిచెప్ప నీరజవైరీ.

౪౩

క విడువక తలపయిం గొన్నా
ళ్ళిడి చూచి కళంకి వగుట యొఱింగి మహేశుం
డుడుకుచు దక్షాధ్వరమున
నడుగునం బడవైచె దాన నడంగవు చంద్రా.

184

41

You were born from milk,*
but that doesn't mean you're good.
Fire is born from water, but it still
burns the whole world
without pity.

42

You're the god of those Turks
who kill cows. It's no wonder
you kill women whose men
are away. That, enemy of the lotus,[15]
says it all.

43

For many days Shiva carried you
on his head, until he noticed
that you have a flaw. Then, furious, he trampled you
under his feet when he ruined Daksha's rite—
and still you didn't die![16]

———

* The Ocean of Milk.

౪౪

క గాండీవము నీ చేతిది
పాండవునిం జేరఁబట్టి బ్రతికితి మా వి
ల్లుండిన నేఁడు నిశాచర
చెండవె యల్లునికిఁ దోడు శితభల్లములన్.

౪౫

వ అని పలికి యక్కలికి తేనియ లొలుకు పూములుకుల
జళుకుఁ బుట్టించు నించువిలుతు నుద్దేశించి.

౪౬

చ తోడిఁబడఁ బాటి పైకుఁటికి
ధూర్జటి కంటి కడిందిమంటలో
నడపాడ గానరాక తెగ
టాటీయుఁ గాలినయట్టి మ్రోడు కై
వడి రతిలోచనాంబువుల
వాన నిగిర్చితె పాంథబాధకై
మడియ కనంగ యవ్వెలఁది
మంగళసూత్రమహత్య మొట్టిదో.

186

44

At first the great Gandiva bow was in your hand. It got
transferred
to Arjuna, and that saved us.[17] Otherwise, you'd have
killed us
with sharp arrows, you and your cousin Desire,
you who prowl through the night."

45

So she said, and then turned her attention to Desire, who
was wreaking havoc with his flowers made of arrows, flowing
with honey.

46

"Unsure and shaky, you rushed at Shiva
and jumped on him, and he burnt you
without a trace with the fire from his third eye.[18]
But you must have sprouted again, like a burnt tree,
when your wife Rati showered you with her tears.
And for what? So you could torment women like me?
Still, I should praise that woman
for her wifely virtues.

౪౽

శా సాహంకారత శంకరుం దలిగి నే
త్రాగ్నిం బయిం బంపినన్
స్వాహాకాముకుఁడౌట నిన్నతఁడు గా
వం బోలు మోమోడి సం
దేహంబేని రతీశ నీవు మగుడన్
దేహంబుతో నుండు కై
ట్లాహో దైవము దోసకారులకె తో
డై వచ్చు నెప్పట్టునన్.

౪౮

చ జడ నొక యింత లేని నెఱి
చక్కదనంబుల నెల్లఁ గూర్పఁగాఁ
బోడ వయినట్టి ధన్యఁడవు
భోగివి పూవిలుకాఁడ విట్టి నీ
వెడపక నిష్ఠరత్వమున
కెట్లలవాటుగఁ జేసి తక్కటా
పడఁతులమీఁద నేయ రతి
పయ్యెదకున్ ననుపైన చేతులన్.

188

47

Angered by your pride, Shiva shot fire from his eye
against you, but Fire was himself totally in love
with Svaha, his wife—and therefore,
god of love,
he didn't kill you. There's no doubt about it. Otherwise,
how could you still have a body? Bad guys
have all the luck.

48

All forms of beauty have come together
in you. There's nothing dull about you.
You're lucky. You live in luxury.
You wield flowers as your weapons.
How could a person like you do such cruel things
to women? Your hands should be playing
with Rati's breasts!"[19]

౪౯

తే అనుచు నిందించి వలవంత యినుమడింప
నవ్యరారోహ విదళిత హల్లకముల
కమ్మపుప్పొడి పై దుమారమ్ము రేచు
మలయ మంథర పవనుపై నలుక వొడమి.

౫౦

ఉ అక్కట గంధవాహ తగ
వా హరిణాంకునిc గూడి పాంథులం
బొక్కcగc జేయc బావకుని
పొం దొనరించి జగమ్ము లేర్చు నీ
యక్కొఆగామి మాన వది
యట్టిద చుల్కనివృత్తి దుర్జనుం
డెక్కనిc జొచ్చి క్రిందుపడు
నొండ్లకుc గీ డొనరింపc గల్గినన్.

49

She went on blaming him, but she felt
twice as bad as before. So, young woman
that she was, she turned her anger
against the wind from the south,
which was dusting her with pollen
from the red lotus in full bloom.

50

"Wind, is it fair to team up with the moon
to torture helpless women like me?
You haven't given up your useless
old habit of fanning flames
so that together with Fire
you burn up the whole world.
But that's how it is. A man who is bad
to begin with doesn't mind stooping lower
by assisting some other villain—
as long as he can still harm others.

౹౧

క నాలుకలు రెండు నిన్నుం
గ్రోలనె కల్పించె నలువ ఘోరాహికి న
న్నాలి గ్రహ మిపుడుఁ దెగఁ దినఁ
జాలద మృదుపవన విరహిజన దురితమునన్.

౹౨

వ అని పలికి యక్కలకంతకంతి దీపించు తాపంబు
పెల్లున మూర్ఛిల్లినం దోడిపల్లవోష్ఠ లల్లనల్లన
హల్లకంబుల హిమాంబుపూరంబులం గర్పూరపటీర
కర్దమాసారంబులం జెంగావుల మృణాళభంగంబుల
నంగంబులకుం జలువ పుట్టింప నెట్టకేలకుం దెలిసె
నంతఁ బ్రభాతసమయం బగుటయు నొక్క పువ్వుబోఁడి
వరూధినితో నిట్లనియె.

౹3

ఉ పాటన సేయమిం గురులు
పైఁబడి శీర్ణపటీరపంక లా
లాటికమై దరస్మిత వి
లాసపుఁజంద్రిక డొంకి వాడుటం
దేటం దొఱంగి విన్ననగు
నీ మొగమో యన మాసి చంద్రుఁడే
పాటలగంధి వ్రాలె నదె
భానురుచిం దన కందు మీఆఁగన్.

192

51

God thoughtfully gave two tongues to snakes
so they could eat you up.[20] But even the fiercest
of snakes weren't able to finish you off,
gentle wind—
because of our
bad luck."

52

Unable to bear the blazing heat of her loneliness, the young woman, her voice melodious as the cuckoo, fell into a faint. Her girlfriends applied cooling devices such as red lotus flowers, ice water, showers of sandal paste and camphor, red cloth, and bits of lotus stems. In the end, she came to. By then night was ending. One of the girls said to her:

53

"Look at the moon, my dear.
He's just like you.
Your black hair is all over your face, uncombed.
The dot on your forehead is smudged and smeared.
Your sweet smile has lost its light, your face
its luster. As for the moon, he's sinking,
turned pale, so all you can see
is his dark stain.

౭౪

సీ సకుటుంబముగ వీఁగి చరమశైలముఁ జేరు
తుహినాంశు దుముదారుదొర యనంగ
నాసీరమై వచ్చు నలినబాంధవు డెక్కి
యంబుపై దీపించు నద్ద మనఁగ
నరుణాగ్రనిబిడ వాద్యములలోఁ గనుపట్టు
సమయశాంఖికుచేతి శంఖ మనఁగ
నినుఁ డప్పు డజుఁ డౌట మునుమున్న పడివాగె
గొనివచ్చు రాయంచ కొదమ యనఁగ

తే నుదయగిరిమీఁదఁ గోపురంబుండి నిగుడు
నహిత రవిరశ్మిచే బద్ధఁ డగుచుఁ దోఁడి
బలఁగ మైనట్టి చుక్కల వలస త్రోవఁ
జూప నేతెంచె నన వేగుఁ జుక్క వొడిచె.

౭౫

మ సకలాశాగతి నర్మకోపవిరతి
    శ్రౌతక్రియారంభణా
త్మక వర్గత్రయికిన్ మదుచ్చరిత శ
    బ్దజ్ఞానమే మూల మిం
తకుఁ బోలన్ వినుడంచుఁ దెల్పుగతిఁ జెం
    తం గొండపై పల్లెలం
గృకవాకుల్మొరసెన్ గృహోపరిఁ ద్రిభం
    గిన్ ఘుగ్ఘుకంఠధ్వనిన్.

54

And here's the morning star,
like a rearguard for the moon, who is
fleeing with his family to the Western Mountain.
Or like a mirror set on the flag that heralds the arrival
of the vanguard in the army of the sun.
Or like a conch in the hands of Time the trumpeter
in the orchestra that goes before the morning sun.
Or a royal white goose ready to be mounted
by the rising sun, who is Brahma at that moment.[21]
Or like a scout attacked by the enemy army
that is sunlight, but who stays at his post
to show his soldiers the road to retreat.

55

Cocks are crowing from the rooftops
in villages beyond the hills
as if to say, 'Listen to us!
When we cry out in our three distinct tones,
some of you set off for work, to make money.
Couples quit quarreling and make love.
Others turn to their morning prayers,
        as the texts command.
We know the time for life's three goals.'*

---

* Profit (*artha*), desire (*kāma*), and piety (*dharma*).

ఴ౬

మ ఇనుఁ డస్తాద్రికిఁ బోవఁ గొల్లకొని నేఁ
డేతేరఁ దద్దీప్తి నం
జనసంబంధజ బాంధవంబున రతి
శ్రాంతాంగనానేత్రకో
ఇనికాయంబుల డాఁచి తద్ధవళిమం
దాఁ బూనెనో చొప్ప మా
ర్ప ననన్ వెల్వెలఁ బాఆ దీపకళికా
వ్రాతంబు శాతోదరీ.

ఴ౭

శా వాలారుం గొనగోళ్ల నీ వలసతన్
వాయించుచో నాటకున్
మేళంబైన విపంచి నిన్నమొదలున్
నీ వంటమించజేసి యా
యాలాపంబె యవేళఁ బల్కెడుఁ బ్రభా
తాయాత వాతాహతా
లోలత్తంత్రుల మేళవింపఁగదవే
లోలాక్షి దేశాక్షికిన్.

196

56

Look at this row of pale lamps:

Yesterday, at sunset,
they stole the sun's red glow.
Now he's coming back,
so they've hidden it in the corners
of the eyes of women worn out
by a night of love and taken their pallor
in exchange. These eyes were happy to do
this friendly favor—they get eyeliner
from the lamps.[22]

57

Last evening you were idly playing your vina,
which you tuned to an evening raga.
Since then you haven't touched it.
Now it's playing the same raga
when the dawn breeze strikes the strings.
It's the wrong time. Dear friend
with dancing eyes, won't you tune it
to a morning mode?[23]

౫౮

చ పలుకులు నేర్పు వేళఁ గల
భామిని నీ విటు లుండఁ బంజరం
బుల నరగన్ను వెట్టి ముఖ
ముల్చరణాగ్ర నఖాళీఁ గ్రేఁకుచున్
నిలుగుచు నావులించుచు వ
నీవిహగోత్క్ర మెట్లు వల్కు న
ప్పలుకులె యజ్జు లెత్తి విని
పల్కెడు వింటివె కీరశారికల్.

౫౯

మ ఉరుసంధ్యాతపశోణమృత్క్షలితమై
యొప్పారు బ్రహ్మండ మ
న్నరడిం గలపుహొంతకాఁడు చరమా
గస్కంధముం జేర్చు ని
బ్బరపున్ సంగడమో యనన్ శశి డిగెం
బ్రాగ్భూమిభృత్క్రతవే
తరబాహాగ్రపు సంగడం బనఁగ మా
ర్తాండుండు దేఁచెన్ దివిన్.

58

These parrots and myna birds, half asleep
in their cages, scratching their beaks
with their claws, stretching and yawning,
hear the harsh sounds of the wild birds
in the forest—and repeat them. Can't you hear them?
This is the hour you should be teaching them to talk.

59

The moon is setting,
as if the wrestler who is Time, exercising
with weights in the gymnasium that is
the universe, had thrown a huge white ball
from his left shoulder, Sunset Mountain, onto the red soil
of sunrise. Now he's raising the ball of the sun
to his right shoulder, Mountain of Dawn.

౬౦

చ కరకరి గూఁటఁ గట్ట యిడఁ
గా మొఉవెట్టెదులీల బాలభా
స్కర కరకాండకందళవి
ఘట్టన నించుక వాయివడ్డ తా
మర మొఉ వెట్టి వెట్టి పలు
మాఉును వాకిలి దాఁటి యాఁగుచున్
మొరయ విపంచి మీటుగతి
మ్రోసి యఱుల్వెడలెం గొలంకులన్.

౬౧

చ అడరు నవీన భానుకిర
ణానల మంటినఁ గూడుకొన్నపు
ప్పొడికొలు చెల్ల మోచికొని
పోయెడి సంభ్రమమొప్పఁ గంటివే
పడఁతి భవద్విహారవన
పద్మసరఃకుముదాలయంబులన్
వెడలు మిళిందబృందములు
వీఁపు పిశంగిమ కైతవంబునన్.

200

60

Like baby birds crying
when some cruel person pokes a stick into their nest,
bees are moaning as the rays of the sun
strike through half-opened lotus flowers.
Again and again they emerge
from the entrance, hesitant to move on,
and finally fly away, humming
like the strings of a vina.

61

Can you see those bees rushing
out of their homes in the lotus flowers
in the ponds where you play, as if these houses
had caught fire when the sun's rays hit them
and the bees were carrying away the golden pollen
that is their stored wealth? Notice
their yellow backs.

౬౨

చ కొలకొలఁ గూయుఁ బై నొఆగుఁ
గుత్తుకఁ గుత్తుకఁ జుట్టుఁ బాఆు చి
ల్పల క్రియఁ గానరానిగతు
లన్ మయి మైఁ బెనఁచున్ జనించు న
ప్ర లఆుత నొత్తు సోలు నిలు
చున్ విధిచాతురిఁ గూడియున్ రతిం
దలఁపవు కంఆె పాసిన వె
తల్దలఁపించుచుఁ గోకదంపతుల్.

౬3

ఉ ఇందునిభాస్య వాఁడనఁగ
నింద్రుఁడొ చంద్రుఁడొ యా యుపేంద్రుఁడో
యిందులకై వగం బొగుల
నేఁటికి నేఁటికి నందుఁ బోదమా
నందనభూమి భూమిసుర
నందనుఁ డుండకపోఁడు రమ్ము నీ
చందము నందముం గనిన
జవ్వని యొవ్వని వెఱ్ఱిఁ జేయదే.

62

Look:
They call out joyfully.
One falls onto the other.
Like snakes, they twine their necks.
They weave their bodies together in ways
you can't predict. They wipe away
each other's tears of joy with their necks.
They lose themselves in ecstasy.
For a second they stand still.
Though they've found each other again
by sheer luck, thinking only about how much
they missed each other, these *cakravāka* birds
are in no rush to make love.[24]

63

My beautiful friend—
come to think of it, who is he? Is he an Indra
or a Chandra or the lord supreme?
Why grieve over him?
Let's go now to that garden.
We're certain that Brahman
will still be there. Can any man see you
even once
without going crazy
for you?

౬౪

ఉ ఏల దురంతవేదన మె
     యిం బొరలాడెదు తాల్మి దక్కి మే
     లే లలితాంగి యెంత పని
     లెమ్మిది విప్రవరుండు గేలయిన్
     బాలుఁడు గాన నప్పటికిఁ
     బైఁ బడఁ గొంకెను గాని వానికిన్
     గా లోకచోట నిల్చునె వ
     గన్ మగుడన్ నినుఁ జూచినంతకున్.

౬౫

క రా రమ్మనుటయు దివిష
     న్నారీరత్నంబు నికట నాకధునీ క
     ల్లారాంభోరుహమధురస
     ధారా చంద్రకిత సలిల ధౌతాననయై.

64

Why toss and turn in pain?
Does it do you any good?
Get up.
It's not such a big deal.
That Brahman is young
and inexperienced. That's why
he hesitated instead of falling
in your lap. He's probably pacing
up and down in that garden, hoping
to see you once more.

65

Come now." She finished speaking,
and the woman of the gods washed her face
in the fresh waters of the heavenly river, which were
dancing with many colors, like a peacock's tail,
and sweetened by the nectar of red lotus flowers.

౬౬

సీ ఘనసార పంక మొక్క లతాంగి దెచ్చిన
ముట్టి వ్రేలనె చుక్కబొట్టు పెట్టి
యింత యొక్కతె పూవుపెత్తు లెత్తినఁ జూచి
విసువుతో నొకకొన్ని విరులు దుటీమి
పడఁతి యొక్కతె రత్నపాదుక లిడ నిల్చి
తొడుగ కవ్వలికిఁ బో నడుగు వెట్టి
బాగాలు వెస నొక్క పద్మాక్షి యొసఁగిన
వెగ్గలం బని కొన్ని వెడల నుమిసి

తే సగము గొటీకిన యాకును సఖులు పిలువ
సగ మొసఁగు నుత్తరముఁ దెల్వీ సగము మఱపు
సగము నయి చింతచే సగ మగుచు నరిగె
నవ్యరూథిని యంతికోద్యానమునకు.

౬౭

వ ఆ సమయంబున దేవజాతిత్వజనిత
విమలజ్ఞానపాటవంబునం దద్వృత్తాంతంబు సమస్తంబు
నెఱుంగుటంజేసి.

66

One of her girlfriends brought her fresh camphor.
She dipped her finger in it and quickly
    dotted her forehead.
Another girl brought her bunches of flowers.
    With some impatience,
she picked a few and tucked them in her hair.
Someone brought her jeweled sandals.
She didn't even put them on.
She wanted to go barefoot.
They brought her betel leaves to chew, but she complained
they were too many and spit some out.
She bit off half a leaf. She half-answered her friend.
She was half awake and half
lost in thought. She went to the garden nearby.
She wasn't quite herself.

67–68

Now there was a certain gandharva who had once been
    taken
by her beauty and had fallen in love with her,
but whom she had rejected. He suffered agonies
of unrequited passion. Skilled in the science
of making love, he still wanted her. At this time,
because he was endowed with the lucid powers
of a god, he had seen everything that had happened.
He said to himself:

౬౭

శా. ఏ గంధర్వుఁడు తద్విలాసములు ము
స్నీక్షించి తా నెంతయున్
రాగాంధం డయి కోరి హత్తక గడున్
రారాపులం గంతుఁ డు
ద్వేగం బందఁగఁ జేయ నెవ్వగల ను
వ్విళ్ళూరుచున్ వేఁగువాఁ
డా గంధర్వకుమారుఁ డంగభవవి
ద్యాపారగుం డాత్మలోన్.

౬౮

ఉ. ఒక్కకవేళఁ బద్మముఖు
లొల్లమి సేయుదు రొక్కవేళఁ బె
న్మక్కువ నాదరింతురు క్ష
ణక్షణముల్జవరాంద్రచిత్తముల్
పక్కున వేసఆం జన దు
పాయములం దగు నిచ్చకంబులం
జిక్కఁగఁజేసి డాసి సతి
చిత్తముఁ బట్టి సుఖింపఁగాఁ దగున్.

౬౯

క. అని తలఁచి యవ్విలాసిని
యనిశముఁ గ్రీడించు పుష్మితారామంబున్
ము ను కలుగఁ జొచ్చి యొక చం
దనభూజము నీడ నిల్చి దంభం బమరన్.

69

"Women are fickle. Sometimes they turn their face away,
sometimes they fall all over you. They change their minds
every other minute. One shouldn't lose patience.
One needs to think up some strategy, and a little flattery,
to make them come to you. If you follow their moods,
you'll have a good time."

70

With this thought, he went
to the flower garden where Varuthini always played.
He got there ahead of her and, standing
in the shade of a sandalwood tree, he set to work
with his magic.

౭౧

సీ అర్ధచంద్రునితేట నవఘళించు లలాట
పట్టిఁ దీర్చిన గంగమట్టితోడఁ
జెక్కుటద్దములందు జిగి వెల్లువలు చిందు
రమణీయ మణికుండలములతోడఁ
బసిఁడి వ్రాఁత చెఱంగు మిసిమి దోఁపఁ జెలంగు
నరుణాంశుకోత్తరీయంబుతోడ
సరిలేని రాకట్టు జాళువా మొలకట్టు
బెడఁగారు నీర్కావి పింజెతోడ

తే ధవళధవళము లగు జన్నిదములతోడఁ
గౌశికాముద్ర యిడిన యుంగరముతోడ
శాంతరస మొల్కు బ్రహ్మతేజంబుతోడఁ
బ్రవరుఁ డయ్యె వియచ్చర ప్రవరుఁ డపుడు.

౭౨

క ఇట నవ్వరూథినియు నొ
క్కొటఁ గతిపయసఖులు దన్నుఁ గొలిచి నడువఁగాఁ
జటుల ఝుళంఝుళరవ పద
కటక సమాకృష్ట కేళి కలహంసిక యై.

71

On his forehead, brighter than a half-moon:
a dot made from mud of the Ganga.
Earrings of crystal, reflecting off his cheeks,
smooth as mirrors.
A shawl red as the rising sun,
with a brilliant gold border.
A belt of matchless gold, and neatly tucked into it,
pleats of a rose-colored dhoti.
Brahman threads, clean and white.
A ring marked with the seal of Kashi.
A gentle, godly glow on his face—
the gandharva that he was became a perfect Pravara.

72

Meanwhile, Varuthini walked into the garden
with a few of her girlfriends, the tinkling of her anklets
calling to the geese, her other playmates,
to gather round.

౨౩

సీ ఉరగపూత్కార ధూమోగ్ర గంధముc బాసి
పొలయుంబో యాతావి మలయపవనుc
డనలాక్షు పెడబొబ్బ నలమిన తలదిమ్ముc
బాయుంబో యా తేంట్ల పాట మరుండు
ఘర్మ సామీప్య సంకలిత దాహస్ఫూర్తి
నాంగుంబో యీ నీడనల్ల మధుండు
గరళసోదర్యాత్తకర సుధాకటుకత్వ
ముడుపుc బో యీ తేనె నోషధీషుc

తే డనంగc జంపక కురవక పనస తినిశ
నిచుల వంజుల దాడిమీ విచికి లామ్ర
పాటలీ పూగ కేసర ప్రముఖతరుల
సొబగు మీఅు నుద్యానంబుc జొచ్చి యచట.

౨౪

మ పవమానప్లవమాన పంకజ రజః
పాళీ పిశంగచ్ఛవీ
భవదభ్యర్ణ విక్రీర్ణకృత్రిమ సరి
త్వాథస్తరంగాహతం
దవపాషాణవితర్ధికాతలమునన్
నాళీకపత్త్రాక్షు లు
త్నవ మొప్పన్ విహరించుచున్ సరసవా
చాప్రౌఢిమల్మీఅంగన్.

73

There, in that garden,
a sweet breeze from Malaya Mountain was blowing,
free from the caustic odor
from the hissing breath of snakes,[25]
and the music of the bees cured the love god
of the headache he got when fire-eyed Shiva
roared at him, and Spring, fearing the thirst
he would soon feel when summer arrived,
found comfort in the shade of trees, and the moon
sweetened his immortal rays with honey from flowers
to wash away the sharp taste of the poison born, with him,
from the sea. Everywhere there were flowers:
champak, *kuravaka, tiniśa, nicula, vañjula,*
jack-fruit, pomegranate, jasmine, mangos, areca,
and many others.

74

The girls moved onto a platform made of moonstones,
washed by waves from little man-made streams, the water
golden-green and glowing with the pollen of lotus flowers
borne by the wind. They were vying with one another, as
    on a holiday,
seeing love everywhere.

౯౫

చ బటువయి విట్టివీఁగి పరి
పాటిగఁ బూచి పరాగపుంజ మొ
క్కౌటఁ గలయంగఁ బర్వఁ గొన
కొమ్మను గోయల మించనొప్పెఁ జెం
గటి యెలమావి హారరుచి
గందవోడిం గనుపట్టి నీలతా
స్పుటతర చూచుకం బగుచుఁ
బొల్చు వనేందిరగుబ్బ చన్ననన్.

౯౬

తే వెలఁది యిచ్చుటి సంపెంగ విరులు గహన
దేవతల యిండ్ల నెత్తిన దీపశిఖలు
గాక యుండినఁ బంచబంగాళ మగుచుఁ
బాఱునే మత్తమధుకర పటల తమము.

౯౭

చ అపరిమితానురాగ సుమ
నోలస య్యై చిగురాకుఁ జేతులం
దపసిని గౌఁగిలించె వని
తా యిదె రంభ దలంప రంభ దా
నపరిమితానురాగసుమ
నోలస య్యై చిగురాకుఁ జేతులం
దపసిని గౌఁగిలించు టుచి
తంబె కదా యన నవ్వె రంభయున్.

214

75

"Look at this mango tree. It's round and full
and proud, with flowers springing up all over
and a thick layer of pollen, and there's a cuckoo
sitting on a high branch. It's like the breast
of the forest goddess covered in pearls
and sandal powder, with a dark, sharp nipple
on top."

76

"Look, my friend. These champak flowers
are lamps lit in the house of the forest gods.
If they weren't, why should the heavy darkness of bees
flee in panic?"[26]

77

"Here is Rambha, the banana plant.
It's flowering red, as if in love, and with its delicate leaves
that could be hands it's embracing the tree
we call 'sage.' There's nothing strange about that.
That's what our Rambha always does. She hugs
a sage with her hands, heavy with love."
Rambha heard them and laughed.[27]

౭౭

ఆ కొమ్మ కన్నుగవకుం గోరగింపంగం బూచి
తఱుచు జొత్తు గ్రక్కు దాసనంబు
గవియు నీతమాల గహనాంధకార వి
తానమునకు నుదయభానుండయ్యె.

౭౯

తే శ్యామలోపరినిబిడపత్త్రాభ్రములకుం
గొండమండంబు దిగు వానకఱ్ళు గాంగం
బంకరుహనేత్ర వర్షర్తుశంక నొసంగు
పోంకబోదియ నవకంబు మొకం గంటె.

౮౦

ఉ చూతమె డాసి పక్వతర
శుక్తిపుటాంతర దృశ్య మౌక్తిక
వ్రాతములై వెలుంగు గరు
వంపుం గొటారుల నొప్పు తామ్రప
ర్ణీతటమట్లు జీర్ణదళ
బృంద సమావృత పాండురప్రసూ
నాతిమనోజ్ఞ మూలముల
నర్ధి నెసంగు మధూకసాలముల్.

78

"The *dāsana* tree, flowering red,
dazzling to the eye, is like sunrise in
the vast darkness of the black
tamāla trees."

79

"See the areca trees, their leaves dark as rainclouds,
and their smooth, white trunks flowing downward
like streaks of rain.
From here it seems
the monsoon has begun."

80

"Like heaps of pearls showing through oyster shells
that litter the banks of the Tamraparni River,
white flowers enclosed in dry leaves
blanket the roots of *madhūka* trees.
Come see them."

౮౧

క పంకజముఖి విరహులపయిం
గింకన్ నిజసైన్యకోటికిని సెలవిడు మీ
నాంకుని కరతల మన నల
కంకేళిం జిగురు గాలిం గదలెడుం గంటే.

౮౨

చ నునుంజిగురాకు మేయుతటి
నోరికెలంకులం దేంటి గుట్టినన్
వనతరు శాఖలం గువకు
వధ్వనిం బాఱు పికాంగనం బికం
బనునయ మొప్పమాన్పు గతి
నాత్మముఖంబు ముఖంబుం జేర్చి చుం
బన మొనరించె సందుసుడి
మాయలుగా మగవారికృత్యముల్.

౮3

క అని పొగడుచు నొయ్యారపు
టనువున జడ లల్లి జిలుంగు లగు పయ్యెదలం
జనుకట్లు గట్టి గట్టిగ
ననిమిషకాంతలు లతాంత హరణోత్సుకలై.

218

81
"Look at the red leaf of *kaṅkeḷi*
waving in the wind
like the hand of the love god
commanding his army to attack
lonely lovers."

82
"The cuckoo was happily
chewing on a tender leaf
when a bee stung her on her beak.
She cried out in pain, trying
to fly away. The male pretended
to console her, pressing his beak
to hers, and stole a kiss.
That's how men are—always looking
for some sly way to get
what they want."

83
They were enjoying the garden.
Gracefully, they braided one another's hair,
tightened their saris over their breasts,
and went off to pick flowers.[28]

౧౪

రగడ.

నేర్పుమై నల్లయది నెఱులం దొలుపూం దుటీమె
దర్పకున కర్పింపం దలంప దెంతటి పెరిమె
యింతి పాపురపురొద యేల విని దారజము
వింతయే విరహిఱుల వెతం బెట్టు బేరజము
సురపాన్నక్రొన్ననల్ సొచ్చి నలుగడ వెదకు
తఱుంగ దందుల తావితందంబు క్రొవ్వేదకు
నటీమి ననుం జివురునకు నగునె కంటక మాడం
జుఱుకు మనె వేఱొక్కచేటం గంటక మాడం
గుందములు నీ కొసంగం గూర్చితిని గైశికము
నిందులకు వెల యదుగ నేల విడు వైశికము
చిఱుందేంట్ల కొసంగె గుజ్జెనంగూళ్ళు గొజ్జంగ
నెఱుంగ కది పూ వంద నేల యిటు రజ్జంగ
నెదిరింపం బోలు నీ వింతి రతిపతిం దెగడం
బొదలం జిగురుల తుదలం బూచి యున్నది పొగడ
పుడుకు మల్లన గందవొడికి నీ ప్రేంకణము
దడయ కిటు నీకిత్తుం దగ రత్నకంకణము
నెరసి పోం జూచెదవు నిలునిలువుమా కనము

84

"Look at how deftly she's picked the first flower
to stick in her hair."
"She didn't offer it to the love god.
It's not fair."

"Why listen to the cooing of the dove?"
"It tortures anyone in love."

"Look for fresh *surapŏnna* flowers."
"Put them in your hair, the fragrance lasts for hours."

"You've pushed me to the edge, made me step on a thorn,
now you yell at me with scorn."

"I made a garland of jasmine to give you for free.
Don't ask how much it costs. It's from me."

"The *gojjanga* bush makes soft honey for baby bees.
This girl didn't know that when she picked the flower.
Don't be displeased."

"You insulted the love god, and he's going to get you.
He's ready with red *pogaḍa* flowers, and he'll never
    forget you."

"Pick the *preṅkaṇa* flower and make perfumed dust.
I'll give you in return a bracelet from my wrist."

గురియు తేనెల జీబుకొన్న దంతట వనము
కా దల్లయది పుల్లకంకేళి పన్నిదము
మొదు గోడిన నీదు ముత్యాలజన్నిదము
ఏటవా లైనయది యీ యరంటిబాలెంత
చేటునకె యగు చూలుచేం గలుగు మే లెంత
నెలంత యీ గేదంగి నీకబ్బె బుక్కాము
చిలుకు నీ పుప్పాళ్ళు చెంచెతల బుక్కాము
మితిలేని తేనె నామెత చేసి విరవాది
యితర లతికల మరిగి యేంగు నది పరవాది
కలిగెట్లు ప్రాంకువేడ్కలై నీకుం దఱిచెదను
నలినాక్షి కడిమిగండమున కే వెఱచెదను
గురువెంద నడి గిలుబుకొనియెం బయ్యెరదొంగ
విరులం గరికుంభకుచ వెఱంజూ మై యర గ్రుంగ
మెరమెరని కొలనిదరి మీలంచు లకుముకులు
మరగె నీకనుదోయి మాయింపు చకచకలు
ఏకాంతమని తొలంగె దిందు నీవఱె వేఱు
చేకొనవె మున్నాడి చెలువ యా వటివేరు

222

"Where are you running away to? We can't see you.
Darkness dripping with honey, the forest will swallow
you."

"That's no *kaṅkeḷi* tree, I said.
It's a *moduga,* just as red."

"Look at the banana plant. It's all bent.
That's what happens when you're pregnant."

"This *gedaṅgi* powder will give you a thrill.
You'll look like a Cencu girl from the hill."

"The *viravādi* flower offered the bee a feast of fresh honey,
and still he runs to other flowers—and there are many."

"You're eager to climb the tall *kaligoṭṭu* trees over there.
I'm too scared to climb even this stubby *kaḍimi* right
here."

"The southern wind has stolen a stack
of *gurivĕnda* blossoms. Bend low
and steal them back."

"Kingfishers think your eyes are fish.
Turn away. Don't let them flash."

"Why are you going away? Aren't you one of us?
Take this cooling root, don't make a fuss."

అరిది యా యేడాకులరంటి నగుకప్పురము
సరిరాదు దాని కల శశియొడలు కప్పురము
పాళ కల్లది పోంకం బ్రాంక బందము దెగియె
నాళి యది దిగజూఱునట్టి చందము నగియె
మలయపవనునిం బిలిచె మావి బళి యా వేళ
మలయు కోవెల పంచమస్వరం బను నీల
సులభమై దొరకె మంజులవాణి చంపకము
చిలుకవన్నెప్పుం బొదలు చేరి యింక వంపకము
చనకుం డింక దవ్వలకు సఖులార పువ్వలకు
ననుచు నలరులు గోసి రతివ లల్లన డాసి.

౮౯

క   నాళీక మధాన్మృత్త మ
    రాళీ ముఖరాళి సుఖకరం బగు కొలనం
    గేళీలాలసగతి డిగి
    యాళీనివహంబు లోల లాడెడు వేళన్.

"The seven-leafed banana gives cool camphor that is rare.
The moon, with its black stain, can't compare."

One girl was crawling up an areca tree
with her feet held together by a string—
which broke as she struggled.
Down she slid, and her girlfriend giggled.

The mango tree is summoning the south wind
with the cuckoo's call.
Let's finish this *ragaḍa* once and for all.

"You found champak flowers at the garden's end.
They're green as parrots. Don't make them bend."

"Enough flowers! Don't go farther,"
the girls cried to one another.

85

Then all of them entered a pond murmuring
with bees and geese drunk on lotus honey—
and, shouting with joy, gave themselves to play.

౮౬

ఉ   వాడిన మొముదమ్మి తెలి
     వాలిక కన్నులు విన్నఁబోవఁ దే
     నాడక నెన్నొసల్కరము
     నం దిడి తీరనిషణ్ణ యై జలం
     బాడఁగఁ బిల్చువారి నొక
     హస్తపు మ్రొక్కున నాడుఁ డంచుఁ దాఁ
     జూడక చూచు చూడ్కి నల
     జోటి దిశల్పరికింప నొక్కచోన్.

౮౭

మాలిని.

     రవిరుచిఁ ద్రసరేణు
     వ్రాతముల్మించు వాత్యా
     నివహనిహతిలో నిం
     దిందిరశ్రేణు లాడం
     గువలయ ఘనకుల్యా
     కూల వల్లీవనీ సం
     భవము లగుచు మింటం
     బర్వ పుప్పొళ్ళలోనన్.

226

86

But Varuthini, her face a fading lotus,
her long white eyes weary, without luster,
didn't feel like playing with them. She covered
her forehead with her palms as she sat on the bank.
They called to her: "Come join us!" "You play,"
she said, folding her hands, begging off,
as she stared into space.

87

Bees were flying in the brilliant sunlight
through motes of dust stirred by the wind,
and the air was thick with pollen from vines
on canal banks, dark with blue lilies.

౧౭

సీ పసిఁడితోరముతోడి బాహు వల్లన యెత్తి
సారెకుఁ బొదలపైఁ జాఁచి చాఁచి
బింబాధరంబు గంపింప నొయ్యన విపం
చీ స్వరంబున జట సెప్పి చెప్పి
దిశల మార్గాన్వేషి దీర్ఘలోచన దీప్తి
గణముచేఁ దోరణగట్టి కట్టి
కమనీయ తనుకాంతి కనకద్రవంబున
నారామరంగంబు నలికి యలికి

తే యానితంబవిలంబి కాలాహికల్ప
ఘనకచగ్రంథి నచటిభృంగముల కసిత
దీధితులు వడ్డికొసఁగుచు దేవపూజ
విరులు చిదిమెడి కపటభాసురునిఁ గనియె.

౧౯

ఉ కాంచి కలక్వణత్కనక
కాంచికయై యొదు రేఁగి యప్పు డ
క్కాంచన కేతకీకుసుమ
గాత్రి వయస్యల డించి తన్నికుం
జాంచలవీథిఁ దాఁఱుచు ఘ
నాంతచలచ్చపలాకృతిం గలం
గాంచిన వస్తువుం దెలిసి
కాంచిన యట్లనురక్తిఁ గాంచుచున్.

88

And there he was—lifting his arms high
over and over, above the bushes, exposing
golden bracelets, chanting Veda in the braided style[29]
in a voice sweet as the vina, his red lips quivering,
while his eyes, looking this way and that,
wove fiery garlands in the sky,
and his glistening body, like molten gold,
lit up the whole garden, and his long hair,
which could have reached his thighs,
tied into a knot, was dark
as a snake, so dark the bees could borrow its hue
on interest. He was picking flowers for the god,
false Brahman that he was,
and she saw him.

89

She saw him. Went toward him, her golden belt
ringing sweetly, her skin glowing like a golden
ketaki flower. Alone, without her girlfriends.
Tiptoed along the path at the edge
of the garden, like a streak of lightning
at the edge of a dark cloud. Looked at him
with longing, like finding for real
something seen in a dream.

౯౦

ఉ ఆ కమలాక్షి యింపున దృ
గంచల మించుక మూసి హర్షబా
ష్పాకులకోణ శోణరుచు
లగ్రమునం జనఁ జూచు చూపు తీ
రై కనుపట్టఁ దమ్మరస
మంటుకొనన్ వెడవింటివాఁడు క్రో
ధైకధురీణతం గఱచి
యేసిన సింగిణి కోలయొ యనన్.

౯౧

సీ తొలుదొల్త వానిఁ గన్నులఁ గాంచినప్పుడ
పల్లవాధరగుండె జల్లు మనియె
నట రెండు మూఁడంజ లరుగునప్పుడ కాళ్ళఁ
బంకజాక్షికిఁ దొట్రుపాటు గదిరె
దాయంగఁ జనునప్పుడ ముఖాంబుజంబునఁ
గంబుకంధరకు దైన్యంబు దోఁచెఁ
గదిసి నిల్చిన యష్ట కనుదోయి తెప్పల
లలనకు మిగులఁ జంచలత బెరసెఁ

తే గటకటా యనునప్పుడ గద్గదిక వొడమెఁ
జెఱఁగు వట్టినయప్పుడ లేఁజెమట గ్రమ్మె
సొలసి మాటాడ నుంకింపఁ దలఁచి మోముఁ
దోఱికొనఁ జూచునప్పుడ కన్నీరు వొడమె.

230

90

Her eyes slightly closed, and red in the corners
from tears of joy, she was shooting looks
like arrows shot by the love god in fury
after he bit them on their tip with his teeth
red with betel.[30]

91

At the very first sight of him, the heart of that young
    beauty
missed a beat.
She took two or three steps toward him,
lost her balance.
As she drew near, a little self-doubt showed
on her face.
As she stood beside him, her eyelids
started quivering.
She cleared her throat, her voice shaking, and
when she touched the edge of his clothes, her hand
was wet with sweat. Lost in him, she lifted her face
to speak, and her eyes, wide open,
filled with tears.

౯౨

క   పాటిత కరిదంతద్యుతి
పాటచ్చర గండఫలక భాగంబులపైఁ
గాటుక కన్నీ రొలుకఁగ
మాట వెడలఁ గ్రేటుకొనుచు మానిని పలికెన్.

౯3

ఉ   ఏలర యీ చలం బుడిగి
యేలర బాలరసాల మాలతీ
జాలములో శశాంకకర
జాలములో వలవంత నఙ్రువుల్
జాలుగ నాల్గుజాలు నిఁకఁ
జాలు భవం బనునంత కాఁకకుం
బాలయి రాత్రి పంచశరు
బారికిఁ జిక్కితి నీకు దక్కితిన్.

92

Tears black with mascara came rolling
down her cheeks that had stolen the color
of an elephant's tusk freshly
split open. She cleared her throat
and spoke.

93

"Why keep saying no?
Take me now
among these jasmines and the young mango
trees. I was crying, caught in the moonlight,
missing you all four watches
of the night. Burning
with longing so bad I didn't want
to go on living. I was tortured
by desire, but I lived,
and I'm yours.

౯౪

శా రా వైరాగ్యముఁ బూని నీవు కడు ని
ర్దాక్షిణ్య చిత్తంబునన్
రావై తేఁ జవి గాని యిందులకు హో
రాహోరిగాఁ బోరి యే
లా వాలాయము సేయఁగా బ్రదుకు నీ
వాచారవంతుండవై
చావో యెక్కుడి నీ యొడం బొడము వాం
చన్ భూసురగ్రామణీ.

౯౫

క కట్టిఁడితనమున కిట్లాడి
గట్టి మనసు చాయి సేసి కరఁగవు మటి నీ
పట్టినది విడువ వీఁక ని
న్నిట్టట్టన నేల మా యదృష్టం బుండన్.

౯౬

వ అనిన నక్కుహనాభూసురకుమారుండు.

234

94

Come.
If you don't,
if your pitiless mind chooses
to give up on joy, why should I
keep on bothering you, fighting
for you against your will?
Live a long life, young Brahman, you
and your rituals. As for me,
love for you will kill me,
or worse.

95

You're determined to be cruel.
You've made your heart
hard as rock. Nothing
will move you. You are
stubborn, aren't you?
But why blame you?
It's my bad luck."

96

At this, the pseudo-Brahman

౯౭

సీ   కొనసాఁగి కామినీ గోష్ఠి బ్రోఢములైన
          యుదుటుఁజూపుల తెప్ప తుదల నాఁచి
       సంతసంబున ముఖాబ్జమునందుఁ జిఱునవ్వు
          కందళింపక యుండ డిందుపఱిచి
       పొంగారు మైఁ దేఁచు శృంగారచేష్టల
          తమిఁ దెచ్చికోలు మొగ్గమున డాఁచి
       పాడము రసావేశమున వచ్చు నర్మోక్తు
          లొదవి నాలుకకు రాకుండఁ గ్రుక్కి

తే   మస్తకము వాంచి యుసురని మౌనముద్ర
       నేల బొటవ్రేల వ్రాయుచు నిలిచి కొంత
       సేపు వెడవెడ చింతించి శిర సొకింత
       యెత్తి సన్నంపు ఱెలుంగుతో నిట్టు లనియె.

౯రు

శా   తల్లిం దండ్రియు నన్నుఁ గానని మన
          స్తాపంబునం బొక్కఁగా
       నిల్లా లార్తిఁ గృశింపఁగా సవనవ
          హ్నిశ్రేణి చల్లారఁగా
       నిల్లున్ శూన్యత నొంది సొంపు చెడఁగా
          నిచ్చోట నేఁ జిక్కి యో
       పుల్లాంభోరుహనేత్ర యే సుఖమతిన్
          భోగించెదం జెప్పవే.

97

held back at the edge of his eyelids
the telling looks that he'd perfected
by flirting with women.
Smothered the smile that was almost dancing
on his face.
Covered up the passionate movements
that were visible on his body
with a pretended innocence.
Stifled the intimate hints
that were on the tip of his tongue.
Bent his head with a sigh and scratched the ground
with his toe in total silence.
Appeared for some time to be deep
in thought. Finally, lifted his head
a little and said in a faint voice:

98

"Just imagine. Father and Mother are grieving for me
back home. My wife is worn thin
with waiting. All the fires have gone cold.
The house looks empty, and I'm
stuck here. Do you think, lady with eyes
wide as the open lotus, that I can
give myself to you
with ease?

౯౯

ఉ ఓ సరసీరుహాక్షి విన
    వో రతిం గొంగిట నీవు చేర్చు నిం
    పా సురభర్తకైనం గల
    దా వలదంచుం బెనంగ నేను స
    న్నూ సినె యొక్కటే త హాత
    హాన్ మన సాగ్గదు కేళిపై 'ననా
    శ్వాసిత దుఃఖితే మనసి
    సర్వ మసహ్య' మనా నెఱుంగవే.

౧౦౦

క ఐనం గానిమ్ము భవ
    ద్దీనతకై వ్రతము విడిచితిం బరులకు మే
    లైనం జాలు శరీరం
    బైన నుపేక్షింపవలయు నది యట్లుండెన్.

౧౦౧

క తివురక యిం కొక్కటి విను
    కవయునెడన్ వలయుం గన్నుంగవయును మూయన్
    ఘువి నిది యస్మద్దేశ
    వ్యవహారము కన్నుం దెఱవ నఘు మగుం దెఱవా.

99

Listen, my beauty. To be held in your arms,
to make love with you—not even the king of the gods
has that joy. I've not given up the world.
I wouldn't say no. Only one worry
makes it hard for me to turn my heart
to you. You know
that everything looks gloomy
to a mind sunk in grief.

100

But let that be. For your happiness
I'll give up my principles. One should sacrifice one's body
for the good of others. But there's something more.

101

Listen carefully, young lady. When we're really close,
making love, you must close your eyes. This is how we
do it in our country. Opening your eyes
would offend the gods.

౧౦౨

శా ఈ మర్యాదకు నీ వొడంబడిన మే
లీ భంగి గాదేని మా
భూమిం జేరంగ నెట్లు నీ యొదలితోఁ
బోఁవంగ లేనే కదా
యా మందాకిని పొంత నీ మునులతో
నీ వృక్షవాటంబులో
భామా యేఁ దపమాచరింతు విధి క
బ్రహ్మణ్యముం బెట్టుచున్.

౧౦౩

తే ఇంక నొక్కటి వినుము పూర్ణేందువదన
వ్రతము చెడ సౌఖ్యమైనను వలయుఁ గలుగ
వాంఛితము దీర నను నీవు వదలఁ జెల్ల
దేను నిను సమ్మతిలఁ జేసి యేఁగు దనుక.

౧౦౪

వ ఇంత యేమిటి కంటేనిం జెప్పెద నేను వైదేశికుండ
బంధుమిత్రకళత్రంబులం బాసి దైవయోగంబున
నింత దూరం బేఁగుదెంచిన వాఁడ మీద భవదర్థంబు
ప్రార్థితుండనై వ్రతహోమాద్యనుష్ఠానంబులు
విడువంగలవాఁడ నగుటం జేసి యంతరంగంబునన గల
తెఱంగు తేటపడం బలుకవలసె నాకర్ణింపుము.

102

It will be good if you accept
this condition. If you don't, I anyway
can't get back to my country in this body,
as you know. So I'll stay here, in prayer,
on the banks of this river, among these sages,
under these trees, cursing fate.

103

And one more thing.
If I lose my principles, I should at least
gain in pleasure. Once you've got your wish,
you can't leave me—until *I* leave you,
with your consent.

104

You might wonder why I'm telling you all this. I'm from
another country. Fate took me away from my family and
friends and wife and brought me here, to this far place. On
top of that, for your sake, at your request, I'm going to give
up my rituals, fire offerings, and meditation. I simply had to
speak my mind. Listen.

౧౦౫

ఉ నీ చనుదోయి సంకుమద
నిర్భరవాసన మేన నూన న
య్యో చిరసౌఖ్యముల్గనుట
యొండెఁ దపంబొనరించి పాపముల్
రాచుట యొండెఁగా కిహప
రంబుల కూరక దూరమై వయః
శ్రీచన రెంటికిం జెడిన
రేవఁడ నొదునె నీరజేక్షణా.

౧౦౬

క అని యాస గలుగఁ బలికిన
విని వేలుపువెలఁది మోము వికసిల్లంగఁ
దనచేతిచెఅఁగు బిగియం
బెనఁచుచుఁ దల వాంచి నగవు బెరయఁగఁ బలికెన్.

౧౦౭

శా హో నీ నిష్ఠురవృత్తి మాని కరుణైఁ
కాయత్తచిత్తంబునన్
మానం జాల నటంచు నేఁడు శ్రవణా
నందంబుగాఁ బల్కుటన్
సూనాస్త్రున్ వెలవెట్ట కేలితి సుఖా
ర్ణోరాశిలో గ్రుంకితిన్
నా నోములఫలియించె నా వయసు ధ
న్యంబయ్యె విప్రోత్తమా.

105

There are only two ways. Either I find
lasting joy by embracing your fragrant breasts,
or I'll wear away my bad deeds in prayers
and meditation. I don't want to waste my youth
and lose out on both
like the washerman in the proverb."[31]

106

When he finished speaking, raising Varuthini's hopes,
her face opened up. Tightly twisting the end
of the sari she held in her hand,[32]
she bent her head, smiled, and said:

107

"It's so good that you've given up your harsh tone
and speak now with a mind full of kindness. You've said
you can't leave me: those words
are a feast to my ears. From now on
the love god is my slave. I'm floating on
waves of joy. My prayers
have borne fruit. My youth is fulfilled,
my lovely Brahman.

౧౦౮

వ   నీ వెట్లు చెప్పి తట్లు సేయంగలదాననని యతని
     నొడంబఱుచు సమయంబునం దోడి నెచ్చెలు
     లచ్చకోరాక్షిం గూడుకొని.

౧౦౯

సీ   అకట నిర్దయబుద్ధి వని దూఱెం గడు రంభ
     యాహా వివేకి వా దనియె హరిణి
     చేఁదు మ్రింగెద వంచుఁ జిలికి నవ్వె ఘృతాచి
     మాయలాఁడని తిట్టె మంజుఘోష
     న్యాయనిఘ్ఘరములఁ బ్రార్థించె నూర్వశి
     జంకించె రమ్మంచుఁ జంద్రరేఖ
     చెలి నేఁచి తని దిసంతులు గొట్టె మేనక
     విడువు మాయ లటంచు నొడివె హేమ

తే   గొంట వనియెం దిలోత్తమ గుర్కిఁ గొసరె
     ధాన్యమాలిని పుంజికస్థల యదల్చె
     దివిజకామిను లీరీతిఁ దిరుగువాటీ
     గువ్వకోల్గొంచుఁ దమలోన నవ్వుకొంచు.

244

108

Whatever you say—I'll do your bidding." Her friends turned up, just as she finished convincing him.

109

"You're a cruel man," Rambha reproached him.
"And very wise too," added Harini.
"You're going to swallow a bitter pill," said Ghritaci
    with a laugh.
Manjughosa accused him: "You're a trickster."
Urvashi welcomed him, in tones harsh but just.
"Come here!" said Candrarekha, in a threatening voice.
Menaka blamed him with a telling gesture:
"You put my friend through a lot of grief!"
Hema said: "Enough playing games."
"You're wicked," said Tilottama.
Dhanyamalini was a bit kinder.
Punjikasthala yelled at him.
These women of the gods crowded round him, laughing
    and teasing.

౧౧౦

క ఆ కుహనాభూసురుఁ డప్పు
డా కాంతల సరససమ్మదాలాపములం
గైకొనుచు ముదితహృదయుం
డై కేళీవనము వెడలి యరిగి కుఞఁగటన్.

౧౧౧

సీ మృగనాభినికరంపు బుగబుగల్గలచేటఁ
జదలేటి తుంపురుల్ చెదరుచేట
వకుళవాటీగంధవహుఁడు పైకొనుచేటఁ
గర్పూరతరుధూళి గప్పుచేటఁ
బసమీఱు సెలయేఱు లిసుక వెట్టినచేటఁ
జిగురుమావుల సంజ నిగుడుచేట
నవమాలికల తీవెనంట్లుట్టిపడుచేట ³
మాణిక్యదీపముల్ మలయుచేటఁ

తే బ్రమదమునఁ దేఁటు లెలుఁగెత్తి పాడుచేట
శారిక లనంగశాస్త్రముల్ చదువుచేటఁ
గీర కలకంఠములు క్రొవ్వి కేరుచేటఁ
బాపురము లారజంబులు పలుకుచేట.

౧౧౨

తే ఆ వరూథిని మణిమండితాలయంబుఁ
గాంచి యనురాగమునఁ బ్రవేశించినంత
వారి నిరువురఁ గూర్చి యవ్వనజగంధు
లాత్మగృహముల కేఁగి రనంతరంబ.

110

The pseudo-Brahman enjoyed these delightful
    reproaches.
Happy at heart, he led the way out of that garden to a place

111

where the sweet fragrance of musk flowed in waves,
and fine spray was scattered from the river,
and the wind carried the scent of *vakula* trees,
and camphor trees shed their pollen,
and mountain streams fashioned sandbanks,
and budding mango trees cast long shadows at sunset,
and jasmine was growing in profusion,
and jewels shone like lamps,
and bees were singing in joy,
and the myna birds were reciting the laws of love,
and peacocks and cuckoos were going wild,
and doves were murmuring sweet nothings.

112

He came to Varuthini's gem-studded house
and entered it eagerly. Her girlfriends made sure
the two lovers were together, and left
for their homes.

౧౧3

క పుల్లలవలీ నవైలా
వల్లిమతల్లికలతోడ వాసంతిక లు
ద్యల్లీల నల్లిబిల్లిగ
నల్లికొనిన యొక లతాగృహాంతరసీమన్.

౧౧౪

క ఆ గంధర్వకుమారుఁడు
నా గజగమనయుఁ బ్రపుల్ల హల్లకతల్పా
భోగంబున రహి మిగులఁగ
భోగింపఁడెడంగి రాత్మ బొంగెడు కాంక్షన్.

113

There, in a pavilion enveloped by vines—
moonlight creepers, cardamom, and wild licorice
intertwined—

114

on a wide bed covered with open red lotuses,
the handsome gandharva and the woman
elegant in movement began to make love,
wanting each other inside.

౧౧౭

వ   ఆ సమయంబున.

౧౧౮

సీ   సహసా నఖంపచ స్తనదత్త పరిరంభ
మామూల పరిచుంబితాధరోష్ఠ
మతిశయప్రేమ కల్పిత దంతసంబాధ
మగణితగ్లాని శయ్యానిపాత
మతివేల మణిత యాచ్ఞార్థ గల్లచపేట
మతిదీన వాక్సూచితాత్మవిరహ
మంకుర తుప్పలక జాలావిద్ధ సర్వాంగ
మానంద కృతహారవాననాబ్జ

తే   మాక్రమక్షీణ నుతివర్ణ మానిమీలి
తాక్ష మాస్విన్నగండ మాయత్త చేష్ట
మాస్తిమితభూషణారవ మావధూటి
ప్రథమసురతంబు గంధర్వపతిఁ గరంచె.

౧౧౯

క   అన్నునఁ గనుమూయుట రొద
సన్నగిలుట కౌఁగిలింత సడలుట నేర్పుల్
సున్నగుట వరూధిని రతి
కన్నెతికపు రతియుఁ బోలెఁ గడు నింపొసఁగెన్.

115–116

They embraced. Her warm breasts pressed against him.
They kissed, deeply taking in each other's lips,
biting each other in the vehemence of wanting,
falling onto the bed, giving in to each other,
and he was slapping her cheeks, begging for her moans.
Helplessly they sought more and more of each other,
bodies coming alive as cries of ecstasy
burst from their throats, their words of praise becoming
        fainter
and fainter, eyes closing, cheeks wet with sweat, their
        movements
quieter, the ringing of their jewels now silenced.
That was their first time, and each melted
into the other.

117

Because she closed her eyes, entirely absorbed,
and her voice was faint, and she was holding him
lightly, not showing all her skill, making love to Varuthini
was like making love to a virgin—a total delight.

౧౧౮

క ఈ విధమున నయ్యిరువురు
భావజతంత్రైకపరత బహుకాలము సా
ఖ్యావహలీలల నుండం
గా వేలుపుముద్దరాలు గర్భముc దాల్చెన్.

౧౧౯

క నడ జడనువడియె నా రే
ర్పడియెం జనుమొనలు నల్లవడియొన్ వడియం
బడియొc గడు నొడలు పడcతికి
బడలికయును నిదుర యరుచి బహుళం బయ్యెన్.

౧౨౦

మ పలుచంబాఱుటc గోమలస్మితరుచుల్
పైcదేcచె నా గౌరకాం
తుల గండద్వితయంబు పొల్చెc బ్రమదా
ర్లోరాశి ఖేలన్నవో
త్కలికాభంగపరంపరేపరి సము
ద్యత్వాcడుడింఢీర పం
క్తులు నాc జిట్టుము లుల్లసిల్లెc దఱుచై
తోఢ్డేc గురంగాక్షికిన్.

118

They made love for a long time, giving themselves
to joy, thinking of nothing else, and in the course of time
the woman of the gods became pregnant.

119

Her movements became slow.
The hair on her loins grew darker.
Her nipples turned black.
She was easily tired.
She slept a lot, and lost her taste for food.

120

Her face grew thin and her cheeks became pale,
as if a gentle, white smile were shining through.
There were constant bubbles on her lips, like a thin foam
playing on waves of happiness and unknown cravings,
welling up from inside.

౧౩౧

తే   నాకజలజాక్షి నిఱుపేద నడుము బలిసి
యల్ల నల్లన వళిసీమ నాక్రమించెఁ
బేర్చి దివసక్రమంబున బీద బలిసి
బందికాఁ డైనఁ బొరువులు బ్రదుకుఁ గనునె.

౧౩౨

క   పాటల సుగంధి పాటలు
నాటలు లే కప్పు డొప్పె నలసతఁ బధికో
త్పాటన జయ పరిశాంత
జ్యాటంకృతి చలన మదన చాపముఁ బోలెన్.

121

Her waist, no longer small, grew fat
and occupied the folds of skin on her belly.
When a poor man gradually grows rich
and turns into a bandit, how can his neighbors survive?

122

Fragrant as a flower, she was too tired
to sing or dance. She was like the bow of the love god,
its string now silent and still after shooting down
lonely travelers.[33]

౧౨3

సీ	మనసు కక్కుఁతీతి మెల్లన లేచి చేతులఁ
గాంతుని జబ్బుగాఁ గౌఁగిలించు
నలసత మృద్గంధియైన కమ్మని నోర
నధరంబు నెడనెడ నాని కూర్కు
మణితాది పవనధారణశక్తి చాలమి
నొయ్యన నర్మోక్తి నుబ్బైనర్చుఁ
గాంక్షితక్రీడ కంగము పంపు సేయమి
నొడ్డుగా నిట్టూర్పు లొలయఁ బొగులు

తే	నిచ్చ యొటీఁగిన రతికేళి మెచ్చి పొగడు
నప్పు డక్కాంత రతిపరిహాసవేళ
జీవితేశ సమేళంపుఁ జేఁత లుడుపుఁ
బ్రార్థనాపూర్వ దీనసంభాషణముల.

౧౨౪

క	అంత వియచ్చరుఁ డభిమత
మంతయు సమకూఱుటయును నచ్చర గర్భ
శ్రాంత యగుటయును గనుఁగొని
యింతట నిచ్చోటు వాయ కేఁగనున్నన్.

123

Somehow she would get up and gently
embrace her lover, wanting him in her mind
even though her body wasn't able,
and she would kiss him lightly, her mouth fragrant
from fresh earth,[34] and fall asleep.
She didn't have enough breath to moan in loving,
but still she would play with him, teasing him with words.
She would sigh deeply, lying crosswise on the bed,
unable to act on his desire. And whenever she saw
her lover wanting her, she would flatter him
for his skill in bed, but if he started,
she would beg him not to and tenderly
hold him back.[35]

124

The gandharva had got what he wanted.
Seeing that this woman was too pregnant,
he thought, "I should leave her now.
If I stay any longer,

౧౨౫

క వంచన యెఱింగిన మతిశఠి
యించునొ సురకాంత చెప్ప కేగినం బ్రేమం
బంచశర శరపరంపరం
బంచత ప్రాపించి మీందం బాపం బిడునో.

౧౨౬

వ అని వితర్కించి యక్కపటవిప్రుం డెఱింగించి
యనిపించుకొనియ పోవువాండై యప్పు డప్పువ్యంబోండి
డాయం బోయి బుజ్జవంబొప్ప నిట్లనియె.

౧౨౭

తే ఎవ్వండేం బాదలేప మొక్కింత నాదు
పాదములం బూయ నింతేసి పనులు పుట్టె
నమ్మహాయోగి బహుయోజనాధ్వగామి
యా గిరికి నేంగుదెంచె నే డేంగి కంటి.

125

she'll figure out the trick I played on her
and might curse me. If, on the other hand,
I leave without telling her, she might die
from the pangs of love, and the blame
will be on me."

126

The pseudo-Brahman wanted her to agree to his leaving, so
he approached her and spoke to her in cajoling tones.

127

"You know that great siddha who applied a little ointment
to my feet, setting in motion all these big things? He travels
thousands of miles, and today he turned up on this moun-
tain. I saw him.

౧౨౮

క అతఁడు మణి తీర్థయాత్రా
ప్రతవశమున వచ్చి మాపురంబు తెరువుగాఁ
గతలుగ మా సంసార
స్థితు లెల్లను జెప్పె నేమి సెప్పుదు నబలా.

౧౨౯

సీ పై పరామరిక చొప్పుడమిఁ బక్వము దప్పి
పండఁబాటీన పొల మెండఁబాటిఁ
గట్టఁ గాపింప దక్షత లేమి నూరూర
బందెలఁ బడిపోయె బహుగణంబు
వంచనామతిఁ బ్రాడ్వివాకులై వటువు లో
జల కొప్పగించిరి చదువు లెల్లఁ
గికురించి రిచ్చి పుచ్చుకొను చోటులవార
లాఁకకు లోనుగా కప్పు లీక

తే గ్రహణ సంక్రమణాదుల రాచనగరఁ
గాసు వీసంబు వెడలమి గ్రాసమునకు
నాధి వెట్టిరి క్షేత్రంబులందుఁ గొన్ని
లెస్స యుందునె గృహకర్త లేని బ్రతుకు.

260

128

He happened to visit my hometown
on his way to the holy places.
He told me at length what's been going on
with my family. What can I say?

129

Because there's no one to oversee the harvest,
our farmland has gone dry.
All our cows have been captured and penned
in the villages around—because no one could take them
to graze and bring them back.
All my students have given up learning
and are running gambling joints.[36]
Those who owe us money are defaulting, since no one
makes them pay.
Whatever little we used to get from the palace
on days of eclipses and planetary transits
has stopped coming in. We've had to mortgage
some of our lands just to survive.
Without a master, can a family thrive?

౧౩౦

క అది గా కేనిట వచ్చిన
యది మొదలుగ౦ జింతచే నహర్నిశమును నా
కెదురెదురె చూచు చిద్దఱు
ముదుసళ్ళును బుత్ర మోహమున నగునార్తిన్.

౧౩౧

క తడిగంట నెపుడు౦ దఱు౦గక
కడి దఱు౦గ౦గ వడియు౦ దఱీ౦గి గాసిం బుడమిం
బడిన౦ గనరాక మంచపు౦
దొడుగఱ లైరఱ్ఠై రుజలతో నేమందున్.

౧౩౨

క కావున వారల౦ జూడం
గా వేగమ చన౦గవలయు౦ గమలదళాక్షీ
నీ వెఱు౦గని ధర్మధ
ర్మావస్థితి గలదె దీనికై యడలకుమీ.

130

Worse still, from the day I came here
my old parents, sick with worry
for their son, have been waiting to see me,
day and night.

131

Their eyes are never dry. They hardly eat.
They've grown so weak that if they fall
to the ground, no one can tell them apart
from the grass. They're stuck to their beds
like dry wood.

132

I have to go see them, as fast as I can.
You know what's right for a son to do.
Don't take it to heart, my dear.

౧33

క వడి గాచి కాచి యుండం
గడవలనీ రినుము ద్రావు కైవడిం బైపైం
బొడమెడు కోర్కులచేం బై
ల్లుడికిన మది భోగముక్తి కూటిట గనునే.

౧3౪

ఉ కావున నెన్నడుం డెగని
కాంక్ష నెపం బొకం డెన్ని రోసి నేం
బోవం దలంతు నేని వల
పున్ ననుపుం దగవుం బ్రియంబునున్
నీవలనన్ సమగ్రములు
నిల్చిన సంపంగెపువ్వుందేనె క్రొ
త్తావికిం దేంటి చిక్కిన వి
ధంబునం జిక్కనె లోలలోచనా.

౧3౫

ఉ ఎవ్వడు మీం దెఱుంగక య
ఛేచ్చసుఖైకరతిం జరింపంగా
నవ్వల వంశహాని వ్రత
హాని యశోధనహాని పుట్టుం దా
నవ్వేడం గమ్మనుష్యపశు
వయ్యవివేకి చెడున్ జగంబునన్
నవ్వంగం బాలు రౌరవము
నం బడం బాలును నిందపాలునై.

133

Like a red-hot iron that sucks up
pots and pots of water,
a mind aflame with desire is never sated
with pleasure.

134

If I really wanted to leave you,
on the pretext that I was sick of my desire
that never ends, I'd look for some fault—
but the love you give me is perfect,
as are your friendship and respect.
If I stay, I'll be stuck like a bee that is lost
in the fragrance of a champak flower.[37]

135

Whoever gives himself totally to pleasure,
lost in his senses, not thinking of what is to come,
will lose everything—family, principles, fame,
and money. Such an idiot, such a human animal,
such a moron will be ruined. He'll become a laughingstock
and will end up in the lowest of all hells."

౧౩౬

మ అనినం జిత్తము జల్లనన్ సారుగు న
య్యంభోజపత్రాక్షిలో
చనగోళంబులఁ జిమ్ములై చిలుపలై
జాలై తరంగంబులై
చనుదీయిం గొన బొకురంగమద చ
ర్చల్ జాటీపొ నొక్క మెం
దున బాష్పాంబురురంబు లుప్పతిలెఁ బో
టుంబాటుగా నెంతయున్.

౧౩౭

క అత్తటి గంధర్వవిఘం
డత్తామరసాక్షి వదన మక్కునఁ గృపతో
నొత్తి మొగమెత్తి యశ్రులు
మెత్తనఁ గొనగోరఁ బాఱి మీటుచుఁ బలికెన్.

౧౩౮

శా ధీరస్వాంతపు వంత నీకుఁ దగునే
దివ్యాంగనల్కోవిదల్
గారే యోగవియోగముల్ సతములే
కర్తవ్యముల్ సేయరే
పోరే రారె ప్రియంబు గల్లినజనుల్
పోరామి పోఁ బోవునే
పో రాకుండఁగ నేమి కాళ్లు దెగినే
ఫుల్లాంబుజాతేక్షణా.

136

She felt a shock. She nearly fainted.
Tears spilled from her eyes, wide as lotus petals—first a
    few drops,
then a trickle, then a stream washing the dark musk
off her breasts, then wave after flooding wave.

137

The gandharva man caressed her cheeks,
kindly pressed her to his heart and, lifting her face,
softly flicked away her tears with his fingernails as he said:

138

"You're a strong woman. You shouldn't cry.
Women of the gods know everything, don't they?
Do people stay together or stay apart forever?
Don't they have other things to do?
Lovers come and go. If I leave for a while,
will our friendship disappear? I still have my legs—
I can always come back to you, my young
and lovely woman.

౧౩౯

తే మూలముట్టుగ దెల్పె నమ్మినవరుండు
ప్రార్థితం డయి నాకు నప్పరమవిద్య
వచ్చుచును బోఁవుచుండెద వదల నిన్ను
శుకకలాలాప ననుఁ ద్రిశుద్ధికిని నమ్ము.

౧౪౦

తే అని వరూధిని నూరార్చి యచటు వాసి
పోయెఁ దనయిచ్చ గంధర్వపుంగవుండు
తప్పరాదు ఋణానుబంధంబు దెగినఁ
బ్రాణపదమైన వలపును బాసి చనదె.

౧౪౧

వ అనుటయుం దరువాతి వృత్తాంతంబు గృపాయత్తం
బగుచిత్తంబున నానతీవలయు నని యడుగుటయును.

139

That siddha taught me this skill
from beginning to end when I asked him.
Now I can come and go anytime I want.
I won't leave you. Believe me
in thought, word, and deed.
Goodbye."

140

He left her with these words of comfort
and went his way. That's how it goes.
Even a love strong as life
comes to an end
when the debt is paid.

141

That's what the birds said, and Jaimini asked: "Could you
kindly tell me what happened next?"

౧౪౨

శా హిందూరాజ్యరమాధురంధర భుజా
హ్రిగ్రామణీ కంచుక
త్కుందస్వచ్ఛయశోగుళుచ్చ యవన
క్షేణీధవస్థాపనా
మందీభూతకృపాకటాక్ష యసకృ
న్నాద్యత్కళింగాంగనా
బందీగ్రాహవిగాహితోత్తరకకు
భ్ఠాటీ సమాటీకనా.

౧౪3

క తిరుమలదేవీ చరణో
దరలాక్షాకల్ప కల్పితస్థల కమల
స్ఫురదిందీవరబంధుర
హరిహయమణివలయకూట హర్మ్యవిహారీ.

142

So it was, great king.
Your shoulders, firm as the first snake,
bear the burden of the land called Hind,[38]
and your fame, white as jasmine,
clothes those shoulders like the serpent's skin.
Your immense kindness has reestablished
the Yavanas' king in his kingdom.[39]
You went north to invade Kalinga
and punctured that king's pride
by capturing his wives—time and again.

143

In your high circular palace,
on floors inlaid with sapphires
shaped like the blue lotus, land lotuses bloom
wherever your wife, Tirumala Devi, walks,
her soles painted red.

౧౪౪

ఉత్సాహ.

వర్ణనీయకీర్తివైభవా ప్రభూతభూతిద్య
క్కర్ణకుండలా వితీర్ణి కర్ణదీర్ఘహృద్భ్రమ
ద్దుర్ణయారిమానహారి దుర్భరానకార్భటీ
ఘూర్ణమాన కొండపల్లి కొండవీడుమండలా.

గద్యము.

ఇది శ్రీమదాంధ్ర కవితాపితామహ సర్వతోముఖాంక
పంకజాక్ష పాదాంబుజాధీన మానసేందిందిర
నందవరపుర వంశోత్తంస శఠకోపతాపస ప్రసాదాసాదిత
చతుర్విధ కవితామతల్లి కాల్పసాని చొక్కయామాత్యపుత్త్ర
పెద్దనార్య ప్రణీతంబైన స్వారోచిషమనుసంభవం బను
మహాప్రబంధంబునందు(ద్వితీయాశ్వాసము.

144

You are worthy of all praise.
Your fame is everywhere, like God's.
You are a Karna[40] when it comes to giving.
Your battle drums break the hearts of the bad kings
of Kondapalli and Kondavidu and leave them reeling
and confused.

The great poem called "The Birth of Svarochisha Manu" was
written by Allasani Cokkayamatya's son Peddanarya, known
to all as the "Creator God of Telugu Poetry," who comes from
a family of Nandavara Brahmans, whose mind hovers like a
bee around the lotuslike feet of lotus-eyed Vishnu, and who was
blessed by his guru Shathakopa with the ability to compose all
four kinds of fine poetry. Chapter 3 ends here.

చతుర్థాశ్వాసము

౧

క శ్రీకృష్ణరాయ గుణ ర
త్నాకల్పా కల్పకద్రుమాధిక దాన
శ్రీకుతుకాగత లోకా
లోకాంతర సకల సుకవి లోకస్తుత్యా.

౨

వ అవధరింపుము. జైమిని మునీంద్రునకుఁ
బతంగపుంగవంబు లిట్లనియె.

Chapter 4

1

Krishnaraya:
Your virtues are the jewels
that adorn you. Good poets from all over the world
sing to you. They know you fulfill
all wishes, better even than the gods' tree.
Listen, now.

2

Here's what the birds said to Jaimini.

3

సీ మున్ను విప్రాకారమున౦ గూడుచో శంక౦
గనుమూయ౦ బనిచె నా ఖచరభర్త
యవ్వరారోహాయు నాసక్త గావున
నిచ్చలో నటు సేయ నియ్యకొనియె
నా ప్రతిజ్ఞాపూర్తి యయ్యో దనంత న
వ్వనితకు రతిపారవశ్యపటిమ
నపుడు తత్పువర దేహసమిద్ధశిఖిదీప్తి
శాంబరీ మహిమచే సంగ్రహించి

తే నట్టి గంధర్వమూర్తి సౌఖ్యానుభూతి౦
జలన మేదిన మానసాబ్జమున నిలువ
వెలసె౦ దేజోమయం బైన వృద్ధి నట్టి
మేటిగర్భంబు నెలలు తొమ్మిదియు నిండె.

౪

వ అనంతరంబ యొకానొక పుణ్యదివసంబున.

3

You know that the gandharva, making love to Varuthini
in the body of a Brahman, asked,
out of fear, that she keep her eyes closed.
And that young woman, being in love,
readily agreed. Then, in the depth of her desire,
that promise fulfilled itself. In that moment
of intense happiness, the image of the gandharva who,
by his magic, had captured the flame
from Pravara's body, was fixed
in her mind. She became pregnant with it.
Nine months passed.

4

Then, on an auspicious day,

౫

శా తేజం బబ్బభవాండగేహమునకున్
దీపాంకురచ్చాయమై
రాజిల్లన్ గ్రహపంచకంబు రవిఁ జే
రం బోని లగ్నంబునన్
రాజీవాక్షి కుమారుఁ గాంచె సుమనో
రాజన్యమాన్యున్ జనుల్
జేజేవెట్టఁ బ్రసూనవర్ష మమర
శ్రేణుల్ప్రవర్షింపఁగన్.

౬

క స్వరుచిస్సురణను శశిభా
స్కర పావక తారకాప్రకాశము లెల్లన్
విరళములు సేయ నతనికి
స్వరేచి యనునామ మిడి రచటి మును లెల్లన్.

౭

చ మటియును నతండు సంయమిస
మాజ వినిర్మిత జాతకర్ముఁడై
నెటీఁ బరివర్ధితుండు నుప
నీతుఁడునై వివిధాయుధంబులం
గటికరియై రణస్థలుల
గద్ధటియై నిగమార్థవేదియై
నెటితనకాఁడునై మెటిసె
నిర్మలకాంతివిలాస రేఖలన్.

278

5

when the five planets* were nowhere near the sun,
she gave birth to a boy who deserved the praises of Indra
and who lit up the world like a lamp.
People sang blessings, and the gods
rained down flowers.

6

He was so bright that he dimmed
the moon, the sun, fire, and all the stars,
so the sages there called him Svarochi,†
"Brilliant in himself."

7

The Brahmans performed his rituals of birth.
When he reached the proper age, he was initiated
into adulthood and became skilled in all kinds
of weapons. Expert on the battlefield,
he also learned the meaning of the Vedas.
He became a striking young man.

---

* Moon, Mars, Jupiter, Venus, and Saturn.
† Skt. Svarochis.

౬

ప్రగ్ధర.

గ్రుద్ధున్ గోత్రాచలంబుల్ గులగుల లయి పో
గోతముల్గ్రుద్ధులీలన్
ఖద్దిం జెండాడు మ్రాకుల్ కవుగిటికొలఁదుల్
కత్తి నొక్కొక్క ఘాతం
బ్రోద్ధామప్రౌఢి వాతాద్భుతగతిఁ బఱచున్
భూమి జవ్వాడఁగా ని
ట్లద్దేవీనందనుం డత్యనుపమ బలుఁడై
యౌవనారంభవేళన్.

౯

క   వేదండము తొండము సరి
కోదండముఁ దివియు నెడమఁ గుడి నిబిడజ్యా
నాదము రోదసి నిండఁగ
భేదించున్ గండశిలలఁ బృథుబాణములన్.

౧౦

క   అతఁడు మఱి తనకు మంథ
క్షితిభృత్తటి విశ్వకర్మ చేసిన నగరిన్
వితతాటవికచమూ సే
వితుఁడై సామ్రాజ్య మనుభవింప నొకతఱీన్.

8

He would smash huge mountains with his fists
as if they were punching bags.
He would cut through the trunks of immense trees
with a single slash of his sword.
He would run with the speed of wind, the earth
shaking under his feet.
No one could rival the strength of Varuthini's son
when he came of age.

9

He would draw his bow, thick as an elephant's trunk,
with either of his hands, and the twanging of the
    bowstring
filled the sky as his long arrows split open big boulders.

10

One day, as Svarochi was ruling in his palace
built by the architect of the gods, Vishvakarma,
on the slopes of Mandara Mountain, and an army
of wilderness warriors was serving him,

౧౧

క కరకా చిటపటరవ భీ
కరమై పెళపెళనినాద ఘనమై ఱుంఱూ
మరుదుజ్జితబిల మంద్ర
స్వరమై యక్కొండ నొక్క వర్షము గురిసెన్.

౧౨

క తెలతెల వేగిన నగ్గిరి
జలజలఁ బ్రవహించు సెలల చప్పుళ్ళు శిఖా
వలకుల కలకేకా కల
కలములు గల తలపొలంబుఁ గనుఁగొనువేడ్కన్.

౧3

ఆ అన్నగాగ్ర మెక్కి యం దెక్క శశికాంత
వేదిఁ గతిపయాప్త వేష్టితుండుఁ
గుటజ విపిన పవన నట దలకభరుండు
నగుచుఁ బ్రొద్దు జరపు నవసరమున.

౧౪

ఆ ఒక్క యెఱుకుతేఁడు నక్కకొమ్మును నిట్టి
గోఱజంబు జున్నుఁ జాఱిపప్పు
బీలిగఱుల యంపకోలలు సెలవిండ్లుఁ
గానుకిచ్చి కరయుగంబు మొగిచి.

11

there was a storm over the mountain:
hail came crashing down like rocks, and clouds
were thundering like hell, and the wind
came whistling through the caves.

12

When the sky cleared in the morning, the young man
wanted to see the water rushing down the mountain
and hear the haunting cries of peacocks
swarming in the valley.

13

He climbed the mountain and took his seat
on a flat moonstone, his friends surrounding him,
the curls on his forehead dancing in the wind
that blew from hill-jasmine groves. At that time

14

the king of the hunters bowed and brought him gifts:
fox horn,[1] fresh musk, honey, forest lentils,
arrows with feathers from *pikili* birds,
bows made from *sela* wood.[2]

౧౫

వ యుగ విగమసమయ సముద్భూత
జీమూతపటలంబునుం బోలెc గైలాసగిరినితంబప్రాంత
కాంతారపర్యంతంబు నిరంతరంబై కాఱుకొన్నయొక్క
గహనరేఖం గరాంగుళిం జూపి భూపతి కి ట్లనియె.

౧౬

క అల్లదె కంటె పొనపొనన్
దెల్లని గట్టుఉత మబ్బుదేఱెడు పొలమం
దెల్లెడc జూచిన ధరణీ
వల్లభ సీరాముసేన వాలుమెకంబుల్.

15

The hunter pointed with his finger at a dark forest spreading
unbroken all the way to the slopes of Mount Kailasa, like the
massing clouds that arise at the end of time, and said:

16

"Look! In the dark forest stretching
all the way to the White Mountain, wild boars
are roaming wherever the eye can see,
outnumbering Shri Rama's[3] army.

౧౩

సీ. కండూతిఖైక రాయుఁ గర్కశం బగుతుంటిఁ
బీఁటవెట్టిన ప్రాను పెల్లగిల్లఁ
జెవి దార్చి విని చీమ చిటుకన్న నొకపారి
సెలవి వెంపరలాడుఁ జిట్టలెల్లఁ
జప్పరించు వెదుళ్ళు సట లుబ్బ దంష్ట్రాగ్ని
చొంగపైఁ బడి చుంయి చుంయి మనఁగఁ
జంత్రనిప్పులువోలెఁ దీండ్రించు కనుమించు
లెసఁగ నొండింటిపై నెక్కఁబాఱు

తే. వెట్టదినముల మడుఁగుల మట్టి గలఁప
బుడబుడధ్వనివెడలు బుద్బుదములందుఁ
జిలుపచిలుపని నేతుల జిడ్డు దేఱు
నేమి చెప్పుదుఁ గ్రొవ్విన యేకలములు.

౧౪

చ. బల మీఁక నేమి చెప్ప వినఁ
బండువెదుళ్ళవలీల మొఱ త్రోఁ
బులఁ బడఁ జొప్ప వంచికొను
పోలిక వంచి తదగ్రధాన్యముల్
సెలవుల ఘైన ముట్టిపడ
జిట్టలతోడనె చప్పరించు న
ప్పోలము వరాహపోతములు
భూవర తొండము లేని యేనుఁగుల్.

17

They're rough and fat.
They rub their flanks on the hard bark of tree trunks,
and the trees are torn up by the roots.
They hold their ears close to the ground to detect even
the slight peep of an ant and then rush to dig up the
    bamboo clumps
with their snout, chewing them up, ants and all,
and their hair bristles on their back,
and their tusks hit against one another,
and sparks fly as their spit hisses in the flame.
Their eyes burn like firebrands as they try to mount
one another. On hot days they enter ponds
and stir up the mud, and foam bubbles up,
greasy from boar fat.

18

You want to know how strong they are?
They bend back thick stalks of bamboo
with their snouts, as if they were flimsy as maize,
and chew up the ears of wild rice growing on top,
their mouths foaming. They're like elephants
without trunks.

౧౯

క పొడిచిన కైదువునకుఁ జమ
రిడఁగా వల దగ్గికాఁక యించుక యిడినం
జెడుగఱ్ఱల గ్రుచ్చిన నం
జుడు మంటలఁ దగిలి నెయ్యి జొటజొట వడియున్.

౨౦

తే వలదు కుక్కల విడువంగ వలవ దేయ
నడచి మొలపిడియమ్మునఁ బొడువవచ్చుఁ
బంకము గొరిజ దిగఁబడఁ బఱవలేవు
మన్ను లివ్వేళ రేగటి మన్నులందు.

౨౧

క పొడ చెదరి బోద చఱచిన
యొదళ్ళతో నాల్గు రెండు నొకటియుఁ బ్రంగల్
వెడలిన కొమ్ముల బరువున
నడుగిడఁగా లేవు బలిసి యందలి దుప్పుల్.

288

19

You don't have to oil the sharp edge of the spear
you use to kill them. If you skewer their meat
and let it touch fire, it sizzles and the fat
comes dripping down.

20

As for gayals, you don't have to set the dogs on them.
You don't need to shoot them with an arrow.
You can sneak up on them and slash them
with a dagger. Their hooves stick in thick mud,
so they can't run here, in this black soil.

21

The antelopes, spots all over, their bodies
fat and heavy, stagger under the weight of their horns
branching first into two, then into four,
to the point that they can barely walk.

೨೨

ఆ చలము లొదవ ముండ్లు గల మ్రాకుదీములఁ
గెరలి తాఁకి కొమ్ము లురులఁ దగిలి
వాని లేవ నీఁచి కానకే కొనిపోవుఁ
బోతరించి యిట్టిపోతు లచట.

೨3

ఆ కప్పవెట్టి వెన్ను కందమ్ముఁ సమముగాఁ
బొదలి జోళ్ళుగట్టి పొరుచుండి
మలయుఁ గాని పోవు మానిసిఁ బొడగన్న
నేమి చెప్ప వాని యాసు లధిప.

೨౪

క కట్టియఁ జేకొని డేగం
బట్టి యుబుసుపోకఁ బొలము మట్టినఁ జాలుం
దొట్టిన క్రొవ్వులు గలయవి
చెట్టడిచినఁ జేఱెఁ డేమి చెప్పం బులుంగుల్.

22

Stubborn stags foolishly attack the hunters'
wooden decoys. Their horns stuck in the snare,
they still escape into the forest, dragging the decoys
along with them. That's how strong they are.

23

They're dark, and so fat that their backs and humps
form a straight line. They pair off and fight with each
    other,
so intent on this struggle that they pay no attention
when they catch sight of a man. Need I say more
about their fury?

24

And there are so many juicy birds.
You can take a stroll with a stick and your hawk:
if you hit a tree, a whole bunch of them will fall down.

౨౫

తే ఉడుము గరిమిడికొక్కు దండడియు వెల్ల
యెలుక కల్లెల్క తఱుచును నేమి చెప్ప
నడవి నెల్లెడC జూచిన నవనినాథ
జల్లెడయుC బోలె లాCగల నుల్లసిల్లు.

౨౬

క అనుటయు మృగయాకౌతుక
మునC జిత్తము చెంగలింప భూధర శృంగం
బుననుండి డిగ్గి నగరికి
ననిమిషకాంతాకుమారుC దరిగి రయమునన్.

౨౭

వ నగరు సొచ్చి యచ్చటం గక్యాంతరశాలాంతరాళంబుల
నందంద తండతండంబులై వ్రేలునత్తెంబులం
జమ్ము రంటు పలలఖండంబుల మండితంబు లగు
నిడుద వెదురు దండెంబుల బర్వి బర్వ నిబద్ధాగ్రంబులై
కొమరారు దోరెపుCద్రాళ్ళతేడం దిరుగుదుల
వెడంగువడి వడిదప్పునట్లు త్రాళ్ళం గట్టువడి పొట్ట
లదురంగ నిక్కి పరిసెనంబుల వేయునవియును,
నపహసితశార్దూలకుటిలనఖకోటిపాటవంబులగు
శ్రోటీపుటంబులం జటకసరటాది జంతుకళేబరంబులం
జరణనఖరాంకురంబుల నిటికి చీరుచుం
గేరునవియును, నాCడునాCటికిం బాటించి వేCటకాం
ద్రదనెటింగి మేపు మేపుల చమత్కారంబుల నిరాకరించి

292

25

Iguanas, bandicoots, white rats, mountain rats—
there are too many of them to count.
You'll find them wherever you look
in the forest, which is riddled with their holes
like a sieve."

26

The hunter finished speaking, and Varuthini's son
felt, in his mind, an eager wish
to go hunting. He came down
from the mountain and quickly went to his palace.

27

Entering the palace, he saw in the pavilions inside each
sector large numbers of hawks of many kinds tied by ropes
to bamboo rods, which had chunks of fatty meat and hand
guards hanging from them, and the rope ends were deco-
rated with peacock feathers, and the hawks were circling
round the rods, making the ropes smaller and smaller, until
they could hardly breathe.

They caught sparrows and lizards and held them tightly in
their claws and tore their flesh with their beaks, which were
sharper than tigers' claws. This was their fun.

When the hunters brought them food at the proper time
and coaxed them to eat, the hawks turned their backs and

వీఁకునం దిరిగి తిరిగి యోఁక దీర్పుకొనునవియయును,
బద నగ్గలించి కూయుచుం గడుపు నకనకంబడం
గనుకట్టుతోడ మొములు మలంచుచుం బంజరస్థిత
కీర శారికా పారావతాదుల పలుకు లాకర్ణించి యొగసి
యొగసి నిజావస్థితతాదృగ్వీధాధర వేణుయష్టులకుఁ
జట్టుపలు చెదరం బ్రదక్షిణభ్రమణంబులం బరిభ్రమించి
మగుడ నెట్టికేలకు మట్టుకొనునవియయును, మేర మీఆం
దిన్నయొరల నన్నుకొని యరగన్ను వెట్టి బోరకడం
బోటమరింపం గూరుకుచుం గుతికీలంబడునవియయును
నై పఆఁగు పలుదెఆంగుల డేగమొత్తంబులను,
గుత్తంబు లగు మిగులమెత్తని జలపోఁత తేలుపఱ్ఱెడలు
మెడల నమరం బసుపార్చి కట్టుఁగంబంబులకుం
దార్చి బంధించిన కుందనంపు గొలుసులు గల్లుగల్లు
మనంగ నొడళ్లు జాడించికొనుచుం గొనసాగి సోగలై
ముంగిసమొరలుంబోని మొరలు సారెసారెకు నెత్తి
బయలు పసివట్టుచుఁ గట్టెదుటి వాజిశాలలం గట్టిన
పొట్టేళ్మకై యాదిగొని నీళ్లి కాలుద్రవ్వి ఘనఘనాఘన
ఘర్ఘరధ్వానసమధ్వనులు చెలంగ మ్రోఁగుచు నింగిఁ
బ్రాఁకుచు నింగలంబు లుమియు నయనగోళంబుల
నాభీలంబులై వివృతవదన గహ్వారవిలంబి
జిహ్వాపల్లవంబులకుం గూరతరదంతకోణ
కాంతికలాపంబులం గోరక స్తబక యోగంబు గల్పించుచు
నల్పేతరగ్రస్త కీలాలపలలజాలగ్రాంబులు నెన్నుడుము
సన్నుదనంబున నట మిగుల డిగ్గి చన కునికిం
గతితటంబులకంఆెం దారె పుటపుటనయ్యె ననం
దేరంబు లగు బోరలఁ గందంబుల నందంబులు గని
బిరుదు లంకించి తమ్ము నుపలాలించు పరిపాలకుల
సంస్తవంబులకుం జెవిదార్చె ననం గర్జకిసలయంబులు
ప్రాలంబడి వెండిగుండులుంబోలెఁ గన్నులపండువులై
గండభైరవ పూజవారువంబు లన మెండుకొనియుండు

preened their feathers, indifferent. But when their mealtime was long past and their stomachs were growling with hunger, they twisted their heads along with the hoods covering their eyes and, stirred by the calls of parrots and mynas in their cages, they jumped up, trying to catch these birds, and their wings fluttered against the bamboo rods to which they were tied, and they kept revolving around the rods, again and again, until, at last, they settled down. After they had eaten more than their fill, they took a nap, their eyes half closed, their bellies protruding.

And he saw hunting dogs, huge as the horses that Ganda Bhairava, the lord of hunters, rides.[4] The dogs' necks were snugly fitted with soft, gilded leather collars. After bathing them in turmeric and water, their keepers tied them with golden chains to posts, and the dogs shook their bodies so that the chains clanked and clattered, and they stretched their graceful muzzles, tapering like the snout of a mongoose, over and over to sniff the air. Eyeing the rams that were tied in the horse stables opposite them, they stretched out and pawed the earth, growling like heavy rain clouds, and tried to jump into the sky. Their eyes red like burning coals, their cruel fangs gleaming, white as soft buds covering tongues hanging like new leaves from their wide-open mouths, they were heavy in front and thin behind, as if the red meat they consumed in huge quantities never went past their waist. Their ears bent like tender leaves, as if they were listening as their trainers called them by their titles, cajoling them, marveling at the beauty of their bodies. They were like heavy silver balls, a feast for the eye.

Svarochi pointed at his servants and ordered them

జాగిలంబులనుం గాంచి యందునందును వేఁటకు
సుఱివైనవాని నేర్పఱీంచి తెచ్చుటకు ననుచరుల నీవు
నీ వని నియమించి తానును నాఖేటకోచిత పరిపాటి
సన్నద్ధం డయ్యె నయ్యవసరంబున.

౨౦

సీ॥   పచ్చని హురుముంజి పనివాగె పక్కెర
        పారసిపల్లంబు పట్టమయము
        రాణ నొప్పారు పైఠాణంబు సింగిణి
        తళుకు లకోరుల తరకసంబు
        మిహి పసిండి పరుంజు మొహదా కెలంకుల
        రావు గుజ్జరి సేఁత కేవడంబు
        డాకెలంకున సిరాజీ కరాచురకత్తి
        కుఱిఁగటం గ్రొవ్వాఁడి గొఱకల పొది

తే॥   పీలికుంచె తలాటంబుఁ బేరజంబు
        మణుల మొగముట్టు వన్ని సాహిణి యొకండు
        కర్త యెదుటికిఁ గొనివచ్చె గంధవాహ
        బాంధవంబగు నొక మహా సైంధవంబు.

personally to select the best hawks and the best dogs, while
he dressed himself for the hunt.

28

A horse trainer brought in his great horse, faster than
    wind,
ready for the hunt:
reins studded with emeralds from Hormuz,
a blanket of silk under a Persian saddle,
a bow made of elegant Paithan horn,
arrows so sharp they shone in their quiver,
a long sword with a hilt of fine gold,
a hand knife in the best Gujarati style,
on the left a sharp Siraji* dagger,
another quiver on the other side, filled with short iron
    arrows,
a bunch of red feathers from the *pikili* bird to crown this
    steed,
and a string of emeralds across its face.

───

* Perhaps from Shiraz.

క తెచ్చుటయు నిచ్చ మెచ్చి మ
రుచ్చుటులకురంగ రయనిరోధిస్యద గ
ర్వేచ్చం బగు నత్తేజి సు
హ్యాచ్చక్రం బలర వేగ యెక్కి వెడలినన్.

30

చ జడలు మలంచి చొళ్ళాముగ
సన్నపు బాగ లడంగ జుట్టి చ
ల్లడములు పూని మీదం బది
లంబుగ గట్టిన మట్టికాసెలం
బిడియము లంట దోపి పృథు
భీషణబాహుల సాఘవంబుల
న్నడవి కెరల్చుచుం జనిరి
నాఘుని మ్రోల నృపాలనందనుల్.

29

Pleased, he mounted the horse, proud
that it was swifter than the deer
that the wind god rides—
and his companions cheered.

30

With their hair woven into braids and twisted
into a circle, held in place by fine cloth,
and with their daggers tucked to the hilt into a tight
    reddish cloth
tied round their waist over the short pants they wore,
young men of royal families walked before him,
crying out in excitement and caressing with their hands
hawks perched on their fearsome shoulders.

౩౧

సీ ఇవి కంఠపాశంబు లింత దుస్సిన మీఁదఁ
బడి దిశాకరినైన గెడపఁ జాలు
నివి మింటఁ బఱచు పక్షీంద్రుఁ జూపిన నీడ
బడి వాలునందాఁకఁ బఱవఁ జాలు
నివి గాలి గనిన మూకవరాహదనుజేంద్రు
నైన జుఱ్ఱెంటిలో నాఁగఁ జాలు
నివి కాటు కొల్పిన వృద్ధకూర్మము వీఁపుఁ
జిప్పైన నెఱచిక్కై చింపఁ జాలు

తే నన గ ఘర్ఝర గళగర్త జనిత భూరి
భూభృదురుబిల భరిత భౌభౌ భయంక
రార్ఝటీదీర్ఘ దిగ్బిత్తు లగుచుఁ జెలఁగె
సరిపెణలఁ బట్టి తెచ్చిన జాగిలములు.

౩౨

చ పులియఁడు బూచిగాఁ డసుర
పోతలరా జనుమంతిగాఁడు చెం
గలువ సివంగి భైరవుఁడు
గత్తర సంపఁగి వెండిగుండు మ
ల్లెలగుది వాయువేగి చిటి
లింగఁడు సాళ్వఁడు వత్సనాభి యే
కలములమిత్తి గబ్బి యనఁ
గాఁ గలవాని గ్రహించి యుద్ధతిన్.

31

As for the dogs, if you let their leashes loose even a little,
they would jump on the elephants that hold up the world
and kill them.
If you were to show them only the shadow of the great
    eagle in the sky,
they would chase it until the bird finally came to rest.
If they were to get no more than a whiff of the fierce
    wild boar, the demon Muka,[5]
they wouldn't let him move an inch.
If you would sic them on even the tough back
    of the First Tortoise,
they would tear it to pieces to get to the meat.
The growling and snarling and howling from deep
    in their throats
roared through the mountain caves and cracked the outer
edge of space.

32

And they had names like Tiger, Goblin,
Buffalo King, Big Monkey, Red Lioness, Blacky, Scissors,
    Champak,
Silver Ball, Jasmine, Faster than Wind, Little Lingam,
Hawk, Lethal Herb, Boar Killer, and Stinker.

THE STORY OF MANU

33

ఉ కట్టిన నీలిదిండ్లు సెల
కట్టియవిండ్లును విండ్లగాసెనల్
చుట్టి నొసళ్ళపై నిడిన
జుంజులుఁబల్లసిగల్కటీతటిం
బెట్టిన మొటకత్తులును
మేనులఁ గార్కొనుకప్ప లేర్చి చేఁ
బట్టిన వేఁటయమ్ములును
బాగగు వాగురికుల్మహాధ్వనిన్.

౩౪

సీ సట లెత్తుకొని యొత్తు కిటినైన మోటాస
పడి యేయఁ బొడుతు నీ పాద మాన
కలగుండు వడఁ జెండు కరినైనఁ జెవిపట్టి
బలిమిమైఁ దెత్తు నీ పాద మాన
సెల నెప్పుకొని రొప్పు పులినైనఁ బీడించి
పడవైతుఁ జొచ్చి నీ పాద మాన
తెరఁదూఱీ వెఱఁబాఱు గురుపోతుపై నైనఁ
బడియెక్కి పొడుతు నీ పాద మాన

తే యితర దుర్బల మృగపంక్తు లేమి లెక్క
కండగరువంపు మాటలు గావు సుమ్ము
చూడు మమ్మని పంతంబు లాడుకొనుచు
నవ్వరూఢినిసుతుఁ గొల్చి యరిగి రపుడు.

33

Padded black waistbands, bows of *sĕlakaṭṭi* wood
wrapped in cloth, bushy red hair twisted and tied
over their forehead, rough daggers tucked into their waist,
darkness seeping from their skin, choice arrows
in their hands, strong hunters skilled with nets
were making a lot of noise:

34

"Believe me. I'll spear any boar that comes rushing at me,
bristling with rage. I won't take cover and shoot an arrow."
"Just watch. I can drag a stampeding elephant by its ear
and hand it over to you."
"I can steal up on a tiger roaring by the riverbank,
torment it, and knock it down. I promise."
"I can mount any wild ox that invades our enclosure
and impale it as it tries to escape, I swear.
"Why mention other, weaker animals?
We're not boasting just because we're so tough.
Put us to the test!"
They bowed to Varuthini's son
as they made their vows.

౩౫

ఆ మువ్వ గదల నత్తెములనుండి యొగురుచుం
బదను మీఆ నెరల వెదకు డేగ
పదువు పట్టి దండపాణులై నడచిరి
విఘుని గెడల డేగ వేఁటకాండ్రు.

౩౬

ఆ గూనివీఁపు లదుర గొణఁగి తిట్టుచు నేకుం
గఆచినట్టి కుక్క గండ్లనంగ
మూతి నరపమీసముల బోయ ముదుసళ్లు
పంది వలలు మొచి పఆచి రపుడు.

35

Falconers walked on both sides of the king
with poles in their hands, wearing wrist guards where
the hawks perched, hungry, for their mealtime had passed
and they were searching for food, trying to fly,
bells jingling.

36

Their backs bent and shaking, cursing their bosses,
old Boya* men with white mustaches ran with heavy nets,
like fierce dogs with a cotton roll[6] between their teeth.

---

* Wilderness warriors.

౩౨

వ ఇట్లరిగి యమ్మహారణ్యంబు సొచ్చి విచ్చులవిడి నచ్చుటం
బచ్చిక బయళ్ళ మచ్చిక లచ్చుపడం దటిచ్చుటులం
బగు లోచన ప్రభాపటలంబు దిక్తటంబులం
బర్వ దాఱుమాఱు పడ నిడికొనిన మొగంబులతో
నేఱేజిహ్వాపల్లవోల్లిహ్యమానాంగంబు లగు సారంగంబుల
ఖురళీకారంగంబులనం గనుపట్టు చెలికపట్టులును,
బిఱ్ఱైసంగు నాకటం దట్టువడి పొట్టకై పుట్టకూటికిం
జీమలకుం జెదలునకు నెలుంగులు గులగులం బుట్టలు
నిశితనిజనఖర కులిశకోటులం గోఱడ నాదందల గాచుకొని
యుండి వెడలి చను విషవిస్ఫురద్భుజంగంబుల
నల్లదం గబళించి గెంటకుండ దంటు చప్పరించు
గతిం జప్పరించుచు నొండెంటికిం బేఱెంబులు వాటీ
కుప్పించి తప్పించుకొను దుప్పుల ఖురజ రజఃశ్వటల
నెసక మెసంగు మసకమసకల మఱుంగుపడియుండు
గండీపలంబులును, బరిహసిత సితేతర
పాషాణపాటవంబు లగు విషాణపరిఘంబు లొండెంటిం
దాకి కఱిల్లు పెఱిల్లుమనం బోరుకారుపోతుల
కోలాహలంబులం బ్రతిశబ్దంబు లీను కోనలును,
మదమొదవ నెడపదనునం బొదలు పెట్టలకుం
జుట్టంబులై చిల్లర సలుగులం బిల్లలం జల్లరంబుల
సాగనిచ్చి గమికి వెనుకవైఘ మలయుచుం బిఱుందం
దిరుగు చిఱుగున్నలకు వెన్నాడు తేడేళ్ళ సివంగులం
దిరిగి తిరిగి మొత్తి పోనొత్తి చరియించు నేకచరంబుల
ఘుర్ఘురధ్వానంబుల ఘూర్ణమానంబు లగు పరిగె పక్కి
పలుమేరు రేగు వేము పులుగుడు గురివెంద యాదు
గేదంగి మోదు గొఱు కోరింద కనుము కానుగు మొదలగు
పొదలం బొదువగు నానావిఫిన పాదపకలాపంబులును,
మాటిమాటికి మానిసికాటు మరగి తెరువులు గాచికాచి
డగ్గుత్తిక పడం దిను పెద్ద పొలవలనం బుటపుటనై

306

37

Entering that deep wilderness, he saw great grassy expanses, like playgrounds for deer, male and female, carefree, full of affection for each other, their faces turned in opposite directions, the doe licking the body of the stag with her long, leaflike tongue, their eyes so bright they illumined all space, like flashes of lightning.

Bears, crazy with hunger, hunting for honeycomb, ants, and termites, were clawing at the teeming anthills with their sharp claws, while the stags were lurking close by on all sides, waiting for snakes to emerge. They would catch them in their mouths, not letting them slip away, and chew them as if they were stalks of maize; then, their bellies full, they would frolic, jumping over one another, stirring up clouds of dust that screened huge boulders.

There were glades in the forest echoing with the harsh clashes of a herd of wild buffaloes, warring with one another, their horns colliding, hard as heavy black rocks.

Wild male boars, while lusting for the females in heat, lingered at the back of the herd to make sure the piglets and baby boars and the newly weaned passed safely. Ferociously, they drove off the wolves and lionesses waiting to grab easy prey. Their deafening grunts and gurgles resounded through the trees of the forest, *parigě, pakkě, palumeru, regu, vemu, pulugudu, gurivěnda, īdu, gedaṅgi, modu, gauru, korinda, kanumu, kānugu,* and many others.

Accustomed to human flesh, tigers lay in ambush on the paths, so full they could hardly roar, so fattened on meat their hair had grown thin, but still aggressive, still capable of pouncing. The forest farmers, tired of the destruction, put

త్రుప్పుళ్లు దుల్లి త్రుళ్లి గంతులిడు గబ్బి బెబ్బులుల
నలఁగుడుల దొడ్డజనంబులు మంత్రించి పొరక
దిగిచిన నీరు మేపుదిగి గిరులు గ్రక్కదల వాపోవుచుం
దిరిగి తిరిగి వాకట్టు విడిచినప్పుడు దప్పిక్రై పొటీ
సెలయేటిఔంకులం బాఱిఅమ్ములు ఔమ్ము కెలంకులం
గాఁడ గాంద్రగాంద్రమని రొప్పి నొప్పి కుప్పరంబుగా
వియత్తలంబునకు విల్లెత్తుపొడు వెగసి నెత్తరులు
గ్రక్కుచుఁ గూలు క్రోల్పులల ఘర్ఝరధ్వనుల
గుండియ లవిసి కలగుండు వడు కారండవంబుల
పక్షపుటపటాత్కారంబుల బోరుకలంగు సెలయేటి
ఔంకులును, మేఁతవెంబడిం బొలము పల్లంబులం
దిరిగి తిరిగి పెంట్రికలు వెట్టు పెంటపట్టునకు
వచ్చి యచటం గుచ్చి కానరాకుండ మునుమున్న
మృగయుండు బిసయొడ్డి సంఘటించిన కాలిబోనులం
బడి బెగడక యద్దారు వీడ్చుకొని యారములఁ
దఱీయంబడి యవ్వలికై వెడలి చనలేక గెడసి తన్నుకొను
మన్నుమెకంబుల యాక్రందనంబులం గ్రందుకొను
విషమప్రదేశంబులును, జిఱుతగంద్రగమిచేత
దైవికంబున దాప్రక్క మీఁదు వడ దాఁటువడి యవి
గొంతుక్రొన్నెత్తురులెఁ క్రోలి విడిచి చన మార్మెదలు
వడి మశకవనదంశమ్ములు మూఁగ మాఁగంబాఱిన
కొండగెఱీయ ముఱుగుడు బొందులకు సందడించు
కంకగృద్రా వళుల మొల్లంబుల ముసుంగువడు
పల్లంబులును, మేయుతఱి వీఁ పెక్కి తేఁ చొకటి
మూఁపురంబు గఱిచి కఱిచి యొఱిచి పడ వైవం దోడి
యొక రెండుమూఁడు వెనుకముందఱి నందంద కాళ్ళం
బెనంగుచు నత్తునుక లేఁటి యేఁటి తినఁ గాలెడలిన
యొడ మందుతద్వేదనకం గాక మట్ట లెత్తుకొని
యొత్తుగల పొదరుటడవులు చొఱం బాఱు పిడికడితి
కదుపు నురవడికి విఱిగి పడిన విటపి విటపంబులం

a charm on a handful of straw and threw it outside the yard, so the tigers that chewed on it could no longer eat or drink and cried out in frustration, making the hills echo. And when the charm finally wore off, the tigers, thirsty now, ran to the streams nearby only to be impaled on wide, sharp arrows planted there and, roaring in pain, they would jump straight, a bow's length, into the sky, vomiting blood until they fell, and ducks in the stream, their hearts broken by the growl of these dying tigers, and frightened too, flapped their wings, the rustle mingling with the rush of water. Gayal, wandering through the low-lying fields, returning to their grazing grounds where they had left their dung, were caught by their feet in the traps that hunters had hidden there; unafraid, they dragged the wooden contraption with them into the bushes where, unable to jump across, they stumbled and fell, wailing, filling the uneven forest terrain with their pain.

Hill sheep were attacked by herds of cheetahs that bit into the left side of their throats and drank their blood, leaving the decomposing carcasses, necks twisted, for swarms of forest flies and mosquitoes, and hawks and vultures haunted those low grounds.

Female elk were grazing, and hunting dogs jumped on their backs and bit into them, tearing off meat and dropping it for other dogs in the pack, which were moving among the animals' legs to pick up these choice pieces. In unbearable pain at every step, the elk lifted their tails and tried to run into the tall bushes and trees, and the trees fell under their weight as if to form a fence in that wild space.

Tens, hundreds, thousands of elephants were moving through the thickets, bending back the bamboo stalks and

దడుకు వొడిచినగతి నొందు నెడలును, బదులుపదులు
నూఱులునూఱులు వేలువేలు గుములు గట్టి దట్టం బగు
నెయ్యంబున వెదురుబియ్యంబు లొండొంటికొసంగ
గరివర కరేణువులు వంప ముంపుచెడి యిట్టట్టుపడి
తిట్టలగు జిట్టల సంకటంబు లగు డొంకలు నీక్షించి
హర్షించి యెక్కుడుం దమి నొక్కయెడ నడుగు
వెడలని టెంకిం గని వాఱుగవులనకు మెకము
దిగ దని యొన్ని మన్ను దూఱ్పెత్తించి గాలి పరికించి
దిగువ దెస దొడ్డివల పన్ని యెగువ పొలిమేర బాఱది
యగు దూరం బేంగ బోంగువాఱీంచి యత్తఱాట వల
మొవం దెర లెత్తి యెత్తి నత్తెఱం దుత్తుమురుగాం
జించుకొని పాఱీనం బోనీక బారిసమరుటకు
వలచుట్టునుం జెట్టు దండగొని నిలువ నలువుగల
పుళిందులం గొందఱ నిలిపి యమ్మంది పిఱుంద
జాగిలంబుల తోడ వాగురికుల నిలువ నియమించి
తెఱకు లోనగువాని నందుం బడంగెట్టించియు
గట్టువెంట దట్టంబుగాం బ్రజ నెక్కించి మటీ కలయ
గహనతలంబున నెల్లం బెల్లుగా విల్లువేంటకు నేటుదప్పని
మేటివిలుకాంద్ర మృగములు వెలు వడుటకు
హరిచ్చదచ్చటాపృతశిరఃకటిధనుష్కోటులై కొట్టికానిం
జూపెట్టుకొని యొదురు మాటులు గాకుండ నుండి చెదరి
పొరదెరువులం బఱువకుండ నీరమల సందుసందులం
దమతమ కట్టిన మోటకత్తుల నొండొండ ఖండితంబు
లగు మందగల కంపమండలు ద్రోచి మునుములం
గనుమ లోనరించుకొనం బంచి తాను నొక్కెక్కయెడం
బాదచారియు నొక్కెక్కయెడం దురగాధిరూఢుండును నై
యెల్లెడల మెలంగుచుం గూంత లెగయం బణవ మృదంగ
దుందుభి ప్రముఖ తూర్యంబులు గొట్టించియు గాహళులు
వట్టించియు నగ్నియంత్రంబులు ముట్టించియు రెద
మిన్నుముట్టం జోపు వెట్టించిన.

offering each other, out of affection, the grains inside; so the dense growth thinned out, and the broken stalks, thrown in heaps here and there, littered the pathways and made them impassable.

He saw all this and marveled at it. He spotted an area difficult to cross, and since animals wouldn't come there if they smelled a human presence,[7] he had dust poured from winnowing baskets to see the direction of the wind and then had a large net spread on three sides, open away from the wind. He had screens hung on ropes over the net, and in case any animal tried to tear its way out, he had forest men stationed near the trees to hunt it down, and behind these men were others skilled with the noose, and hunting dogs. On a hillock he put many other hunters, and all over the forest were archers who never missed, camouflaged with green leaves covering their heads, waists, and bows, who had cut their way with thick swords through the undergrowth to tunnel the animals into the trap and had closed off any possible escape route for their prey; they kept their eyes on the spotters,[8] making sure their view was unobstructed.[9] He himself was everywhere, sometimes on foot, sometimes on his horse, and he ordered many kinds of drums to be beaten and trumpets to blare and muskets to be fired so that a vast noise shook the heavens.

౩౮

మ   చకితైణాహుతిదావ మావళితపు
    చ్చస్వల్ప గచ్చత్తర
    క్షుక మద్రిగ్రహయాళుభల్లుకము వ
    క్షోభాగ నిక్షిప్త డిం
    భక వల్లత్ప్లవగీకదంబము ప్రాదాం
    భః ప్రొత్తితక్రోడనా
    యక మాభీలముఖద్విపిస్థపుటితం
    బయ్యెన్ వనం బత్తటిన్.

౩౯

క   నెల వెడలియు నెటి సడలియుఁ
    జల ముడిగియు నిదుర సెడియ జంట లెడసియుం
    గలహము లడఁగియుఁ బఱచెం
    బులి కిరి కరి మన్ను దున్న మొదలగు మెకముల్.

38

Deer were so frightened that they ran into the fire,
like offerings. Lionesses slowly walked away,
folding their tails behind them. Bears crawled
into the mountains. Monkey mothers held their babies
to their breasts as they jumped. Wild boars emerged
from the ponds, and terrifying tigers
ran helter-skelter through that wilderness.

39

They left their homes, lost their power,
lost their courage. Shaken from sleep, separated
from their mates, they stopped fighting
one another as they fled, all of them,
tigers, boars, elephants, gayals, wild buffalo,
and the rest.

౪౦

ఉ అత్తఱి వే౦పికా౦డ్రు యము
నా౦బుతర౦గ పర౦పరాకృతిన్
ముత్తర మైన సూకరస
ముత్కరముం గని మొటుకా౦డ్రు వి
ల్లెత్తకమున్న రాజుమది
కెక్కెడునట్లుగ దీని మిత్తికిం
బుత్త మట౦చు౦ బట్టెడలు
బోరన డుయ్య భయ౦కరార్భటిన్.

౪౧

క జాగిలములు మొఱసడములు౦
జాగె౦ గలసి చాపముక్త శరగతి న౦ దా
జాగిలము లెదిరె౦ బ౦దుల
కై గోధాదికము గాలి కడరె నితరముల్.

40–41

Suddenly the hunters with dogs caught sight of a herd of
    wild boars
moving in waves like the dark waters of the Yamuna River.
Eager to kill them and gain the king's attention
even before the bowmen could shoot,[10] they unleashed the
    dogs,
and in one great, frightening surge the huge hunting dogs
and the little ones rushed off like arrows shot from a bow—
the big dogs going for the boars, the little ones sniffing out
iguanas and other prey.

౪౨

సీ॥ ఎగుచుకూఁతలు ముట్టె యొత్తి బిట్టాలించి
గమికిఁ గన్నాకయి గాలి యరయు
వడీఁ గుక్క లంటంగ వచ్చిన మెడ ద్రిప్పి
ఘుర్ఘురించుచు బయల్ కొమ్ముఁ జిమ్ముఁ
దారసించిన చోట దారునఁ జొరఁ బాఱి
యొకటి రెంటిని దెబ్బ లురల నడుచుఁ
బాలచేరులు వట్టి తూలింప బలిమి నీ
డ్చుకొని డొంకలఁ దూఱి చుట్లఁ బెట్టు

తే॥ నీఁటె పోటులఁ బడి ప్రేవు లీఁదులాడఁ
బోయి పోలేక దగ దొట్టి పాదలు సాచ్చి
బెండువడియును జొరనీదు పీఁటవెట్టి
చూపులనె యేర్చుఁ బ్రజ నొక్క సూకరంబు.

౪౩

క॥ అట్టియెడ నొక వరాహము
బిట్టడిచిన మొఅసెఁ గుక్క ప్రేవులు దంష్ట్రం
జుట్టుకొని రొంపిఁ గలఁపఁగ
నిట్టలముఁ దగిలినట్టి యెఱ్ఱలు వోలెన్.

42

One wild boar, hearing the hunters' voices, raised his snout and, taking charge of the herd, sniffed the wind. As the dogs came near to attack, he turned his neck aside and, grunting, warded them off with his tusks, but they came at him again, and now he bit off chunks of flesh from one or two of them. The dogs caught his testicles and shook him, but fiercely he dragged them into the thicket, worrying them, turning them round until he was pierced by spears and, with his intestines hanging out, trying to run away but unable to, tortured by thirst, exhausted, settled on his haunches, still burning the hunters with his eyes.

43

Another boar pierced a dog with his tusk
and stuck its snout into the mud, stirring it up,
the dog's guts still wound tightly around the tusk
like a string of earthworms.

౪౪౪

మ హరిణం బొక్కటి కుక్కతండముం బుళిం
దానీకముం ద్రోచి యు
ర్వరం గా లూందక దాంట నేటలవికిన్
వాహంబు నడ్డంబు నూం
కి రసావల్లభుం డేసె ఛల్లమున నిం
గిం గాళ్ళు జోడించుచో
గొరిజల్నాలుగుం ద్రైవ్య సేన వొగడెం
గేదండ పాండిత్యమున్.

౪౪౫

క పఅచు నొక కడితిం బతి ముకుం
జెఅమలకై యేయం జిప్ప చినుంగంగ నది యు
క్కఅం గాండి దుస్సి పాటిన
నఅీముటీం జాపరువు వాఅీ యల్లటు వడియొన్.

44

Its feet high in the air, a deer jumped over the hunting
     dogs
and the whole army of Pulinda hunters,
while the king moved his horse into position
for a good shot—and, as the deer
brought its feet together just before landing,
he cut off all four hooves with a single arrow,
to the soldiers' applause.

45

The king shot an arrow aimed at the nose
of a Sambur deer; the arrow broke through the skull
and came out on the other side. The Sambur ran for its life
with one last burst of strength
and fell dead.

౪౬

మ   గవిలో బెబ్బులి డాఁగి గ్రుడ్లు మెఅయం
గాఁ గాంచి రా జేసె నే
య వడిన్ బాణము వెంటనే నిగిడి పై
కట్టేచి రా నేసె రెం
డవకాండంబుఁ దదస్తముం గొనక డా
యన్ వచ్చి కొక్లేయక
ప్రవిభిన్నం బయి నేలఁ గూలెఁ బవిధా
రాభిన్న శైలాకృతిన్.

౪౭

తే   క్రొవ్వి నడగొండ కయివడి గునుకు నొక్క
యొంటిగాని మహీనాథుఁ డెదిఁగి యేయ
గొరక మే నుచ్చి ధరఁ గాఁడ శిరము విసరె
లే దస్యక్వాన మనుచుఁ దెల్పెడు ననంగ.

౪౮

తే   ఒక్కఁ డడుగెత్తి గొఅకఁ వేయుచును డాఁచి
నట్టరిగి ఆెంకీఁ గని వీఁకఁ బట్టుటయును
మృగయు లందఅు సని వెల్వరించి నిశిత
కాండములఁ జెండి రొక పెద్ద కారుపోతు.

46

A tiger was hiding in its dark lair, but the king
detected its glowing eyes. He shot an arrow, and the tiger
jumped at him, straight into the line of fire.
He shot a second arrow; the tiger
was still not stopped. As it closed in,
the king cut into it with his sword,
and it fell like a mountain split
by Indra's diamond bolt.

47

A boar was moving slowly, like a walking mountain,
when the king, stepping aside, shot an arrow through its
    body
so that it hit the ground on the other side. The boar fell,
shaking its head, as if to say, "No, you haven't hurt me."

48

One hunter, making buffalo sounds, crept forward
and found a big buffalo in its resting place, as if he'd hid
it there himself. All the hunters
swarmed around, forced it out,
and killed it.

౪౯

ఉ   ఆ సమయంబునం జకిత
మై మెక మెవ్వని మీఁదఁ బాఱ వాఁ
డేసినయమ్ము వమ్మయి మ
హింఁ బడ కొక్కటి కొండ చాలి వీ
తాసులఁ జేయ మెచ్చి వసు
ధాధిపముఖ్యుఁడు మొట్ల నున్న బా
ణాసనభృత్యులిందులకు
నర్థి నొసంగె నభీప్సితార్థముల్.

౫౦

క   వలఁ బాఱినవానిని భటు
లలుఁగుల పాలాడి రధిపుకై పట్టిరి బె
బ్బులి మహిష మెలుఁగు కిటి దే
డెలు మొదలగువానిఁ గొన్నిటిని వేఁటకరుల్.

౫౧

తే   మున్ను జాగిలములఁ గూడి చన్నయట్టి
యుడుపకుక్కలు కుందేళ్ళ నందురువుల
నుడుముల గ్రహింపఁ బుట్టల కడలఁ బొదల
గిరుల సటీయలఁ బసివట్టి తిరుగుచోట.

49

At that moment, every hunter killed,
with a single shot, the animal he was luring
with a decoy shaped like a man. Not even one arrow
was wasted. The king acclaimed the Pulinda bowmen
and happily gave them whatever they asked for.

50

Soldiers put to death all the animals that escaped
their nets. The ones caught in the nets
they took alive as gifts to the king—tigers, buffaloes,
bears, pigs, wolves, and all.

51

In one spot where the little dogs were following the
  hounds,
sniffing out iguanas, rabbits, and rodents from anthills,
bushes, and holes hidden in the hills,

౫౨

చ బరవస మొప్పఁ గాలితడఁ
బాటు మెయిం గవిఁదూటీ యొక్కకు
ర్కరము దమంబులో వెరఁజి
కోఅలచేఁ గబళించి పొట్టపెం
జైర నుడు మంచుఁ దెచ్చి కని
చేవ దెఅంగక ద్రుంచివైచెఁ ద
ద్ధురుబిరుదప్రమాదముల
కుం బతి మొదవిషాదశాలి గాన్.

౫3

క ఒడ లుబ్బి నిక్కి ముందటీ
యడుగులు ధర నూఁది చిందు నలబలమునకున్
జడియ కొక గబ్బిగం డె
క్కుఁడుఁగడిమిం దివిచెఁ గ్రుంగి కొమ్ములయుడుమున్.

౫౪

తే కంపతోడు గీఁచినట్లేఁదు గానఁ జన్న
తెరు వెఅుంగుచు నొకఁ డేఁగి పరువుతోన
పడి యడఁగి యుండఁగాఁ బటపటన ముండ్లు
గాలిఁ గదలుట గని పంట్రకోలఁ బొడిచె.

324

52

one small dog entered a cave and, in the darkness, led
    astray
by a smell, mistook a poisonous snake
for an iguana. With its teeth it bit into it and brought it out
into the open, where it saw the mistake. Still, it
wouldn't give up and tore its prey to pieces. The king
    watched it all,
both the courage and the error, happy and sad
at the same time.

53

A big dog stretched its body,
dug its front legs firmly into the ground,
and, paying no heed to the hubbub all around,
bent down a little, jumped on a horned iguana,
and killed it.

54

A porcupine was moving through the forest, like a thorny
    bush
in motion. A hunter ran after it and—though the
    porcupine now lay hidden
and still—the hunter heard its quills quivering in the wind
and pierced it with a three-pronged spear.

౩౩

వ అత్తటిం దత్తఅంబున మొత్తంబయి చోపుడుంగోలలు
గొని కెలంకుల పొలంబులం బులుంగులం జోపుచు
డేగవేటకాండ్రు వేఱుపడి వేటాడం దొడంగి రందు.

౩౬

ఉ లీలం బులిందుం డొక్కడు గ
ళిందసుతోర్మి సరోజినీదళాం
దేళిత కోకరేఖం దన
తోరపు నల్లని దీర్ఘ బాహుపై
హాలహాలంబపోలె విడి
యత్తమునం దల యెత్తి చూచు బల్
సాఱువమున్ వడిం జను శ
 శంబుపయిన్ విడిచెన్ మహోద్ధతిన్.

౩౭

క మొలదట్టిచెఱింగుం జెక్కుచు
బలుదిట్ట కిరాతుం డొకడు పటు వగుముష్టిన్
సెలకట్టెం బట్టి వేఱొక
సెలకట్టెం గొట్టి వైచెం జెమరుంగాకిన్.

326

55

Now the falconers got excited and went into action, each one
poking a tree with long sticks so as to set the birds in flight.

56

Like a ruddy goose on a lotus leaf carried on the waves
of the dark Yamuna River, a hawk was looking upward
    from its perch
on the leather strip that covered the thick, black arm
of a Pulinda hunter, who let it loose, cruel
as the first poison, against a rabbit running away.

57

Tightening his waistcloth and tucking it in securely,
a strong hunter held on to his hawk with his clenched fist
while with his other hand he struck at a black crow[11]
with his stick, and killed it.

౩౭

సీ   పెనుదవ్వు దగ దొట్టఁ జని రెట్ట వడఁ గొట్టి
       నుడువీథి బెళగువ్వ నొక్క యెణజు
       తెక్కఁతాఁకున స్రుక్క నిక్కి ప్రక్కలు నొక్కి
       నుఅక కల్లేటి నొక్కొరణంబు
       పొదఁ దూఱు నొకమేటి పూరేటి వెలికిఁ బోఁ
       దేలి కైకొనె నొక్క తేఁచిగాఁడు
       తను నేలుదొర చిత్తమున మెచ్చఁ దీతువుఁ
       జని పట్టె బిట్టొక్క జాలెదేఁగ

తే   విజ్ఞవిజ్ఞానఁ దన్నుంగ విడువ కెలమిఁ
       గఅకుటంబ్ముల నిఱికించి గజ్జె గదలఁ
       గఱికి నెఱినెఱి కోఁలెమ్ముకయును విఱుగ
       విఱిచె వడిఁ గైజు నొక పెద్ద వేసడంబు.

౩౮

క   నింగికయి కుంచెయెత్తి వే
       సం గే యని యార్వఁ బక్ష సంహతిగాడ్పుల్
       తీంగని మ్రోయఁ గుజగ్రపు
       గొంగల నొక లగుడు డిగ్గికొట్టె నిలఁబడన్.

328

58

An *aṇuju* hawk, thirsty from flight, pursued a ringdove, shitting in terror, far through the skies until it struck it dead. An *oraṇa* hawk pounded a *kalleḍu* bird with its wings, weakening it before it crushed it. A *tocigāḍu* hawk dragged a quail from its hiding place in the bushes. A *jālĕ* hawk targeted a yellow lapwing and caught it, to the falconer's delight. A big *vesaḍa* hawk caught a *kaiju* quail that struggled to get free from the sharp claws as the bells on the hawk's feet went on chiming until the quail's wingbone snapped.

59

Lifting its tail feathers, flapping its wings,
and whipping up a breeze, a *laguḍu* hawk
descended on the cranes sitting on the upper branches
of a tree and—as its owner egged it on—
hit them hard, so they fell to the ground.

౬౦

వ ఇ ట్లాఖేటఖేలనంబున వివిధమృగవిహగవధం
బాచరించి చాలించి యంచెలంచెలం బంచతాపతిత
చమర స్రమర కిరి హరిణ రురు మహిష పృషదంశక
గేధికా శశ పిశిత ఖండంబు లొండెండ యువ్వెత్తుగా
నాకు బొత్తరలం గట్టియు గుదులు గుట్టియు
జిక్కంబుల నించియు గావదుల నుంచియు సవరించి
దిగదిగన విసరి బగబగన మండు చిదుగు సాదమంటల
కడ్డంబు వట్టి మీసంబులు సూడిచూడి వాడులగు
కత్తులం దిత్తులొలిచి కుత్తుకలు గోసి శితముఖంబులగు
నఖంబులం బెకలించి విపుల వపు రపహసిత
మహాశైలంబు లగు శార్దూలంబుల బొందుల నందంద
పడవైచి యంతంత గాంతారంబున దంతురంబుగ
బడిన దంతావళంబుల దంతంబులు గైకొనియు
దత్కుంభ నిర్గత మౌక్తికంబు లేటీకొనియు గోఅజంబం
జమరవాలంబుల బర్బిబర్బంబులం బరిగ్రహించియు
మరలి యత్తటి గడింది నెత్తురుం బ్రొడ్డగుట వెంచచవం
జఅవ నేడు పెనుమండ్ల బండ్ల సరియలు నెఅీయలు
వాఅీ బోరనం గాఅు ధారాళ రుధిరాసారపూరంబు నాకి
నాకి నాలుకలు దిగవైచి యేచిన మహా తపోష్ణంబునం
దృష్ట వొడమి దగ నిగుడ వగ రఅరి యొదలం
దొదలను మెదలను బెడిదంపు నిదుడ కోఅల సలుగు
లడిచినయొదలం బొడబొడను వెడలెడు నుడుకునెత్తటం
బడలి తూలు కొలేయకమ్ముల యంగమ్ము
లార్ద్రికర్పటంబులం గప్పి దప్పి నిగుడ నప్పాలంబు
పశ్చిమపు దండ నుండు వెండికొండ బండలం జండకర
కరహిందనంబునం బాండుప్రభలు నిండి పఅిచు తఅిచు
సెలయేఅుల సూఅెలం గాఅుకొను భూరుహనికాయంబుల
డాయం జని తద్ఘనచ్ఛాయల నిలిచి యచ్చటంగ్రిచ్చి
గరువు నేలల గుంట లౌనరించి లోన నుమ్మగిలి

60

In this hunter's game, they killed many kinds of animals and birds before they stopped—yaks, big and small, boars, stags, antelopes, buffaloes, wildcats, iguanas, rabbits. They collected the meat from the dead game and packed it in leaves, stacking it in a tall heap. Then they arranged them in smaller piles so they could be carried in bags made of rope on either end of a long pole. They lit wood fires with small kindling sticks and fanned the flames to burn the whiskers off dead tigers' faces.[12] Then they skinned the carcasses with sharp knives and cut their necks, taking out the sharp claws before they threw away the bodies that were bigger than mountains. They took the tusks from dead elephants that were strewn throughout that wilderness and gathered the pearls that had popped out of their temples; they took yellow bile, bushy yak tails, and peacock feathers. Returning at high noon, they found dogs profusely bleeding at the mouth from porcupine quills they had bit on, and they were licking at this blood, their tongues hanging down as they panted, thirsty in the fierce heat, while from wounds caused by the sharp fangs of wild boars to their bodies, thighs, and necks warm blood was flowing, and they could barely walk. The hunters covered them with wet blankets to ease their pain.

Feeling thirsty, they moved westward among the boulders on Silver Mountain. Streams white with sunlight were flowing there with thick forest on either side; they stood a while in the shadow of the trees. Where the land was dry they dug holes and laced them with *āvura* leaves, which, when heated, emit a good smell; they selected the choicest pieces of meat and placed them over a dense, even layer of soft liver, heart,

గబ్బు వలవక కమ్మ తావులు గల నావురాకులు పఱచి
యెఱచిలో మేలేఱీ కారిజముం గందనకాయ క్రొవ్వ
మొదలగు మిగుల మెత్తని పలలభిత్తంబు లందుఁ
గ్రందుకొనం గ్రుక్కి యొక్కువ తక్కువలు గాకుండఁ
గండ గలతింత్రిణీ శలాటు సంఘాతంబు లామీద
నెఱయం బచరించి యొసరుగాఁ దేఁట లగు లేఁటినల్లలు³
గుమ్మరించి లవణకణ సంచయంబు నించి లావుగాఁ
గావు గప్పి యుపరిప్రదేశంబులఁ గారెనుపపెంటపట్ల
నీఱాఱు నేఱుం బిడుకల దాళ్ళిడి నెల్లికొయ్యలు
ద్రచ్చి నుచ్చు లంటించినం బెచ్చుపెరుగు చిచ్చు
లాత్రంపులం దవిలించి చిముడ నుడికిన వెలువరించి
యుప్పు వెప్పునుం గల యప్పిశితఖండంబులు
గనగని నిప్పులం జమురు చిప్పిలం గాల్చిన
కమ్మకఱికుట్లం జట్రాతిపయఁ గాఱ్చెనికిం గుడుపువెట్టి
పిదపఁ బాళ్ళవెంబడిం బంచుకొని తారు నుపయోగించి
తద్దేవతాప్రీతికై తలలుఁ దేఁకలు దెక్కలు నచటి విటపి
విటపంబుల వ్రేలం గట్టి శిశిరమధురసలిలమ్ములు ద్రావి
వాగురికులు విశ్రమింప నిలింపాంగనాసుతుండును
సహసమాగత చతుర వలల కృత పలలఫలమూలాది
శుచిమధుర మృగయోచితా హారంబులం దృప్తి వహించి
పరిజనారచిత పల్లవాసనాసీనుఁడై గండూషమితపుండరీక
మధురసాసారంబు లగు నిర్ధరానిలకిశోరంబు లోలయ
నలయికలు దేఱియున్న సమయంబున.

and fat, adding unripe tamarind fruit in just the right amount and then the clear blood of the deer and crystals of salt. On top they laid dry droppings of the gayal to build an oven and, after gathering sticks of *nelli* wood, they rubbed them together to make fire that, bursting into a flame, was applied to the cakes of dung. When the meat was well cooked, they took it from the fire; other meat was barbecued on skewers, the fat sizzling and dripping. Some they placed on a flat stone as offerings to the forest god; only afterward did they parcel out the rest among themselves according to their rank. After they ate, they hung the heads, tails, and ribs on branches of the trees to please the gods of that place. Refreshing themselves with cool, sweet water, the hunters took their rest.

The son of the gods' woman* ate his fill of meat, fruits, and roots and other dishes appropriate to a hunting expedition, all prepared by skilled cooks he had brought along with him. Relaxing on a seat his attendants had made for him from tender leaves, he enjoyed the light breeze carrying the fragrance of lotuses from nearby streams. At that time,

---

* Svarochi.

౬౧

మత్తకోకిల.

నిండెఁ గావిరి దిక్తటంబుల
నింగిఁ గుండలి చందరు
జ్మండలిం గనుఁగొంచు మ్రోసెను
మాలకాకులమూఁక ల
య్యుండ నిల్చి యదల్చె నప్పు ?
వాళి యూళలఁ బద్మగ
ర్భాండభాండము ధూళిధూసర
మయ్యె నుద్ధతవాత్యలన్.

౬౨

క ఆ కొఱగాములఁ గనుఁగొని
శాకునికుం డొకఁడు లేచి సంభ్రమ మొదవన్
జ్యాకలిత శరాసనుండై
వీఁకను సైనికులఁ దిట్టి విభుతో ననియెన్.

౬3

క తఅచుగ మెకములఁ బొరిగొను
మఅఅపున వచ్చితిమి దవ్వ మనపొల మిట కి
త్తఆ నగునిమిత్తములు నృప
కొఱగా విదె మనకుఁ బెద్ద గొడవగు ననినన్.

61

A smoky darkness engulfed all space.
Flocks of pitch-black crows cawed as they saw the sun
encircled by clouds. Jackals howled, rousing fear,
and Brahma's Egg—the whole world—turned dark
in the dust raised by fierce winds.

62

Seeing those signs, an expert in reading omens
got up and, alarmed, placed an arrow on his bowstring,
yelled at the soldiers, and said to the king:

63

"We were so lost in killing animals
that we forget ourselves and ended up
here, far from home. The omens, O King,
do not bode well. We're in for big trouble."

౬౪

మ అతఁ డాస్ఫాలితసజ్యకార్ముకుఁడు వా
హోరూఢుఁడుం బార్శ్వసం
భృతతూణాహృతచండకాండుఁడు దిశా
ప్రేంఖత్కటాక్షాంచల
ద్యుతిజాలుండును నై పులిందభటసం
దోహంబుతోడన్ మహో
ద్ధతి నండం జయలాభసూచక నిమి
త్తంబుల్మొయిందేఁచినన్.

౬౫

వ ప్రాణరక్షాసంశయంబగు మహారణక్షోభం బొక్కటి గలుగు
మీఁద నెట్టకేలకు మితి వెట్టరాని జయమంగళంబు
లగునని యంతరంగంబున నిశ్చయించి యాఱడిలు
సమయంబున.

౬౬

క ఆ విపినాంతరమున హో
హో వనిత ననాథ నబల నార్త విపన్నం
గావరె యీ పుణ్యమనం
బోవరె యని పలుకు నాఁడుమొఱ విన్ఁబడియెన్.

336

64

The king was ready in a moment. Mounting his horse,
he twanged his bow, then picked up a killer arrow
from the full quiver behind his shoulder.
He looked in all directions from the corners
of his glowing eyes, with the hunters all around him.
Now he felt omens of future victory on his body.

65

In his heart he knew that a fierce battle that would put life
itself in danger was about to happen and that it would end
auspiciously in an endless happiness. He comforted himself
with this thought.

66

Then he heard a woman's cry:
"Save me! I'm a helpless woman,
in deep distress. God will bless you."

౭౨

క ఆమొఱ వేమఱుం జెవి నిడి
భూమండలభర్త కరుణ పొడమంగ నయ్యో
యేమానిని కెవ్వనిచే
నే మాయెనొ యనుచు నచటు నీక్షించుతఱిన్.

౭౭

శా మఱ్ఱెల్మ్రొయంగ గబ్బిచన్నుంగవ గం
పం బంద వేణీభరం
బట్టెఱ్ఱై కటిం జిమ్మచీంకటులు గా
నఫ్రువ్రజం బోడిక
ల్గట్టం జూపులు చిమ్మిరేంగి దివి రో
లంబాళింగల్వింపంగా
మిట్టాడంగ నరుండు లేనియడవిన్
మీనాక్షి దీనాకృతిన్.

౭౯

క ఒక్కతె భయశోకంబుల
వెక్కుచు మెయ్యంగల విలాస విభ్రమలక్ష్ముల్
దక్కుటయును నొక యొఱఱపై
నెక్కొన ధరణీశునెదుట నిలిచి వినీతిన్.

338

67

The prince heard that wail again and again
and was moved. "Someone has done something
terrible to some woman," he thought, looking
in that direction.

68

Toe-rings jingling, breasts shaking,
hair coming undone and enveloping her waist
in darkness, tears flowing from her eyes
that were looking in all directions, like bees
swarming in space, a fish-eyed woman was moving
      helplessly
in that desolate wilderness.

69

She stood humbly before the prince; she was sobbing
in fear and grief. Her naturally elegant movements
were lost, and that itself gave her
a different kind of beauty.

౨౦

క పలుచని వాతెఱ మెఱుంగునం
బలు మెఱుంగులు సందడింపం బాపటపై నం
జలిం జేర్చి జఱుకుంజూపులం
బలుకులం బులకండ మొలుకం బలికెం గలంకన్.

౨౧

శా ఓ రాజన్యమహేంద్ర యో మణిగణ
ప్రోతాసివాతాశన
ప్రారజ్యత్కటిచక్ర యో ముఖరశా
ర్జన్మూరబాహార్గళా
యో రుక్మాచలకల్ప యో కవచిత
వ్యూఢాంగ కావంగదే
యో రాహుత్తశిరోమణీ నిరవధి
ప్రోద్యత్ప్రతాపారణీ.

౨౨

క అనినం దలంపున నింపిన
యనుకంప నిలింప చంపకామోదసుతం
డనునయ మొప్పగ నోడకు
మని నిజవృత్తాంత మడుగ నది యిట్లనియెన్.

70

Her teeth dazzling white between thin and brilliant lips,
she folded her hands on the parting of her hair and,
with frightened eyes, shaken, she spoke words
sweet as candied sugar.

71

"Oh king of kings,
steady as Golden Mountain,
your hips adorned by a jeweled sword
swaying like a deadly snake,
a bow made from horn rustling
on your massive arms,
your body shielded by armor,
best of all horsemen!
You're like the firesticks
that produce endless flames.
Please save me, king of kings."

72

Svarochi, son of a godly woman fragrant as a flower,
felt compassion fill his mind.
"Don't be afraid," he said
kindly. "Tell me your story."
She said:

23

సీ విసుమానములు గాఁగ వసతోడఁ బెనవెట్టి
నెఱ్టెంబుగాఁ బ్రేవుఁ జుట్టినాఁడు
బండికందెన చాయ బైసిమాలిన మేన
మెదడు గందపు రొంపి మెత్తినాఁడు
కునఖంపు డాచేతి పునకకప్పెర నిండఁ
బ్రాణికోటుల నల్లఁ బట్టినాఁడు
కొకిబికి వేసంపు గూని మూఁపులమీఁద
మూఁడు పంగల యాఁకె మోపినాఁడు

తే నిట్టతాడనఁ బొడువుచే నిక్కినాఁడు
నిడుదకోఅల మిడి గ్రుడ్ల నెగడినాఁడు
నరవరోత్తమ నేఁడు మూనాళ్ళనుండి
యుసుఱు గొన వెంటఁ దిరిగెడు నసుర యొకఁడు.

24

క ఏయెడ ననదలమొఅి వా
లాయము వినవలయు 'దుర్బలస్య బలం రా
జా' యన వినవే ధరణీ
నాయకులకు నార్తరక్షణంబులె క్రతువుల్.

25

క మరుదశ్వపుత్తి కిందీ
వరాక్ష గంధర్వరాజువలనఁ బొడమితిన్
నరవర వెలసితిఁ గళలం
దు రమించుటఁ జేసి భువి మనోరమ యనఁగన్.

73

"There's this demon chasing me.
He's tall as a palm tree.
He has fangs and bulging eyes.
Intestines wrapped around his head and packed with
    marrow.
An ugly body, black as axle grease, smeared with filth of
    brains.
A skull teeming with the blood of endless victims held in
    his left hand with its dirty nails.
On his humped back, draped with a hodgepodge of
    clothes, a three-pronged spear.
He's been trying to kill me for the past three days.

74

You should always save the helpless.
You know that the king is the strength
of the weak. Taking care of those in trouble
is how kings worship gods.

75

My mother is the daughter of King Marudashva,
and the gandharva king Indivaraksha is my father.
My name is Manorama, 'Pleasing to the Heart,'
because all the arts please my heart.

౯౬

శా రారాపిళ్ళ భుజంగదంబుల మణుల్
రాలంగ విద్యాధరుల్
గారా మొప్పగ నెత్తికొంద్రు నను నం
క స్థాయినిం జేయంగా
వారిన్ వీడ్కిని సింహపీఠికఁజల
త్వం బొందు మాతండ్రి మం
జీరం బించుక ఘల్లు మన్న నవి దాఁ
జెప్పంగ నిం కేటికిన్.

౯౭

తే దేవ పార్శ్వనిపట్టి కళావతియును
నల్ల మందారవిద్యాధరాత్మజన్మ
యగు విభావసియును నాకుఁ బ్రాణసఖులు
వారు నేనును నొకనాఁడు గారవమున.

76

All the vidyadharas used to try to pick me up, brushing
against each other so that their jewels fell from their arms,
and my father would rise from his throne and dismiss
    them
so he could take me in his lap whenever he heard
my anklets ringing. Why talk of that now?

77

My lord, I have two close friends: Kalavati, daughter of
    Para the sage,
and Vibhavari, daughter of Mandara, a vidyadhara.
One day, the three of us

౭౮

సీ॥ నెత్తమ్ము లేకొండ నెత్తమ్ముఅలం దాడు
విద్యాధరీకోటి విటులతోడ
నెచటిగాడ్పులం బుట్టు విచికిలామోదంబు
శబర కాంతల గుట్టు సఖ్యంబెట్టు
నెన్నగేంద్రపు జఱుల్ మిన్నంది పెన్నంది
కోరాడుం దనగుబ్బకొమ్మలొడ్డి
యెం దుండు గురివెంద పందిళ్ళ పూందేనె
జడి యిందుశిలలందు జాలువాఱు

తే॥ నట్టి కలధౌతశిఖరిం బుష్పాపచయము
సేయువేడుకc బోదరింట్ల చాయలందుc
దిరుగుచుండి యొకానొక దెసc దృణంబు
దళముగా వాత మొలచిన బిలమునందు.

౭౯

ఉ॥ ఊసరవెల్లి చందమున
నొక్కట బీఅినరాలు దేఅింగా
మీసలు గడ్డముం జడలు
మే నుదరంబును వీనులన్ జరా
ధూసరమైన రోమతతి
తోc బెనంగంబడి దూది రాశిగాc
జేసినరీతి నున్న యొక
జీర్ణమునిం గని కౌతుకంబునన్.

౩౪౬

78

went to pick flowers on a mountain
where *vidyādharis*[13] play dice with their lovers,
where the smell of jasmine carried by the wind
lets loose desire in forest women
and Shiva's great bull rams his horns
into the slopes and shakes them,
and honey from *gurivĕnda* vines wound around trellises
drips onto the moonstones.

That's where we went, to Silver Mountain.
Roaming through bowers and bushes,
we came upon a cave with an opening
thickly covered with grass

79

and saw a decrepit sage looking something like a
    chameleon,
the veins visible on his body, and the grey hair on his skin
    grown so thick
it was twined with his mustache, beard, dreadlocks, and
    the hair
in his ears, as if he were a big ball of cotton. Out of childish
    curiosity,

౩౦

ఆ ఇతని వదన కుహర మెద్ది నేత్రద్వయం
బెద్ది కర్ణయుగళ మెద్ది యనుచు
బూచివోలె నున్న వాచంయముని మోము
బాల్య చాపలమునఁ బట్టుటయును.

౩౧

క ధ్యానస్తిమితం డగు న
మ్మౌని మదీయాంగుళీవిమర్శనములచే
మే నెత్తఁగి తొంటి యనుసం
ధానము చెడి కన్ను దెఱచి దారుణఘణితిన్.

౩౨

ఉ ఓసి దురాత్కురాల గృహ
మొల్లక సర్వసుఖంబులున్ నిరా
యాసమునం దొఱంగి మిహి
రాంశు మరుచ్చదనీర నీరస
గ్రాసము దేహధారకము
గా గుహలం దప మాచరించు మ
మ్మీసరణిన్ స్పృశించి నగ
నేమి ఫలం బొనఁగూడెఁ జెప్పుమా.

348

80

I poked his face. I thought he was a ghost.
'Where,' I said, 'is his mouth? Where are his eyes
and his ears?'

81

He was deep in meditation, but he woke up
at my touch. He'd lost his concentration.
Opening his eyes, he said harshly:

82

'You bad girl. I left home and all the comforts
that come with it to discipline myself in these caves,
with only water, leaves, wind, and sunlight
to keep my body together. Now you touch me
and laugh at me. What do you gain by this?

౮3

క తిమిరంపు వయసు గుబ్బల
కొమరాలవు నీకుఁ దగిన గోవాళ్ళ మహిన్
నెమకి నగరాదె ముదిసిన
మమ్ముఁ జెనకిన నేమి కలదు మద మేమిటికిన్.

౮౪

క ముసురుకొను జరభరంబున
నసురుసు రై యన్న మమ్ము నడకించితి వి
ట్లుసురు మనఁ బట్టువడు మొక
యసురకు నీ వనుచుఁ బలికె నాగ్రహ మెసఁగన్.

౮౫

క జననాథ యేమి చెప్పుదుఁ
గనలుచు నవ్వగ్గు తపసి కటము లదరఁగాఁ
దనచేతి నాగబెత్తముఁ
గొని పసరముఁ గొట్టినట్టు గొట్టె నదయుఁడై.

౮౬

క కొట్టువడి యటకు మునుపే
తిట్టుం బడి యేడ్చు నాదు దెసఁ గని మదిలోఁ
గట్టులుక వోడమి నాసఖు
లిట్టినిరి మునీంద్రుతోడ నెత్తిన పెలుచన్.

350

83

You're a girl blinded by youth,
with proud breasts. Why don't you find a young man
to laugh at? Why tease an old man like me?
You're too wild.

84

My body is worn by age.
You're making fun of me.
You'll pay for it. You'll be caught
by a demon.' So he said, very angry.

85

What can I say, my lord? That old man,
his temples throbbing with rage, picked up
his yoga stick and beat me without mercy,
as if I were an animal.

86

First he cursed me, then he beat me.
I was crying, and my friends, seeing this,
were enraged and screamed at that sage.

౯౦

తే ఒండెకఁడవైన నిపుడు నీ పిండి యిడమె
బ్రాహ్మణఁడ వౌట మాచేత బ్రదుకు గంటి
తడవఁ బనిలేదు నిన్ను గౌతముని గోవ
వనుచు వాదించి విడిచిన నాగ్రహించి.

౯౧

క ముసలి శపియించె నపుడ
య్యసితాభ్రేక్షణల రాజయక్షక్షోభం
బెసఁగ నశియింప నగు న
ద్దెసఁ బాఱుఁడు సుగుడి గామి తెల్లమియ కదా.

౯౨

క ఆ రుజ యప్పుడ యయ్యం
భోరుహలోచనలఁ బొందె భూవర నన్నున్
వారత్రయముననుండియు
దారుణగతి నొక్కయసుర తఱిమెడు వెంటన్.

90

If you were anybody else, we'd have beaten you to a pulp.
Because you're a Brahman, we let you live. You're as
    fragile
as Gautama's cow,'[14] they said, and moved away.
He was furious

91

and cursed those black-eyed beauties
to suffer from consumption and die.
It's clear, isn't it, that that Brahman
was no good man.

92

The disease afflicted them right away.
As for me, oh king, for the last three days
that demon has been cruelly chasing me.

౯౩

సీ ఇచ్చెద నీ కస్త హృదయంబు నివ్విద్య
నరనాథ మున్ను పినాకపాణి
యగు రుద్రుc డిచ్చె స్వాయంభువ మనువున
కతc డిచ్చె మటి వసిష్ఠాఖ్యమునికి
నతcడిచ్చెc గరుణ జిత్రాయుధం డను పేరc
దనరు మదీయ మాతామహునకు
నతc డిచ్చెc బెండ్లి యొనపు దరణంబుగా
మా తండ్రి కతc డిచ్చె మమత నాకు

తే సకలరిపునాశకము యశస్కరము నైన
దీని వేవేగ నాచేc బ్రతిగ్రహించి
యడcపుమా దైత్యు వీరు వా రనcగ వలవ
దనఘ సద్విద్య యొందున్నc గొనcగవలయు.

౯౪

క అనుటయు శుచియై నిలిచిన
జననాథునకుం బ్రయోగ సంహారంబుల్
వనిత రహస్యంబుగc జె
ప్పిన నాతcడు నెటీcగె నంత భీషణభంగిన్.

93

Prince: I'll teach you a mantra called 'Heart of Weapons,'
which Rudra the trident bearer gave to the self-born
    Manu,
who gave it to Vasishtha, who in turn gave it to my
    mother's father,
named Chitrayudha, 'Equipped with Marvelous
    Weapons.'
He gave it to my father as a wedding gift, and my father
gave it to me out of love. It kills all enemies
and also makes you famous. Take it, please, from me.
Hurry. Kill that monster. Knowledge should be received
from anyone who offers it, without asking
where it comes from."

94

The prince accepted the offer, purified himself,
and stood before her. She taught him secretly
how to cast, and to withdraw, that weapon.
He learned it all. Now, a terrifying laugh

౯౫

మహాస్రగ్ధర.

గళగర్తక్రోడ నిర్యత్కహకహ నినదో
ద్ధాఢహాసంబు భూభృ
ద్విలముల్మ్రోయింపఁ గాదంబినిగతిని బౌగల్
పెంప మిన్నెల్లమైగాఁ
జలితాస్యక్రూరదంతక్షత రదవసన
క్షారకీలాలవేళ్ల
జ్వలనజ్వాలాభ జిహ్వాంచలుఁ డగుచు గదన్
జాళముల్ద్రిప్పుకొంచున్.

౯౬

ఉ. దానవుఁ డద్ధరారమణుఁ
దాఁకె నుదగ్రపదాగ్రఘట్టన
గ్లాని సపాటమై యచటి
కాన ఘరట్టవిఘట్టితాకృతిం
బూని చెడన్ గిరీశగళ
మూల హలాహలకాలకాంతితో
మేనటికంబు లాడు తన
మేటి త్రిశూలముఁ బూని యుద్ధతిన్.

౯౭

తే. నింగి నొరయు రాకాసిమన్ననీ మేని
నీడఁ జీఁకటిగొనె నవనీతలంబు
చంద్రికలు గాంచె నట్టహాసముల వెడలు
నిశితదంష్ట్రలచేన వనీతలంబు.

95

seemed to come from the depths of a throat, like a hollow
in the earth, echoing in the mountain caves, and the body
of the demon filled the whole sky, like a black cloud,
and like a flame of fire his tongue shot out, bright with
    blood
flowing from his lips, which he'd bitten with his cruel
    teeth.
He was brandishing a mace, twirling it round.

96

He attacked the king. Crushed by the demon's feet,
the wilderness was leveled and turned to dust, as if ground
by a grinding stone. He picked up his trident,
a close cousin of the black poison that Shiva
holds in his throat.

97

The shadow of his huge body rubbing against the sky
darkened the earth, while the forest gleamed white
as moonlight from his sharp, bright teeth
when he laughed.

೯೦

పంచచామరము.

పలాశి డాసి రాజుᛘ జూచి
పల్కె నోరి నోరి కీ
పొలానᛘ బెన్బొలాన లేక
పోవ నీవు దేᛘచి తో
బలా బలాలితోడᛘ బాలᛘ
బట్టి బిట్టు చుట్టి నిన్
హళాహళిన్ హలాహలాభ
యౌ బుభుక్షᛘ దీర్చెదన్.

೯೯

మహాస్రగ్ధర.

అని బాహాస్ఫోట రావాహత పతగకులం
బవ్వనీశాఖి శాఖా
జనితవ్యాకీర్ణజీర్ణచ్చదముల కరణీం
జల్లనన్ రాల భూషా
ర్చి సుదీర్ఘాలాత చక్రాకృతిగᛘ జిఐజిఐం
ద్రిప్పి వైచెం గడన్ వై
చినᛘ దేఙిన్ రాజు గెంటించెᛘ దొలᛘగ నది య
చ్చెంత కాంతార మేర్చెన్.

98

"Hey you!" he cried. "I've been scouring this land
for meat, and now, luckily, you've turned up.
I'll capture you, your army, and this girl
and eat you right now. Hunger is burning me
like a poisonous fire."

99

He slapped his shoulders, and at that thunderous sound
birds perched on the branches of trees fell dead
to the ground like dry leaves. He whirled his mace,
the jewels embedded in it weaving a circle of light
like a torch, and threw it at the king, who spurred his horse
aside, but the forest was utterly destroyed.

౧౧౦

పృథ్వి.

గదాహతికి నాత్మ గొం
కక యొదిర్చి రాగా ని దొ
గదా యనుచు ద్రిప్పి రా
క్షసుడు వైచె గాఢభ్రమీ
నదత్కనక కింకిణీ
నటన జాగ్రదుగ్రార్భటీ
వదావద మహాగుహో
వలభియైన శూలంబునున్.

౧౧౧

శా ఆ శూలం బవనీశమౌళి కులిశా
హంకార హుంకారక్
న్నైశిత్యం బభినుత్య మై నెగడు బా
ణశ్రేణీ జెండాడి వే
కాశశ్వేతగరుత్వరంపరల నా
కాశంబు దుగ్ధాభ్దిసం
కాశం భై వెలుగన్ శరావళులచే
గప్పెం గకుప్పంక్తులన్.

౧౧౨

క అవి యాతని పై తోలును
నవియింపగ లేక మిడిసి యల్లటు వడ జూ
చి వనేచరు లేచిన వెఱ
దవిలిన మతి నద్దరయ్య దయ్యం బనుచున్.

100

When the mace came at him, Svarochi showed no fear.
He fought back. The monster then said to himself,
"This should work,"[15] and picked up his spear,
turning it round and round so that its golden bells
rang out, and their echoes went on ringing
in the deep mountain caves.

101

The king demolished that spear with a shower of arrows
so sharp they could mock Indra's diamond sword,
so white with feathers, like *rĕllu* grass, that they turned
the sky into a ocean of milk to the ends of space.

102

But they couldn't even scratch the monster's skin.
They fell at a distance, and the forest people,
seeing this, were terrified and took to their heels,
crying, "Hey, he's a ghost!"

౧౦3

సీ. పక్కుపక్కున నంఫ్రిపాశములవేసc డ్రెంచి
   డేగ తండముల మింటికిని విడిచి
   గళగళ ధ్వనులతోc గంతశృంఖల లూడ్చి
   సుడివడc గుక్కల నడవిc గలిపి
   గుప్పుగుప్పున మొచికొనియున్న వలలతోc
   బలలంపుc బొత్తరల్ పాఠివైచి
   కంగుకంగున నేలcగై దప్పుగాc బడు
   వేcటమ్ము లేఅక దాcటిదాcటి

తే. తిరిగి చూచుచు దల్లెగcదీసికొనుచు
   దగలు దొట్టి యథాయథ లగుచు విటీగి
   యొకcడు వేయునత్రోవ వే ఱొకcడు పోక
   చెట్టొకcడు గాcగc బఱచిరి చెంచు లపుడు.

౧౦౪

క. ప్రోప్పc దలపోసి నిలువక
   పాపాత్మకమై కిరాత బల మటు పాఠిన్
   భూపతి యయ్యింతి హాయ
   స్థాపితగాc జేసి పలికెc దన్ముఖ్యులకున్.

103

They let loose the hawks, cutting the ropes that bound
    their feet,
and sent them flying.
They unhooked the chains tied to the dogs' collars
and let them run off into the forest.
They threw off the nets they were carrying on their backs
along with parcels of meat.
Arrows fell from their hands, and they didn't even stop to
    pick them up
as they ran, panic-stricken, looking back in fear,
pulling up their clothes, scattering in all directions,
each on his own, one per tree.

104

Ungrateful, unmindful of the service they owed him,
the men of the forest kept on running, their minds dark,
and now the king raised the woman onto his horse
and called out to the leaders:

౧౦౭

ఉ కైదువు సున్న పూజ్యములు
కంకటఖేటశిరస్నిలత్రముల్
లే దరదంబు తత్తడి హు
ఖిక్కి సహాయము సర్వమంగళం
బీ దనుజండు చిక్కె భయ
మేటికి లుభ్ధకులార యాత్మకుం
బీదతనంబు మేలె మటి
మృత్యువు డాఁగెడిచోట లేదొకో.

౧౦౬

ఆ నీడఁ గడవఁ బాఱి నేలకు వెలి గాఁగ
నడుగు వెట్టి తిరుగ నాత్మ మొఅఁగి
యొకటిఁ దలఁప నరుల కొదవిన నొదవ దే
కరణి మృత్యుదేవిఁ గన్నుఁబ్రామ.

౧౦౮

క చావుఁ దలపోసి మానవుఁ
డేవగ దుష్మీర్తి వొరయకే దినములు పాఁ
డై వెడలునట్లు నడవఁగఁ
దైవం బటమీఁద మేలు తాన ఘటించున్.

366

105

"He has no sword.
No armor, no shield, no helmet.
No chariot. No horse.
No allies.
This monster is a sitting duck.
Why, great hunters, are you afraid?
Does it feel good inside?
Won't Death find you wherever you're hiding?

106

Running away from your own shadow,
walking without touching the ground,
thinking of something without your mind—
even if all of these were possible,
you can't hide from Death.

107

Knowing death to be certain, if a man lives his life
without getting a bad name, spending his days well,
the future will take care of itself.

౧౦౮

సీ   బుద్ధీంద్రియక్షోభములకు బెట్టని కోట
విపదంబురాశి దుర్వీకృతి కోడ
ఖల దురాలాప మార్గణ వజ్రకవచంబు
రణ మహీస్థలికి శ్రీరామ రక్ష
శాత్రవ దుర్గర్వ సంస్తంభనౌషధి
మొనయు చింతాశ్రేణి మూఁకవిప్పు
యోగాదిసంసిద్ధు లోనఁగూర్చు పెన్నిధి
తూలు నేకాకుల తోడునీడ

తే   సకల సుగుణప్రధానంబు సకలకార్య
జాల సాఫల్యకరణైక సాధనంబు
ధైర్యగుణ మట్టి ధైర్యంబు దక్కి పోరఁ
దత్తటీంతురె యకట మీ తరమువారు.

౧౦౯

క   అని తెలిపి తిరుగుఁ డనుటయు
మనమున లజ్జించి యొఱుకు మన్నీ లిఁక నీ
జనపతితోడిడ లోకం
బని తమతమ మొనలు ద్రిప్పి రవియును దిరిగెన్.

108

Courage is the only thing that works.
It's the best of all virtues,
a natural fortress against any attack
on the mind or the senses, a boat
to carry you across a sea of sorrows,
armor against the arrows of harsh words,
a god-given defense on the field of battle,
a charm that paralyzes an enemy's pride
and dispels an army of cares,
a buried treasure that gives you all yogic powers,
the one true friend when you're lonely.
That's what courage is. Can people like you
live without it?

109

Come back to fight!"
When they heard this, the hunters' leaders
were ashamed. "Our lives," they said,
"are with this king." They turned their men back.

౧౧౦

వ ఇట్లు తిరిగి యుక్కెక్కి రక్కసుండెక్క డెక్కడ నని
యక్కొటబలంబు లగుడంబులుం గటారు లీంటెలుం
బందీంటెలు విండ్లు గంత్రగొడ్తెండ్రుం జిల్లకోలలుం
బంత్రకోలలు మొఅయ రయసముద్ధూత ధూళిధూసరిత
ధారాధరపథంబగుచు నొక్కపరియ చీమపరి యనం
గవిసె నందు.

౧౧౧

మ శరసంధానముతోనె కొన్ని యడుగుల్
జొజవ్వనం బాటీ య
ద్ధరణీం గాల్కొని ద్రోణముల్దివియు దో
ర్దండంబులం జేండి యే
సిరి బోయల్దిను మంచు నార్చి పరంగం
జిట్టాసలం డాయుచుం
గొరవంకల్మొఅవెట్టినట్లు గుణముల్
ఘోషింప రోషింపుచున్.

౧౧౨

తే ఆ శరావళి నమ్మనుజాశనుండు
లీల మృగదంశకము మశకాళి నౌడిసి
చప్పరించు విధంబున శాతదీర్ఘ
దంష్ట్రికలం జప్పరించి రౌద్రమునం గెరలి.

110

Regaining their strength, saying "Where is that demon?"
the hunters brandished their weapons—long clubs, swords,
spears, boar spikes, bows, axes with curved blades, hooked
lances, and forked javelins—and kicked up so much dust that
it turned the sky grey. They circled the demon like a swarm
of ants.

111

They came running, shaking the earth,
and took their stand before him, bows drawn,
raging. With arms strong from twirling heavy clubs,
they twanged the bowstrings, which shrieked
like myna birds, and closed in on the monster,
ready to give up their lives. Yelling "Take that!"
they shot.

112

The man-eating ogre chewed up those arrows
with his sharp, long teeth, as a dog would casually
eat mosquitoes.

౧౧3

సీ గళితశృంఖల మైన గంధనాగముఁవోలెఁ
      బ్రజలపైఁ బేరెముల్ వాఱి పాఱి
      కలశాబ్ధి మథియించు కైటభాంతకులీల
      జవ మొప్ప జేతులు సాఁచి చాఁచి
      కన లూను కీనాశ కాసరమ్మునుబోలెఁ
      గమిచి తట్టువగుంపుఁ జమరి చమరి
      యమ్మృతాపహరణార్థ మరుగు పక్షిస్వామి
      గతిఁ బులిందశ్రేణిఁ గమిచి కమిచి

తే సెలవులు బిగించి నేత్రదంష్ట్రికలు మెఱియ
      నిడుదమొగ మెత్తి మీసల నెత్తు రొలుకఁ
      బటబటఁ గపాలపంక్తులఁ బగులఁ గొటికి
      బలమునెల్లను గడియలోపలన మ్రింగె.

౧౧౪

క ఆ సమయంబున గీర్వా
      ణీసుతుఁ డయ్యింతినొక్క నికట నికుంజా
      వాసమ్మున నిడి క్రమ్మటి
      వే సురరిపుఁ దాఁకెఁ దురగ వేగము మెఱయన్.

113

Like an elephant in rut breaking out of its fetters,
he stampeded over them, again and again.
Like God Vishnu churning the ocean,[16] he stretched out
    his hands
and, like the buffalo that Death rides, smashed their
    ponies,
and like the eagle Garuda flying down to steal the elixir,
he chewed up the mass of hunters. Tightening his lips,
his eyes and teeth glowing, he cracked open their skulls
and, blood soaking his mustache, gulped them down.

114

Then Varuthini's son set the girl down
in the comfortable shade of some nearby trees
and raced back to attack the demon, as fast as his horse
could take him.

౧౧౭

వ ఇట్లు తలపడి యమ్మనుజ దనుజులు బీరంబులు
దోరంబులుగాఁ బోరుతఱి భూరమణుండు గుద్దండె
సమిద్ధరణీ బద్ధపరంపర యగు నంపఱం బెంపఱం
జంపరాదు నిలింపారాతినని విత(ర్కించి కించిత్తును
గొంచక కాంచనద్రవకంచుకితంబును దరణీఖరకిరణ
కాండచండంబును నయి యాఖండలదోర్దండ
సముజ్జృంభితవజ్రాయుధ చకచకం బకపక
నవ్య వజ్రభేదియలుంగు వెలుంగ మత్తరులకు
నుత్తలంబీడు నత్తలంబును బద్మరాగమణిచూడంబగు
కేడెంబునుంగొని వేడెంబునం దురంగంబు(
బఱపితెఱపి గని తఱటుచేసి యొఱసి చన నుటికించి
కటకుటరిబరి(బఱీయ వడం బోడిచి కడచి నిలిచినం
బెలుచనం బఱిగోలపోటున నాటోఁపించు మత్త కరివృత్తి
నెత్తు రేలుక నక్రంచరం దుదంచితగతి సవ్యదిశకెత్తి
తఱుమ నపసవ్యగతిన్జాఱంబున హాయంబు(
బోనిచ్చుచు నచ్చరకొడుకు దిరిగితిరిగి సింగిణి
నేయుచుం జుట్టుకొని రా మనుజాఱియు నిట్లట్ల వెనుక
వెనుక కడుగిడుచు నడ్డంబుగా నడవి కడ కొత్తికొని
నడచి యొడుదొడు కగుడు బెడిదంపు నడక నడరి
కడకాళ్ళ కోడియం జిక్కె రక్కసునకుం దుఃఖారంబను
నాలోన నడిదంబునం బుడమిపతి పెడవిసరు విసరి
యసురవరు కరాంగుళంబులు దెగనడిచె నడిచిన
సుడివడక మడమలం దాటించిన ఘోటకంబు
వెగ్గలంబుగ మ్రొగ్గియు నగ్గలిక చెదక మోఁకరించుకొని
కొన్ని యడుగులు చని సేకరించుకొని కంచుమించుగం
బఱచుట గగనచరుల వెఱ(గువఱిచె నట్లు పఱచినం
గంధంబు(జఱచి మొగంబు దుడిచి ప్రస్తుతుల(
గుస్తరించి యతిరభస ఫూత్కర ఘోరారావంబుతో
ఘోణారంధ్రనిశ్వాస గంధవాహ ప్రవాహంబు వెడలు

115

The two of them—human and demon—fought furiously. The prince was enraged but, realizing he was unable to kill his enemy even with a rain of arrows, and totally without fear, he picked up a lance sharp enough to cut through diamonds, which mocked the diamond weapon that Indra wields and was bright with liquid gold and sharper than the sun's rays; also holding a spear that burns up even the toughest of enemies and a shield inlaid with ruby, he drove his horse around the monster. Coming close, finding an opening, he made the horse rub against the enemy and, driving the spear deep into his thick skin, went past him and stopped. Like an elephant in rut hit by a spear and bleeding, the demon deftly moved to the left and pressed against the prince, who sidestepped to the right, circling round and round, striking him with his spear. The ogre stepped back, letting Svarochi reach the edge of the forest. Then with a violent movement as the horse slowed down over uneven ground, the demon tried to catch the horse's hind legs and almost did, but the prince quickly swung his sword to the left and cut off his fingers. The demon was not disturbed. He kicked the horse with his heels, and the horse bent forward, almost but not quite losing its balance, and moved ahead a few feet, collecting itself.[17] Then it galloped faster than the eye could see, so that even the gods in the sky were amazed.

After this wild gallop, Svarochi patted the horse on its back, wiped its face, coaxed it on with words of praise, and walked it back and forth to cool its thirst. A heavy breath came rushing from its nostrils along with a frightening, puffing noise. Wanting to see what the demon was up to, the

వాహంబు దగ మట్టువడ నిట్టట్టు మట్టించుచు
నాస్వరేచి నిశాచరు నుద్యేగంబు చూచికొనవలసి
నిలిచి యంతన యతం డెక్క తరువు‍ గరయుగళి
నిటీయంబట్టి పెల్లగింప మల్లాడు నాలోసన గల్లునం
గింకిణులు మొరయ మెఱుంగు మెఱసినగతి మరల
హరిం బఱపియొకటి రెండు మూ‍డు గొఱకల నెఱ‍కులు
గా‍డ గుబ్బకొలందికిం దిగవైచి మ్రాను విడిపించి
యెలయించుకొని బయలువెడలించి దీ‍ప‍చరుండు
పాషాణమ్ముల కెపుడెపుడు వంగె నపుడపు డెల్లం
దురంగంబు నటం దేలి గంటి యిడి వెంటంబడుటయు
గెంటించి లేదు బంతి యన్నయ ట్లల్లంత నుండి వా‍గె
సడలించి పగతుపై నిగిడి వా‍గె‍ గుదియింప ముంగాళ్లు
గగనంబున రా మగిడించి యందెచప్పుడుం గింకిణీ
రవంబును నురుమ గీసినగతిం దే‍టి మ్రోసిన‍క్రియ
నాదా‍ఱిక యే దిక్కు‍ జూచిన నాదిక్కుననే వినంబడ
నెక్కడ‍ జూచినం దానయ్యె నీడ యేర్పడక పార్శ్వంబులం
గట్టుకెంబట్టు లాలసరి సమకట్టు ఠక్కులుగా
యాతుధానుం డను కొండచిలువ నొ‍డియ నేలపట్టుపుగా
నాడు గరుడుం డనం బాయుచు దాయుచు దవ్వలం
బొలసి కు‍ఠింగట‍ దే‍చి కు‍ఠింగట నని చూడ దవ్వలం
బొలసి దవ్వ చేరువ లనిర్ధార్యంబులుగా మెలంగం
దేజికాశ్వంబు మెలంపుచు వెంటనుం బంట్రకోలల
నడిదంబున నత్తలంబున నేసియ వ్రేసియ నడిచియుం
బొడిచియుం గడపలం గానక మిడిసి మృతుండునుం
గాని దానవునిం జూచి వేసరి రోసంబున.

prince stopped still and watched him struggling to uproot a tree that he had grasped in both hands. Before he could finish this, Svarochi turned the horse back toward him and shot one, two, three iron arrows, glistening like lightning and ringing like bells, which penetrated deep, right up to their feathers, into his flesh. These forced the demon to drop the trees, turn toward him, and come out into the open. Each time his opponent bent down to pick up a rock, the prince drove the horse close to him and wounded him again, chasing him and pushing him while loosening the reins on the horse, as if challenging the demon: "You can't catch me!" Then he pulled the horse up short so it reared up with its front feet in the sky before he turned it around, bells ringing together with his anklets as if someone were scraping a drum and bees were buzzing on and on, the sound filling all space, and wherever the ogre looked, Svarochi was there, and not even his shadow could be grasped.

The scarlet tassels tied on either side of the saddle were flying like wings, so he looked like an eagle swooping down on the earth to catch a boa constrictor. He appeared both close and far, or more precisely, when the ogre thought he was far he turned up right beside him, and when he thought he was close, he was far away. "Close" and "far" were indeterminable as he rode the gallant horse. With his bow, iron-spiked bamboo stick, sword, and spear he shot, hit, slashed, and poked at the demon but still saw no end to him; and seeing that he was not yet dead, he grew sick and tired of it all, and very angry.

౧౧౬

క　భూపతి పావకబాణం
బేఫున సంధించి తివిచి యేసిన మెయిం గీ
లాపటలి పాదువ నతండా
రూపం బెడంబాసి భేచరులు వెఆంగండన్.

౧౧౭

లయవిభాతి.

ధగధగని దేహరుచి నిగనిగని కుందనపుం
దగడుం దెగడం జిగురు జిగి నెగుచుమోవిన్
నగవు నిగుడం గురుల పాగరు మగుడన్ నయన
యుగళి వెలిదామరల మగలమగలై డా
లెగయ మృగనాభి భుగభుగ లెసంగం జామరలు
మగువ లిడ మౌళిమణి మిగులంగ వెలుంగం
దెగలు గలహారముల జిగి చెలంగంగాం గొదమ
మొగులం దగు యానమున గగనచరుం డయ్యెన్.

౧౧౮

క　నవనవ సౌరభముల నె
క్కువ కువలయవర్ణ మపుడు గురిసెన్ మొరసెన్
రవరవ మురజ రవంబులు
దివి దివిషజ్జలజముఖులు తెలిసి నటింపన్.

116

So he picked up the mantric weapon, an arrow of fire,
placed it on the bowstring, drew it back,
and let go. Fire engulfed the demon, who took leave
of his body, and to the amazement of the gods

117

he turned into a god of the skies: his body gleaming like
    gold,
lips redder than tender buds breaking into a smile,
eyes whiter than the lotus, so white they pushed back
the black mass of his hair, women fragrant with musk
fanning him on either side, a brilliant jewel on his head,
his chest gleaming with long necklaces. A vehicle carried
    him
through light clouds into heaven.

118

There was a rain of blue water lilies, thick with fragrance,
and drums were beating while women of the gods
who knew what had happened began to dance.

౧౧౯

వ అనిన విని తరువాతి వృత్తాంతంబు వినుటకుం
దివుటమై మదీయమానసంబు కౌతుకాధీనంబయ్యెడు
వినిపింపుడని యడుగుటయును.

౧౨౦

శా శ్లాఘాలంఘన జాంఘికోజ్జ్వల గుణా
లంకార ఘీంకార హే
షాఘోషోద్భట దాటికా గజఘటా
శ్యక్షుణ్ణ విశ్వంభరా
మౌఘీభూత భుజంగ భోగభర సం
ఫుల్లాబ్జపత్రేక్షణా
ద్రాఘీయఃప్రతిభావిచక్షణ త్రయీ
ధర్మైకసంరక్షణా.

౧౨౧

క బహువీర హనన మిళ దఘ
వహనప్రమకృత్కళంక వర్గేగ్రాసి
గ్రహిళ భుజయుగళ గజప
త్యహిపహరణ తార్క్ష్య సజ్జనావనదక్షా.

119

At this point Jaimini asked, "What happened next? I'm dying to know. Please tell me more."

120

Listen, great king: your many merits outstrip our ability
to praise.
Your army of trumpeting elephants and neighing horses
running
all over the earth have raised such a huge cloud of dust that
the burden
carried by the Great Snake on his heads is much lighter.
Your eyes are wide as the open lotus, and your inner eye
can distinguish truth from falsehood. You are the only one
who can save the Vedic order.

121

You've killed so many enemy warriors that the swords
you hold in either hand, stained dark with blood,
almost look like they're carrying the sin of so much slaughter.
You're the eagle who killed that snake, the Gajapati king.
You take care of everyone who's good.

౧౨౨

పృథ్వి.

సుధీ మధురవాక్సుధా
సుముఖ నాగమాంబా సుతా
మధుప్రసవసాయక
స్మయవిరామరమ్యాకృతీ
దధీచ విధు కామధు
గ్ధనద దుగ్ధసింధుప్రథా
వధీరణ పరాయణో
జ్వల వదాన్యతాలంకృతా.

గద్యము.

ఇది శ్రీమదాంధ్ర కవితాపితామహ సర్వతోముఖాంక
పంకజాక్ష పాదాంబుజాధీన మానసేందిందిర
నందవరపుర వంశోత్తంస శతకోపతాపస ప్రసాదాసాదిత
చతుర్విధ కవితామతల్లి కాల్లసాని చొక్కయామాత్యపుత్త
పెద్దనార్య ప్రణీతంబైన స్వారోచిషమనుసంభవం బను
మహాప్రబంధంబునందుఁ జతుర్థాశ్వాసము.

382

122

You're attentive to the sweet words of scholars,
son of Nagamamba! You're so handsome
you've wiped the smile off the love god's face.
You're so generous that you've dimmed the fame
of Dadhīca,[18] *the moon,*[19] *the wish-granting cow, Kubera,*
*   and the ocean of milk.*

The great poem called "The Birth of Svarochisha Manu" was
written by Allasani Cokkayamatya's son Peddanarya, known
to all as the "Creator God of Telugu Poetry," who comes from
a family of Nandavara Brahmans, whose mind hovers like a
bee around the lotuslike feet of lotus-eyed Vishnu, and who was
blessed by his guru Shathakopa with the ability to compose all
four kinds of fine poetry. Chapter 4 ends here.

పంచమాశ్వాసము

౧

క   శ్రీనందన సౌందర్య సు
ధీనందన వితరణావధీరిత బలిరా
డ్వానుజ పరరాజస్య
ర్వానుభుజాహీంద్ర కృష్ణరాయనరేంద్రా.

౨

వ   అవధరింపుము. జైమిని మునీంద్రచూడారత్నంబునకు
నీడేడ్చవంబు లి ట్లనియె.

౩

తే   అపుడు గంధర్వపతి మహి కవతరించి
రాజు విస్మయమున హాయరాజు డిగ్గ
నక్కు సేర్చి ముదంబుతో ననియె దంత
కిరణములు హారకాంతులు సరసమాడ.

384

Chapter 5

1

Listen, Krishnaraya,
handsome as the love god,
a blessing to the learned,
more generous than King Bali and Karna,[1]
with arms that eclipse rival kings
like the snake that swallows the moon.

2

Here's what the birds answered Jaimini, that wonder
of a sage.

3

The gandharva from heaven came down to earth.
The king, utterly amazed, climbed off his horse.
The gandharva hugged him to his chest and said
with a smile that mingled with the whiteness of his pearls:

೪

సీ. భద్రమా నీకు నీ బాహుభృతక్షితిం
 బ్రజలకు లెస్సలా రాచవారు
ధన్యుండ నైతి నీ దర్శనంబునం జేసి
నా దుష్కృతము లెల్ల నాశమొందె
గారాపు మీ తల్లికడవాడం గాని నే
గణుతింపం గడవాడం గాం జుమయ్య

తే. పెండ్లి కొడుకవు మాకు నీ బిసరుహాక్షి
కూర్మినందన యొక మౌని ఘోర శాప
వికృతి మానిసిదిండి నై యకట దీని
ప్రాణముల కల్గం దలంచితిం బాపబుద్ధి.

౫

క. అనునెడ వచ్చి మనోరమ
జనకుని పాదముల కెరంగ సస్నేహమతిం
గనుంగవ నీ రేలుకంగ నం
దనమూర్ధఘ్రాణ మతండు దయం గావించెన్.

౬

ఆ. అపుడు విస్మితాత్ముండై వరూధినిసుతుం
డేమి కారణమున నేతపస్వి
యిట్టి శాప మిచ్చె నెటింగింపు విన వేడు
కయ్యె ననఘ యనిన నాతండనియె.

4

"How are you faring, you and the people you rule
in this land? Is the royal family well? I'm so glad
I got to see you. All my bad deeds
have perished. I'm known in all three worlds.
The dancing women in heaven sing my name,
    Indivaraksha.
I'm your dear mother's younger brother—no stranger
to you. You're my future son-in-law. This woman
with bright eyes is my loving daughter. A horrible curse
by a sage turned me into a man-eater,
and I almost ate her up."

5

Manorama heard him and fell at her father's feet.
With tears in his eyes he embraced her and lovingly
kissed her forehead.

6

Varuthini's son said: "Tell me, why were you cursed,
and who was the sage who did it? I'm more than curious.
You're a good man."

౨

మ   కలం దుల్లోకయశఃపురంధ్రి జగతిన్
గంధర్వ వంశంబునన్
నలనాభాహ్వయుం డేం దదీయతనయుం
డన్ బ్రహ్మమిత్రుండు ౩
మ్యలకుం గంటను వత్తిం బెట్టుకొని
యాయుర్వేద మొరంత ప్రా
ద్ధులం జెప్పన్ వినుచుండి మానసమునం
దుం దజ్జిఘృక్షారతిన్.

౩

తే   మౌనివరుం జేరి భక్తి నమస్కరించి
చెప్పవే నాకు నీ విద్య శిష్యకోటి
తోడం గూడంగ నేం గృతార్థుండ నగుదు
ననుచుం బ్రార్థింప ననుం జూచి యపహసించి.

౬

క   నటవిట గాయక గణికా
కుటిలవచశ్శిధురసముం గ్రోలెడు చెవికిం
గటు వీ శాస్త్రము వల ది
చ్చుట నినుం జదివింపకున్న జరగదె మాకున్.

7

He explained: "In the gandharva clan
there's a man known throughout the worlds.
His name is Nalanabha. I'm his son. A certain
    Brahmamitra
was teaching his students Ayurveda at all hours
of the day or night. I was listening, and I too
was dying to be his student.

8

So I went and bowed to him in reverence
and asked him: 'Please teach me this science
with all your other students. I'll be eternally grateful.'
He looked at me and laughed.

9

'You spend your time getting drunk on the crooked words
of dancers and playboys and singers and whores.
This subject is not for you. It will sound harsh to your ears.
You cannot enter here. We can manage just fine
without you.'

౧౦

తే అనంగ నే నట్టివాడం గాననఘ చరిత
యించుకించుక మీవంటి యొఱుక గలుగు
పెద్దవారల శిక్షలం బెరింగినాండ
నవధరింపుము శిష్యంగా ననిన నతండు.

౧౧

క ధనరాజ్యరమా మదమునం
గనుగాని నిన్ను శిష్యంగాం గై కొనుకం
టెను నేరమి గలదే ననుం
గనలించుచుం బ్రేల కింకం బొకాలు మటన్నన్.

౧౨

క అచటన్ 'ద్వేష్టి గతాయు
శ్చ చికిత్సక' మను నయొక్తి చర్చను నుచ్చా
వచ వచనంబులం గోపము
ప్రచురము గానీక మౌనిపతి కిట్లంటిన్.

10

I said, 'No, sir. I'm not a man like that.
I grew up under the guidance of learned people
like you. I've learned a little. Please take me
as your student.' He said,

11

'I know you. You're blinded by wealth and power.
There can be nothing worse than accepting you
as my disciple. Don't irritate me
with your empty chatter. Get out of here.'

12

I thought of the wise saying, *dveṣṭi gatāyuś ca cikitsakam*,
'You hate the doctor when your death is near.'
So I held in my anger at his rough words. Quietly I said:

౧3

తే నీవు చదివింతు వనుచు నిన్నియును విడిచి
బిచ్చ మెత్తంగ రాదుగా బేల తపసి
కడవ నాడకు చాలు నీ గెడవ యేల
వెజ్జుందన మేల యని మది లజ్జవొడమి.

౧౪

శా కంటే బ్రాహ్మణుం డెన్ని కాఱు లఱచెన్
గర్వించి వీరెల్ల నా
కంఠెం బాత్రులె విద్య కెట్లు నిది నేం
గై కొందునంచున్ మదిన్
గెంటెంపుంజల ముప్పతిల్లం గపటాం
తేవాసి నై శాంబరిన్
గొంటుంజందము మీఱి శిష్యలగెడం
గూర్చుండి చర్చారతిన్.

౧౫

తే కాయ బాల గ్రహోర్ద్వ్యాంగకములు నాల్గు
శల్య దంష్ట్రా జరా వృష సంజ్ఞ నాల్గు
నైన యష్టాంగకము రావు లారం గల్గు
వైద్య మెనిమిది నెలల సర్వమును నేర్చి.

13

'I can't become a beggar just to be the student
of a simple-minded Brahman like you.[2]
Enough said. No more harsh words.
I don't want to have anything to do
with you or your medicine.' Still, I felt
a bit insulted.

14

'Just look at how this stupid Brahman had the temerity
to speak to me. Are these students of his better than me?
Somehow or other, I'm going to learn.' That's what I
        thought,
more determined than ever. I tricked him, disguised
        myself
as one of his pupils, and sat among them, listening
to every word.

15

Internal medicine, pediatrics, psychiatry, ear-nose-and-
throat, surgery, toxicology, geriatrics, rejuvenation—in eight
months I mastered all eight branches of medical science.

౧౬

క ఇరుమూఁడు రుచుల దీపపు
విరసత మానన్ జ్వరాది వృష్యాంతం బై
పరఁగు చికిత్సయ్యెఁ గని శాం
బరిఁ బాసి తపస్వితోడ మదమున నంటిన్.

౧౭

శా తండ్రీ నాకు ననుగ్రహింపఁగదె వై
ద్యం బంచుఁ బ్రార్థించినన్
గంద్రల్‌గా నటు లాడి ధిక్కృతులఁ బో
కాల్మంటి వేహో మదిం
దీంద్రల్‌గల్గినవారి కేకరణినే
నిన్ విద్య రా కుందునే
గుండ్రా డాఁచినఁ బెండ్లి యేమిటికిఁ జి
క్కుం గష్టముష్టింపచా.

౧౮

మ అనినం గన్నులు జేవురింప నధరం
బల్లాడ వేల్తుప్పనః
పునరుద్యద్భ్రుకుటీ భుజంగ యుగళీ
ఫూత్కార ఘోరానిలం
బన నూర్పుల్‌నిగుడన్ లలాటఫలకం
బందంద ఘర్మాంబువుల్
చినుకం గంతుదిద్దృక్షు రూక్షనయన
క్వేళాకరాళధ్వనిన్.

394

16

When I knew how to treat a humoral imbalance
and impairment in any of the six tastes
leading from fever to impotence, I was ready.
I took off my disguise and, filled with pride,
stood before my teacher.

17

'Father, I begged you to teach me medicine, but you
kicked me out and yelled at me. If someone is itching to
    learn,
won't they get knowledge somehow or other? You stupid
    beggar—
can you stop a wedding just by hiding the grinding stone?'[3]

18

His eyes turned red, his lips quivered, and a blast of hot
    venom
issued from his nostrils while his eyebrows rose and fell
    like snakes
spreading their hoods. His forehead poured sweat.
Roaring like Shiva when he turned his fiery eye on Desire,

೧౯

వ   జటిలుండు గిటకిటం బంద్రు గొణికి హుమ్మని కటమ్ము
లదుర ముకుంబుటమ్ములు నటింపం గటకటా
కుటిలాత్మ యటమటమ్మున విద్య గొనుటయుంగాక
గుటగుటలు గురువుతోనా యని కటకటం బడి
కకపాలలోని బూది కేలం గొని యాసురి యగు మాయ
మాయెడం బ్రయోగించి వంచించి యపహసించితివి
గావున నసురవై పిశితంబును వసయును నస్సగ్రంబు
నశనంబులుగా మెసవి వసుధ వసియింపు మని
బసుమంబు సల్ల గుండె జల్లుమని కల్లువడి మునితల్లజు
పదపల్లవంబులం ద్రెళ్ళి యిట్లంటి.

౨౦

శా   నా యజ్ఞానము సైంచి సంయమివరే
ణ్యా కావవే రాక్షసుం
డై యే నెట్లు భజించువాండ దురితం
బయ్యో నృమాంసంబు కూ
డై యే నెట్లు భరించువాండ నుదరం
బార్ద్రాంతరంగుండ వై
యోయయ్యా దయసేయవే యవధి యే
నోపంగదే హింసకున్.

19

that man with matted hair gnashed his teeth and said, 'Hum!', his temples throbbing, nostrils quivering. 'You crook,' he said, 'you stole knowledge from me, and you're even proud of it!' He took ashes from the bag under his arm and cursed me: 'You tricked me with inhuman deceit and made a fool of me. You'll become a demon and live on earth, feasting on meat and blood and fat.' Then he sprinkled the ashes on me. My heart sank. Petrified, I fell at his feet and said:

20

'Forgive my ignorance. You're a great sage. Save me.
How can I live the sinful life of a demon?
How can I fill my belly with human flesh?[4]
Let your heart grow soft with compassion.
Tell me when this curse will end. I can't stand violence.'

౨౧

చ   అనినఁ బ్రసన్నుఁడై ముని క
రాజ్జములన్ నను నెత్తి వత్స మ
త్సునిశితశాపశూలహతి
ప్రుక్కితిగా యిఁకఁ గొన్నినాళ్ళఁపైఁ
దనయను మ్రింగఁ బోయి యొక
ధన్యుని దివ్యశరార్చిఁ ప్రేలి వే
కనియొదు భద్ర మన్నఁ దుర
గంబుపయిం బడి ప్రొద్దు గ్రుంకఁగన్.

౨౨

క   సన్నపుఁదలయేరున మయి
యన్నుఁకొనుచు నాము దిన్న యల్లె రాఁగా
ఖిన్నుఁడ నై పురి కేఁగితిఁ
దిన్నదనం బుడిగి కొన్ని దివియలు వెలుఁగన్.

౨3

క   అంపఁ దగువారిఁ గసరుచు
నంపి నగరు సొచ్చి వెలఁదు లారతు లీఁగా
నిం పఱఁ గఱాభిహతులం
జంపించితి వారి నన్నిఖామధ్యమునన్.

398

21

The sage turned kind, lifted me up with his hands.
'Son,' he said, 'you've been badly hurt by my words sharp
as spears. Within a few days, you'll try to eat your
    daughter.
A great man will burn you with his arrow. Then you'll find
    peace.'
I staggered onto my horse as darkness came on.

22

My head started to ache a little, and I was losing control
of my body, as if I'd eaten poison grass.[5] Very depressed,
I went home, a few lamps burning around me.
I was no longer myself.

23

Instead of dismissing the servants,
I yelled at them; and when I entered
the inner palace and women came to welcome me
with lamps, I had them whipped to death
that very night.

౩౪

సీ అబ్రమండలి మోచునందాఁక నూరక
పెరిఁగినట్లౌ మేను నరవరేణ్య
యవధి భూధరసానువందాఁక నూరక
పఱచినట్లౌ మేను పార్థివేంద్ర
యబ్జభూభువనంబు నందాఁక నూరక
యొగసినట్లౌ మేను జగదధీశ
యహిలోకతలమంటునందాఁక నూరక
పడినయట్లౌ మేను ప్రభువతంస

తే యఖిలజగములు మ్రింగునం తాఁకలియును
నబ్ధి లేడును జెడఁ గ్రోలునంత తృషయు
నచలచాలనచణ మైన యదటుఁ గలిగె
నసురభావంబు ననుఁ జెందు నవసరమున.

౩౫

క రక్కసుఁడ నై నెపం బిడి
యొక్కొక యపరాధమునకు నొక్కొక్కఁడు గా
బొక్కఁగ లోకము పురపురఁ
బొక్కఁగఁ బాడయ్యె నంతిపురమం బురమున్.

24

I felt, oh king, like my body was growing taller,
just like that, until it reached the sky.
And it was spreading, just like that,
as far as the mountains at the edge of the earth.
Soon it was jumping all the way up to Brahma's world
and slipping down as far as the world of the snakes.
I was so hungry I wanted to swallow all three worlds
and so thirsty I wanted to drink up the seven oceans.
I had a sudden urge to move mountains.
That's how it felt, king, when this demonic mind
came over me.

25

Now that I was a demon, on one pretext or another
I started accusing everyone, one by one, of whatever
came to mind—and then I would gobble them up.
My palace and the city were both soon ruined.

౨౬

తే　ఊరు పా దైన౸ గెఱవుల యూళ్ళ కుటికి
మెసవ దొర౸కొంటి౸ బ్రజ మరి మసఁగినట్లు
తీఱె౸ గతిపయదినముల దేశమెల్ల
మల్లె వట్టిన చేని క్రమంబు గా౸గ.

౨౭

వ　ఇవ్విధంబున విధివిధానంబున యాతుధానుండనై
ధారాధరోత్సేధంబును నతినిశితరోమ
సంబాధంబును ధూమసమధామంబును
ధృతాంత్రదామంబును జలితకపాలకుండలంబును
జ్వలితసితదంష్ట్రామండలంబును
నాగాయతత్రాణంబును మస్తకోత్తుంగఘోణంబునునై
యనవరత హింసానురూపంబగు రూపంబు౸దాల్చి
శకటాంగభంగికమ్ముల్లై యింగలమ్ము లోలుకు
నపాంగమ్ములం బిశంగమ్ము లగుచు౸
బశ్యజ్జనాసుమోచనమ్ము లగు లోచనమ్ములు వెలుంగ
బభ్రుకేశమ్ములు దూల సకలభూతభయంకర
మ్మగు పటిమ నిచటి యుటజమ్ముల కుటికి జటి
యనక వటు వనక యతి యనక వ్రతి యనక
గృహి యనక సతి యనక శిశు వనక భక్షించి
భక్షించి కుక్షింభరిత్వంబునం బ్రవర్తిల్లితి నది
యట్లుండె వినుము. తారలకు వర్షధారలకు
నిసుమునకు౸ గసవునకు లెక్క గలిగినం గలుగు౸
గాని మదీయజఠరానలజీర్ణ జంతుసంతానంబునకు
లెక్కయిడ న క్కమలగర్భుండును సమర్థుండుగా౸

402

26

Once the city was ruined, I moved on to neighboring
  places.
There too, I devoured everything alive, like the goddess of
  pox.
Within a few days the whole country was finished,
like a blighted crop.

27

That's how I became a man-eating demon, by an act of fate. I
was tall as a cloud, my body thick with prickly hair and dark
as smoke, garlanded with intestines, with skulls hanging
from my ears and blazing white fangs and a huge nose on my
face. I had the strength of ten thousand elephants. Violence
was written all over me. My eyes, huge and round like chariot
wheels and yellow, shot flames. People gave up their lives the
moment they looked at me. Flinging my yellow hair around
me, with terrifying fury I jumped onto the thatched huts of
sages and ate whoever was there, whether it was a yogi or a
student or an ascetic or a family man or a woman or a baby.
I ate them just to fill my belly. That's how it was. Listen.
You might be able to count the stars or raindrops or grains
of sand or blades of grass, but not even Brahma the creator
could count the number of living beings that were burnt in
the fire of my hunger. My in-laws could see that a demonic
nature had taken me over and, afraid it would get worse, took
away my wives under the pretext of a festival visit and kept
them safely with them. I was looking everywhere for food,

డిట్టి కృత్రిమదనుజభావావిష్టుండ నగు నా
దొష్టంబు సవసవగాఁ దెలిసి ముదురకయ మున్న
మత్కళత్రంబులం బుట్టినింటివాఁ రుత్నవావలోకన
వ్యాజంబున ననిపించుకొని చని నిజగృహంబుల నునిచి
రక్షించుకొని యుండి రిపు డే నశనంబు గానక కానక కన్న
యక్కన్నియం గైలాసకాననంబునం గుసుమంబులు
గోయుదానిం గని కనికరం బుడిగి కడుపుఁ జిచ్చునకు
మ్రింగం దఱుముకొనివచ్చి యిచ్చోట భవదీయ
దర్శనంబున వృజినరుజ వలన విముక్తుండనై
నిజప్రకృతిం బొంది కృతార్థుండ నైతి.

౨౮

క   ఈ యుపకారమునకుఁ బ్రతి
సేయఁగ శక్యంబె జంభజిన్నిభ శఫరా
త్యాయతలోచన రైన మ
దీయాత్మజ నీకు నిత్తు దేవీమణిఁగన్.

౨౯

క   ఆయుర్వేదముఁ గైకొని
యీ యింతిం బెండ్లియాడు మెలమి రమానా
రాయణపరిణయగేయ వి
గాయన గంధర్వ మైన కవ్యపుఁగొండన్.

404

and I came upon my dear daughter—born to me after a long
time—collecting flowers in the forest on Mount Kailasa. I felt
no compassion, wanted only to satisfy the flame in my belly.
But when I saw you, I was released from the burden of my
sins and got my old self back. Now I'm happy.

28

How could I ever repay your good deed?
Let me give you, who are equal to Indra,
my daughter in marriage. She has eyes wide
as fish. Make her your queen.

29

Accept my knowledge of medicine along with my
　　daughter.
Marry her on Mount Mandara, which once served
as the churning rod, where gandharvas sang when Vishnu
married Lakshmi.

30

లయగ్రాహి.

అన్నగముపై జరత పన్నగపతిస్పుటల
నన్నెగసి కోటతుదలన్నెగడుకొమ్మల్
మిన్నగల రాయ రుచిC జెన్నగు విమానముల
పన్నగడ పన్నగC బ్రభిన్న గజఘోట
చ్చన్న గహనాపణములన్నిగనిగద్యుతి ర
విస్నుగుమణిప్రకర మున్న గరిమం బే
రెన్నగల యంగడుల వన్నె గని సంపదల
మన్నగరి యొప్పు బలభిన్నగరి శేవన్.

31

తే అని నిజోదంత మావంత యైన దాCప
కంతయును జెప్ప నద్భుతం బంతరంగ
మంతయును నిండ హర్షించె నా స్వరేచి
యంత రవి యేCగెC బశ్చిమాశాంతమునకు.

30

My city is there, radiant as Indra's.
The ramparts of my fort thrust into heaven
like the spreading hoods of the Ancient Snake,
and there are multistoried buildings that scrape the sky,
and in the markets, crowded with horses and elephants,
shops display precious gems that overshadow the sun,
as everyone knows."

31

Thus he told his whole story, holding nothing back.
Svarochi was amazed, his heart flooded with joy.
Then it was evening. The sun moved to the west.

౩౨

మ	వికసిల్లం బ్రజ చక్రపాలనము గా
	వించెం గరవ్యాపృతిం
	గకుబంతంబుల నాక్రమించెఁ బొసఁగం
	గా నేర్చె వర్ణాళిఁ గాం
	తికిఁ బాపెం బెఆరాజకోటిఁ దుది శాం
	తిం బొందె దైవంబు సేఁ
	తకుఁ దాపం బీఁక నేలనంగ నినుఁడ
	స్తప్రాప్తుఁ డయ్యెం గడున్.

౩౩

తే	అసురవరుఁడైన యిందీవరాక్షు మేన
	నంటుకొన్న స్వరేచిబాణాగ్ని వోలె
	నంతఁ గనుపట్టె శుకతుండ కాంతిఁ దెగడి
	సాంధ్యరాగంబు పశ్చిమాచలమునందు.

౩౪

క	తలచూపె నప్పుడ ఖిలా
	శల దట్టపు టిరులు చిలువ జవరాలు నభ
	స్థ్సల మండపకోపరిసీ
	మల నిడిన సితాండపటలి మాడ్కిం జుక్కల్.

32

It had started its day by ruling the world, to everyone's
    delight,
and by reuniting the *cakravāka* birds.[6]
Its rays filled all space with a regal power.
Colors shone, and people lived, all of them true
to their nature.[7]
The moon lost its brilliance, a weakened rival.
Now, in the end, the sun accepted the law of time
and turned cool as it set, like an aged king.[8]

33

Like the arrow of fire shot by Svarochi
that engulfed the demon in Indivaraksha,
a fiery red enfolded Western Mountain,
brighter than a parrot's beak.

34

Like the white eggs of a huge black boa
scattered everywhere, stars appeared
in the canopy of the nighttime sky.

౩౫

ఆ సాంధ్యనటన చండ చండీశ పదహతిం
దరణిచక్ర మొరగి శరధిం గ్రుంగ
దోరగల్లువడియె భూరభేతర భాగ
చక్రమనంగ నపుడు శశియుం దోంచె.

౩౬

క తమ మను కాలాహి ప్రపం
చము నెరగని యోషధీశ సద్యఃకృత దం
డమున మగుడంగం గ్రక్కెడు
క్రమమున నొయ్యొయ్య విచ్చి కడలకుం దొలంగెన్.

౩౭

వ అనంతరంబ క్రమక్రమంబున.

35

As if under the pounding of Shiva's feet when he danced
his fierce dance at dusk, the chariot that was earth
fell on its side, one wheel, the sun, submerged
in the ocean while the other—the moon—
came out on top. That's what moonrise looked like.

36

Darkness slowly receded to the edges of the sky
like a black snake that has swallowed the world
and then is forced to cough it up by the master
of herbs—the moon.

37

Then, gradually,

౩౮

సీ కలయ వెల్లువగట్టి జలజలఁ బ్రవహించు
శశికాంతవాంత నిర్ఝరముజలము
మలయానిలముచేఁ దుమారంబు రేఁగు సౌ
గంధికంబు రజంబు కఱికుదుమ్మ
నిండార విరిసిన బొండుమల్లెల నుండి
వడియు మరందంబు గుడరసంబు
తొలఁకి మింటికిఁ బొంగు దుగ్ధపాథోరాశి
కఱడులమీఁది మీఁగడల మెఱుఁగు

తే తనకు రసవర్గములుగా సుధాకరుండు
సారెసారెకుఁ గరములు సాఁచి చాఁచి
యచ్చ తెలుపుగ నపుడు బ్రహ్మాండ మండ
పంబు వెన్నెల సన్నుసన్నంబు సేసె.

౩౯

వ ఆ సమయంబునం బరిశ్రాంతం డగునమ్మహీకాంతుం
డెక్క శశికాంతశిలామండపంబున దట్టంబుగాఁ బఱిచిన
చిగురుపఱపుల గంధర్వరాజునుం దానును సుఖాసీనుం
డై యిష్టకథాగోష్ఠి నా రాత్రి గడపె నంత.

38

the moon extended his long hands to whitewash the whole
    world.
He took water pouring from melting moonstones
and mixed it with fragrant red dust stirred up
by the southern wind, added jaggery that was the nectar
from thick-blooming jasmine as well as heavy cream
from the ocean of milk rising in waves
into the sky. Combining these choice ingredients, he laid
a layer of white plaster on every surface.

39

The king, exhausted, sat comfortably with the gandharva
king on thick mattresses of leaf buds spread on slabs of
moonstone. They spent the night talking and swapping
stories. Now

౪౦

సీ   తనుఁ బాసి శశి దవ్వు చనిన నెవ్వగఁ బోలెఁ
దొలిదిక్కు జవరాలు వెలుకఁ బాఆెఁ
బ్రథమాద్రిసభయందుఁ బఱీచిన కెంబట్టు
జముకాణ మనఁగ రాగము జనించె
ధవుఁ గూర్మి కొసరుచున్నవి వోలె ముఖరాళి
వనరహస్యములఁ బద్మినులు తెఆచె
భానూష్మభీతి ముస్పడిన చుక్కలభంగి
దొరలె వేకువగాలిఁ దరుల మంచు

తే   కాలగుణయుక్తి మింటి చక్కటికి నెగయ
వాసవునిపట్టి పొడుపుగా వైచి యాడు
గచ్చు చమరిన దారు చక్రంపు బిళ్ళ
వోలె నొయ్యనఁ బ్రాచి లేఁ బ్రొద్దు పొడిచె.

౪౧

క   ఈ గతి నత్తఱీఁ దెలతెల
వేగిన గంధర్వపతికి వేగుట విని తా
రాగమున కేఁగి కాంచిరి
రాగమ్మునఁ గొలిచి మను పురాతన ఖచరుల్.

40

the lady of the east* turned pale in grief when her lover,
    the moon, left her and went away.
The eastern sky turned red: was it a silk carpet spread in
    the assembly hall on Sunrise Mountain?
Lotuses opened with buzzing bees. Were they begging to
    be loved by their husband, the sun?
Dewdrops fell like stars from trees shaken by the morning
    breeze.
Were they afraid of the sun's heat soon to come?
The sun rose like a red toy made of wood, bound by
the string that is Time, that Indra's boy kicked
    into the sky.[9]

41

Morning came. News spread that the king of gandharvas
was freed from his curse. All his old servants rushed to see
him on Silver Mountain.

---

* The direction personified as a woman.

೪౨

ఉ కాంచినఁ బొంగి వా రొసఁగు
కానుక లర్థిఁ బరిగ్రహించి మ
న్నించి పురప్రయాణ రతి
నిక్క నరేంద్రుఁడు మున్నుగాఁ దటి
చ్చంచలవాహమై మణుల
చాయల దిక్కు లలంకరించు హో
న్నంచు రథంబు చాఁగు బళి
యంచు నకీబులు మ్రోయ నెక్కినన్.

೪౩

క నందనయు నుచితరత్న
స్యందనమునఁ జనియె నర్థి జనకునిబడి న
య్యందీవరాక్షఁ డీ గతి
మందరమున కెగయ గగన మార్గమునందున్.

42

He saw them and was overjoyed. He took the gifts
they had brought. Now he was keen to go home.
Inviting Svarochi to enter first, he mounted his chariot,
drawn by horses faster than lightning, brilliantly studded
with precious stones and golden trim. Attendants cried
before them: "*Cāgu baḷi*! Hurray!"

43

His daughter followed in her own jeweled chariot.
All of them were soon airborne on their way to Mandara
    Mountain.
En route through the sky,

౪౪

సీ మండిగాలిడి దంత శుండాగ్ర హతిఁ జించి
జలధరాంభముఁ గరుల్ చల్లులాడ
నహిమాంశు హయ హేష లాలించి చెవి వంచి
కెరలి వాజులు బయల్ గొరిజఁ ద్రవ్వ
ధ్వజవాతహతి నాఱ వైద్యుతాగ్నులఁ జూఁడి
పగలు దివియలవారు పంజు లెత్తఁ
బెటులు చప్పుడు లాత్మభీరు స్వయంగ్రాహ
పరిరంభ సుఖము ఖేచరుల కొసఁగఁ

తే జామరప్రభ గగనగంగామరాళ
చకచకభ్రమ మొదవింప శంకరాద్రి
కాననముమోచి మందరాగంబుదాఁకఁ
బౌఁజువెట్టిరి తన్మూల బలము దొరలు.

౪౫

క కుంజర శతాంగ హయ భట
రంజితమై పై రజఃపరంపర లలమన్
మంజుల కాంతిఁ గసీసపు
మాంజిష్ఠముఁ బోలె గగనమండప మమరెన్.

44

elephants bent their legs and raised their trunks,
tearing open a hole in the rain clouds and reveling in the
    downpour.
Hearing the neighing of the sun steeds, horses grew
    restless
and pawed empty space with their hooves.
When the wind from waving flags put out their torches,
torchbearers lit them again from the lightning in the sky.
Fiery weapons were exploding, and terrified women
    rushing
into their lovers' arms made them happy beyond thought.
Bright yak-tail fans were golden geese swimming in the
    river
of the sky as the generals drove the army forward
from the forests of Mount Kailasa
all the way to Mount Mandara.

45

The sky became a dark tent painted with elephants,
chariots, horses, and soldiers, while the dust they
churned up colored its top yellow and red.[10]

౪౬

తే   సారిది నీ రీతి దివిc దేడు సూపినట్టి
        దొరలు గొలువంగ ఖచరేంద్రుc డరిగి యరిగి
        మింట గ్రహరాజు తనసగమింట వెలుంగు
        మంథగిరిc గాంచి పలికె నమ్మనుజపతికి.

౪౭

సీ   జరత కచ్చపరాజు చరమాంగ గృహమేధి
        భోగివేష్టన రేఖc బోలుచు జాణ
        కులములోc దరితీపు గలిగి మించినమేటి
        మైనాకు నొరసిన మాసటీcడు
        తొలువేలుపుల వేలుపులపనుల్గొనుతేcడు
        కడలిరాయల లోcతు గన్నగబ్బి
        సురరాజునకుc బాండుకరిc జేర్చు మరకాcడు
        కల్పకంబుల పంట కమ్మతీcడు

తే   గంటె మథిత సుధాధౌత కటక జాత
        చంపకవన ప్రకంపనాకంప విసర
        దఖర ముఖరవ మధుకర ముఖర శిఖర
        నందరస మందిరం బగు మందరంబు.

46

The gandharva king, served by his military aides
in proper order, traveled far until he caught sight
of Mandara Mountain, its lower half lit by the sun.[11]
He said to the human king:

47

"Look at this Mount Mandara.
He's the one who lives on the back of the ancient
    tortoise.[12]
The Snake[13] left traces of his coils on his handsome body.
He's the one in his family who knows the sweetness of
    churning.
He is the wrestler who fought with Mainaka under the
    ocean.[14]
He did the bidding of both gods and antigods.
He plumbed the depths of the ocean—
that's how he retrieved the white elephant and gave it to
    Indra.
Like a farmer, he harvested the fruits of the wishing trees.
On his slopes, washed by the elixir of life, the wind shakes
the champak bushes and bees hover nearby singing
gentle music.

౪౮

శా   వైకుంఠాంగద హేమ మాతత వల
          ద్వాతాశనాకృష్ట రే
          ఖాకారంబులం జుట్టు నంటి మొలనూ
          లై మేటియొడ్డాణమై
          శ్రీకారప్రభ గంతియై శిఖరిరా
          ట్సింహోల్లసత్పట్టమై
          యీ కొండం గనుం గొంటె మాయ దిపుడున్
          హేరాళపుం గాంతులన్.

౪౯

తే   వేదవేదాంతముల వేధ వెదకి కని
          పద్మలోచను శ్రీపాద పంకరుహము
          లబ్జరేఖాంకితము లవే యచలవంశ
          వల్లభుని మేఖలాసీమ నెల్ల మొఱయు.

48

Can you see that radiant gold left behind by Vishnu's
    bracelets?
It's still gleaming on the lines left on his craggy body
by the great snake that look like a loin string
down below and then a belt and then a necklace,
curved like the letter *Śrī*,[15]
and that finally coiled into a crown for the king
    of all mountains.
They haven't faded after all this time.

49

See those footprints? Vishnu left them,
marked by conch and lotus,
all over this mountain. Not even the Creator
could find them
in the Vedas.

౫౦

ఉ నాలుకబంతి వ్రేలఁబడి
నంజునఁ దోఁగి తమాలపల్లవ
శ్రీల హసింప నుబ్బి కనుఁ
గ్రేవల జేవుఱు పుక్కిలింపఁగా
వాలిక మేనిపీఁ చెగయ
వాడిన మాల్యమువోలె నాదిమ
వ్యాళము దీనిపగ్గ మయి
నట్టి యవస్థఁ దలంతు నెప్పుడున్.

౫౧

చ బిలముఖ పంక్తి నీ ధరణి
భృత్పతి వారిధి నిర్భరభ్రమిన్
దలముగ మున్ను ద్రావిన సు
ధారసధారగుణంబునం జుమీ
పలితవికార దూర నిర
పాయసుఖస్థితిఁ గాంచె నాఁగఁ గో
మల విచలచ్ఛిరోరుహ త
మాలవినీలిమరేఖ యొప్పెడిన్.

50

I feel sad for the First Snake. At the end of the churning,
he looked like a used garland—his thousand tongues
hanging loose, soaked with poison, blacker than *tamāla*
    leaves,
his eyes bulging and red, his old skin peeling off like fiber
after all that chafing. That image keeps coming to my
    mind.

51

This mountain drank up the elixir with its cavelike mouths
while churning the ocean. That's why,
despite its vast age, its hair is still black, with no trace of
    grey:
just look at the dark *tamāla* trees on its crest.[16]

౯౨

చ   జడధి మథింప౬ జిక్కి సుధ
    సౌరభ మానుట౬ జావు దక్కి ఆ
    పడ౬కులనుండి దుగ్ధభవ
    పాండిమ బొందుల నందమొంద నిం
    దడవి మెకాలతో గదుపు
    లై చరియించునను మే౬తకై బయల్
    వెడలి ధులీకులీరశకు
    లీమకరీముఖ వారిజంతువుల్.

౯3

మ   అనుచుం జందనపంక పంకిల తలం
    బై కేతురుద్ధాతపా
    ధ్వనిరుష్టం బయి మంచకోపరికుటీ
    వాటీ నటన్నెఱ్తకీ
    జన మై యౌవత సర్వతఃకలితవీ
    క్షాతోరణప్రజ్ఞ్బం
    ధన మై యొప్పుపురంబు సొచ్చి భవన
    ద్వారప్రఘాణంబునన్.

౯౪

క   మంతుల బాంధవభటసా
    మంతుల నాశ్రితుల నిలిపి మహికాంతు నిశా
    కాంతమణి కాంతికందళ
    కాంతం బగు నొక్క దొరనగర విడియించెన్.

426

52

Turtles, crabs, fish, and crocodiles escaped death
when the ocean was churned, since they too had tasted
the flavor of immortal nectar. Their bodies creamy
white from milk, they emerge from crevices in the rock
and set off in herds, unafraid, to hunt for food
with wild animals who live on land."

53

They entered the town, its soil sprinkled with sandal
    water,
roads shaded by flags from the hot sun, girls dancing
on high stages set up in front of the houses. Everywhere
    young women
cast their glances, like garlands, upon the king.
As he entered the gateway to his palace,

54

he ordered his advisers, relatives, generals,
subordinate kings, and suppliants to stand at a distance
and showed Svarochi to his quarters in a palace
glittering with moonstones.

౫౫

వ విడియించి యనంతరంబ యంతఃపుర కాంతాకరాంత
తంతన్యమాన మణిభాజన నీరాజన మంగళంబు
లంగీకరించి ప్రియాంగనల సంభావించి మగుడ నాస్థాన
మండపంబున కేతెంచి మతంగ మంకి మంకణ
మందపాల మరీచి మాండవ్య మార్కండేయాది
మహామునుల రావించి లగ్నంబు నిశ్చయించి గగనచర
జంఘాల కరప్రేషితలేఖతరులేఖాముఖంబులఁ
జిత్రరథ చిత్రాయుధ చిత్ర సేనాదులగు గంధర్వులను
వరాహకర్ణ గజకర్ణ సుకేతు మాణిభద్ర ప్రముఖ యక్షులను
రేవంతప్రముఖ గుహ్యకులను మందారముఖ్య
విద్యాధరులను బిలిపించి వినయపూర్వకంబుగా
విత్తాధిపతికి విజ్ఞాపనపత్రిక లిఖియించి నిజప్రధానులం
బంచి నలకూబరు రావించె నంత.

౫౬

క పసుపుల నలుఁగిడి రైదువ
బిసరుహలోచనలు పెండ్లి పెద్దల యాజ్ఞన్
వసుధాధ్యక్ష బుభుక్షున
కసితాలకభరకుఁ బేరఁటాం డ్రొగిఁ బాడన్.

55

Then the gandharva king was welcomed with the waving
of lamps, row after row, held on gem-studded plates by his
palace women. He embraced his beloved wives, then moved
on to his court. He met with all the sages—Matanga, Manki,
Mankana, Mandapala, Marici, Mandavya, and Markan-
deya, among others—and according to their advice fixed the
auspicious moment for the wedding. With flying messengers
he sent invitations written on leaves of the wishing trees to
Chitraratha, Chitrayudha, Chitrasena, and other gandhar-
vas, to yakshas such as Boar Ear, Elephant Ear, Suketu, and
Manibhadra, to Revanta the guhyaka, and to vidyadharas
such as Mandara. He also sent by way of his chief minister
a personal letter, humbly couched, to Kubera, Master of
Money, asking him to send his son, Nalakubara.

56

The elders in charge of the wedding gave the order,
and beautiful women with wide eyes rubbed and bathed
the king of kings, Svarochi, and the black-haired princess
with a paste of turmeric and lentils to the music
of festive songs sung for the occasion.

ఇ౨

ఉ	మజ్జన మాడె రాజు కృశ
మధ్యమ లింపున వంప గుంపులై
గొజ్జెగనీటి వెల్లువలు
గోవ జవాజుల నిగ్గుఁ జూపఁ జం
చజ్జరఠాహికంచుకము
చాయ మడుంగుల నొత్తఁ జెమ్మనీ
రుజ్జిగిలన్ వహించె మెయి
నూఁదినఁ బాఱు దుకూలచేలముల్.

ఇఠ

చ	గరువున కొత్తఁ జెంగలువ
కచ్చు ఘటించినమౌళిఁ జుట్టెఁ జె౦
దిరిక చెఱంగునం బసిఁడి
తీఁగెలు నించిన జిల్గుపాగ బం
భరసభ వాసనాపవన
పారణఁ దేల నలందెఁ గస్తురిన్
మరకతమౌక్తికాదిమణి
మండనమండితుఁ డయ్యె నయ్యెడన్.

57

Svarochi bathed as teams of young women with tiny waists
poured rose water in thick streams and applied fragrance
    of civet
from Goa. Then they dried him with a robe thin
as a snake's shed skin, and he put on clothes
so fine they would fly away
if you breathed on them.

58

Around his head he tied a turban made of fine red cloth
embroidered with gold and folded like the petals
of the red water lily, opening to one side. The musk
he wore on his body soaked the breeze that made swarms
of bees very happy. He was shining with emeralds
and diamonds.

౫౯

మ   కదిసెన్ లగ్నమటంచు మంత్రులు దొరల్
గంధర్వరాజాజ్ఞ ను
న్మదవేదండ ఘటాభటాశ్వరథ సే
నా జైత్రవాదిత్ర సం
పద మీఆం జనుదెంచి కాంచిముదమొ
ప్పం జేసి రారూఢుఁగాఁ
గదళీకాంచనకక్ష్యలన్ మెఆయు లే
ఖస్వామి చెదంతిపైన్.

౬౦

ఉ   అత్తఱీఁ బట్టణంబు విక
చాంబురుహాక్షులు కౌతుకంబునం
జిత్తము లుల్లసిల్లఁ గయి
సేసి గృహంగణసౌధమాలికల్
హత్తి నరేంద్రవీథిఁ జతు
రంగబలంబులుఁ గొల్వఁగా మరు
న్మత్తగజంబుపైఁ జను కు
మారశిరోమణిఁ జూచి రుబ్బునన్.

59

Ministers and attending kings arrived with royal
    elephants,
infantry, cavalry, chariots, and big drums. At the
    gandharva king's
command, they seated the groom on Indra's four-tusked
    elephant
with golden flags flying, for the moment was drawing near.

60

Just then, the beautiful women of that town
opened their eyes wide in eagerness. Excited,
they adorned themselves and pushed their way
to the front yards and balconies of their houses
where they could catch a glimpse of the young king
riding an elephant down the royal street, the four divisions
of the army around him.[17]

౬౧

ఉ అంచెలు గట్టి కాలి తోడు
సై చననీవు గదమ్మ ప్రోదిరా
యంచ లివేటి సంగడము
లయ్యెను దయ్యమ యేటివేడ్క నా
కంచుౕ బదంబునన్ మొరయు
నందియ యూడౕగౕ దన్నిపోయి వీ
క్రించె లతాంగి యొర్తు మర
జిన్నిఘ సాగరమేఖలావిఘన్.

౬౨

చ వలపులపల్లవుం డొకౕడు
వట్టిచలంబున నేౕప దీనయ్యె
యలుకలు తీర్చితీర్చి యొక
యచ్చుర వచ్చి నృపాలు నన్నగ
ర్వేలువడి చూచెౕ గాముకౕడు
వెంటనె రా నపుడాత్మఘర్మయ్యె
వెలవెలౕబాౕ దన్ముఖము
వెల్వెలౕబాఆ విటాననాబ్జమున్.

434

61

"These pet geese are annoying. They come in rows
and stick to my feet. They won't let me go.
What a nuisance!
I want to see the king of this earth." With this thought
in her mind, one woman kicked off her ringing anklet
to stop them from coming at her
and ran to see him, handsome as Krishna.[18]

62

One apsaras, pestered by her lover, was at pains
to convince him that she wasn't interested
in any other man. Then she came out of her bedroom
to see the king. Her lover followed
after her and found her sweating
with desire. Seeing him seeing her,
she turned pale, and so did he.

౬3

చ చిలుకలకొల్కి కల్కి యొక
చేడియ నాటకసాల మేడపై
నిలువున నాడుచుండి ధర
నీపతిఁ జూడఁ దలంచి యంచునన్
నిలిచి రహిం గనుంగొనుచు
నెయ్యమునం దనువల్లి యుబ్బి కం
చెల తెగిపడ్డఁ గేతనము
చీరచెఅంగున మూసెఁ జన్నులన్.

౬౪

ఉ కీరమనోజ్ఞవాణి యొక
కిన్నరి కిన్నెర మీటి మీటి యొ
య్యారపులీల నేఁగి వసు
ధాధిపుఁ గన్గొనె జిల్లుపయ్యెదన్
హారముఁ జక్కఁ బెట్టెడు కు
చాహితహస్తము పైఁడిగోళ్ళు హిం
సారతి సేయు దర్పకుని
సంపెఁగములుల్కులుఁబోలె మించఁగన్.

63

The corners of her eyes red as a parrot's beak, a woman
was dancing on the terrace of her palace. Wanting
to see the king, she went to the edge and looked down,
exploding with desire. Her blouse split open. Quickly
she grabbed a flag flying nearby and hid her breasts.

64

A *kinnari** with a voice sweet as a parrot's
was playing the vina. She put it down and rushed
to see the king as she was adjusting the sash on her breasts
with her hands, and the golden finger guards were like
yellow champak arrows the love god was shooting
straight at her.

---

* Heavenly musician.

౬౫

చ పరవశదైన్య మాడుకొను
   ప్రౌఢలఁ గానదు ఘర్మవారిచేఁ
   గరఁగి ప్రవించుచిత్రకము
   గాన దనాద్యతవీటిపాటలా
   ధరమున సున్న మంటిన వి
   ధంబును గానదు నవ్వుటాల కా
   భరణము గొన్సఁ గాన దొక
   బాల నృపాలునిఁ జూచి నివ్వెఆన్.

౬౬

చ అలికులవేణి యొక్కతె ర
   తాంతమునం దనయంగవల్లికం
   బులకలు చొక్కు లేఁజెమరుఁ
   బుట్టఁగ నేఁగి నరేంద్రుఁ జూడ నా
   పులకలు చొక్కు లేఁజెమరుఁ
   బోవక యట్టుల యుండె నట్టి దొఁ
   జెలువగువానిఁ గన్గొనిన
   చెల్వకుఁ జూపుల కావె కూటముల్.

438

65

A young girl paid no heed to the older women
who were showing their helpless love, and she didn't see
the dot painted on her forehead melting in sweat,
and she didn't see the white lime sticking
to her careless lips, red from chewing betel,
and she didn't notice that someone had taken
her jewel, just to tease her. She was lost
in looking at the king.

66

One dark-haired beauty had just finished making love,
her body thrilling with joy, full of goose-bumps
and drops of sweat. She rushed to see the king:
that same shiver of joy, those goose-bumps,
those drops of sweat all over again.
For a beautiful young woman, just looking
at a handsome man is making love.

౬౭

చ అలరులబంతి జృంభికకు
నడ్డము సేయుచు౯ గర్భపాళిపై
కలకల౦ ద్రోయుచు౦ దర౦గ
లో ప్రమదాస్రులు గోట మీటుచు౦
జెలి ఘుజపీఠి నొత్తగిలి
చిల్కను దువ్వుచు వాలు౦గన్ను౦ గ్రే
వల కుదధార చేర నొక
వారవిలాసిని చూచె రాసుతన్.

౬౮

చ జిలు౦గుల౦ బెట్టుచు౦ దొడల౦
జెంద్రికపాపడ యంట మైతడిం
బెళపెళ లేనిచీర౦ గటి
బింకపుఁజన్నుల౦ జేర్చికొంచు వే
జలకము లాడియాడి యొక
చాన కరస్థితకేశ యై నృపు
న్వెలువడి చూచె లో౦బడితి
నీ కని బాసకు నిల్చెనో యనన్.

440

67

Yawning, a courtesan covered her mouth
with a bouquet of flowers and gathered
her loose hair behind her ears. She stood there, flicking
tears of joy from her eyes with her fingernails.
Leaning on her girlfriend, patting her pet parrot,
she stared at the king as tears kept falling
from the corners of her eyes.

68

A young woman had just finished her bath. She rushed
to see the king, her red petticoat still soaked and sticking
to her thighs, and she was covering her wet breasts
with a crisp, dry sari that was turning soft
as she held her dripping hair in her hand.
She stood there as if she'd taken a vow:
"I'm your woman."[19]

౬౯

మ ఒకనేత్రాంబుజ మొక్కగల్ల మొకచ
న్నొయ్యారపున్లీల వీ
థికిఁ దోఁపన్ దలుపోరఁగా నొక పురం
ధ్రీరత్న మీక్షించె రా
జకిశోరంబుఁ దదీయలై వెలయుభా
షాలక్ష్ముణం జూచి త్ర్యం
బకభాగంబు మొఅంగి మైత్రికి శివా
భాగంబ యేతెంచె నాన్.

౭౦

మ కలయం గూర్మిఁ జెమర్చునంగములల ల
గ్నంబైన సన్నంపుమం
జుల కౌశేయమునందు మించు కమల
స్తోమంబుచేఁ జూచె నో
క్కలతాతన్వీ చెలంగి పొంగు మదికాం
క్షల్దీఅ మే నెల్లఁ గ
న్నులు గావించి కుమారుజవ్వనము చె
న్నుం జూచుచందంబునన్.

69

A housewife opened the door a crack, revealing
one beautiful eye, one cheek, one breast
as she looked at the young king. It was as if the left half
of Shiva had duped the right half
and slipped away to join Language and Wealth
when she saw they were with him.[20]

70

A passionate young woman was sweating all over
as she stared at the king to her heart's content,
taking in his beauty, and her sari,
printed with lotus flowers, stuck to her body,
as if she were all eyes.

౬౧

వ ఇత్తెఆంగునం గరంగు నంతరంగంబులు గల
కురంగాక్షుల యపాంగంబులం దుఃఅంగలించు
సితేతర తరళతర దృగ్రోచుల నభంగశృంగారరసవీచుల
చాలునం బోలెఁ బొదువంబడి యాలంబిత చీనాంబర
ప్రాలంబమాలికాచిత్రమ్ములగు నాతపత్రమ్ములు
మెఱయఁ బత్తమ్ముల డిగ్గి దుర్గ్గాధిపతు లేమేమ యని
త్రోపు త్రోపాడుచు వీచు వీచొప్పు లచ్చమ్ము లగు కౌముదీ
గుచ్ఛమ్ముల సంతరింప నంతిక వైజయంతికలం
గ్రాలువలువలం బోలయి చిఱుగరువలిం దూలు
నీలాలకల యలక లుభయపార్శ్వసముత్తుంగ
మత్తమాతంగమదసౌరభ సంగిభృంగ సంఘంబుల
నెలయింప నింపారుకలపంబు లబ్బుటునం బేటులెత్తి
యొండొరుల యొత్తిడిం బొడిపొడియై యొగయు
విస్రమరపరాగపూగంబు చదల నెల్లెడ నుల్లెడ గట్టిన
ట్టమర దట్టదట్టమ్ముగ సాగు నాగరుల వాగారవమ్ములు
నిగుడ నెడవడక పొగడు పొగడికల కలకలమ్ములును
బుంఖానుపుంఖ శంఖభేరీపటహకాహళవేణువీణాది
వాదనధ్వానంబును గలమధురకిన్నరీ నిక్వాణంబుల
రాణం ద్రాణఁ జేఱుచు విన్నాణంపుఁ గొల్పు
టెలుంగులును వేల్పుగణాలు పాడు లక్ష్మీనారాయణల
కల్యాణంపుఁబాటలం దీటుకొను తిన్నని రవంబులం
గలసి బలసికొను కోలాహలమ్ము లిమ్ముగ సందడుల నెడ
గలుగం జడియు వేత్రహస్తుల ప్రశస్తతర సాహోనినాదంబు
సంబంధించి పెంపొలయ నత్యంతకాంతంబయి
నిరంతరగతిం గ్రంతనడవ నడదివియలై
మకుటారవిందరాగంబులు వెలుంగ నలుగడల
సామంతసందోహంబు క్రందుకొన మందమంద
గమనంబునం జను బృందారకవేదండంబు
పై నుద్దండ తనుచ్ఛాయాకలాపంబు జంబేటి

71

He was thus engulfed by continuous waves of love flowing from the glowing corners of these women's dark eyes, soft as the eyes of a doe, as their innermost hearts were melting for him. Parasols of Chinese silk with strings of pictures hanging from them were towering over him. Commanders of fortresses climbed down from their vehicles and pushed one another as they competed for the honor of fanning him with yak-tail fans, white as moonlight, while the breeze from the billowing flags nearby shook the black curls of ravishing women as if the bees hovering around the temples of proud elephants had changed places and come forward.[21] The sandalwood paste that people had smeared on their bodies dried and flaked and, since everyone was crushed together, these flakes were ground into dust that rose up like pollen into the sky, as if making a vast canopy.

The unending chatter of the town people mixed with the continuous praises sung by bards and the blaring of conches and beating of drums, big and small, and the notes of trumpets and flutes and vinas and voices singing more sweetly than any lute along with songs sung by apsarases celebrating the wedding of Lakshmi and Narayana, and through the vast cacophony one could hear the guards with batons in their hands crying out "Sāho" in order to make room for people to move as the members of the groom's family were walking in procession to offer gifts to the bride. Subordinate kings were marching on all sides as the rubies in their crowns lit their way. A golden light, like the magical river that turns dust to

జంబాల కదంబకంబు డంబు విడంబింపఁ
దిన్నని రవంబునం గలసి బలసిన కోలాహలంబు
హంసాది విహంగమ హృదయంగమ రావంబును
బెడంగువడ నడచు క్రంత నత్యంత దర్శనీయంబులై
మెఅియు మంగళద్రవ్యంబుల నెడనెడఁ దీండ్రించు
పుండ్రేక్షుదండంబుల కడలుఁ గడలుకొను పసరుటాకుల
డాలు శైవాలంబు నందంద క్రందుగా మండు
చేదివియలు చెందివలునుం గాఁ బార్శ్వద్వయ
సముత్తుంగమణిసోపధవీథికారేదేంతరాళంబున
గంధగజఘటాఘనాఘన కాంతిక కాళి మాగధం
ప్రవాహంబునం గూలంకషంబగు నృపతిపథ
యమునాప్రూదంబు గగన గంగావగహనాభ్యాసంబున
నిండుకొనిపోవునదియ్యునుం బోలెఁ దనరఁ
దన సముద్ధామతేజో భరంబునం జడిసిన
మేరుగిరిమొరులుం బోలెఁ దీరుగల భుజంబులం
దాఁఉమాఅుగా నిడిన తారతారంపుఁ బంచసరంబులు
దేరంతరహారంబులుఁ గేయూరహీరంబులుఁ గరకంకణ
కురువిందకందళంబులుఁ గటికనకమేఖలఘటితం
బగు చేరుకరాచురీమరకతంపుఁ బిడిమెఅుంగులం
దఅీసి వెన్నెల క్రొన్నురువుల బోరన న్నుగు నరపడుగు
జిలుఁగుకంచుకంబున మించి వెలుపలం దీఁప
మంచు గవిసిన రోహణమహీధరంబునుం బోలె
రాజభవనాంగణంబు చేరవచ్చె నంత నక్కుడ.

gold,* radiated from the body of the king, seated on the white elephant of the gods that was slowly, very slowly, moving along. The vast din of the crowd mingled with a murmur that was like the cackling of geese, and amid the parade of auspicious gifts you could see, here and there, bunches of sugarcane with green foliage on top, like algae floating on water, and lamps people held in their hands were like red water lilies in the deep dark flood of people, dark as clouds, heavy as elephants crowding the space between heaven and earth on that street lined on both sides with high buildings adorned with sapphires. In short, the royal street was like the black Yamuna River in spate, rushing to meet the Ganga.

The prince was all aglow, his shoulders so high that they terrified Mount Meru, with five-stringed necklaces falling from them unevenly onto his chest along with other, straighter strings, and he had diamonds on his armlets and *kuruvinda* rubies on his bracelets and a *karācurī* dagger with an emerald handle stuck into the golden belt around his waist, and all these brilliant colors shone right through the fine white robe he was wearing that put to shame the creamy white of the moon. Like Mount Rohana clothed in fog, he arrived at the king's palace.

---

* The Jambunadi.

౭౨

క కాంతా కదంబకిసలయ
కాంత కరావర్జ్యమాన కనకఘటీని
ర్వాంత సుగంధి జలంబుల
నింతి జలకమాడి జిలుంగు లిడి తడి యొత్తెన్.

౭3

చ తళుకు దుకూలశాటిం గటిం
దాల్చి పటీర మలంది హారకుం
దల మణిపారిహార్యరశ
నా కటకాంగుళిముద్రికాది భూ
షలు తొడి పారిజాతవిక
సత్పసవావళీం బూని యొయ్య న
వ్వెలందిం వివాహవేది కలి
వేణులు దేం జనుదెంచె సిగ్గునన్.

౭౪

తే ఇట గృహద్వారసీమకు నేంగుదెంచు
నా కుమారున కిందివరాక్షుం డెదురు
సని మరుత్కరి డిగ్గి వందన మొనర్చి
నతని దీవించి హితమంత్రియుతము గాంగ.

72

Meanwhile, the bride bathed in perfumed water
poured from golden pots that beautiful young women
held in their delicate hands above her head.
Then she dried herself with a fine, smooth cloth.

73

She put on a white silk sari, rubbed sandal paste
on her skin, and adorned herself with a pearl necklace,
earrings, gem-studded bangles, a belt of sixteen bands,
rings, and *pārijāta* flowers in full bloom
for her hair. Thus she came to the wedding dais
with her friends leading the way.

74

Indivaraksha came out to the front of his palace
to welcome the prince, who climbed down
from the white elephant and bowed. His father-in-law
blessed him and, with his ministers and friends,
led him in

౭౫

ప భూసురాశీర్వాదనాదంబులు రోదసి నిండ నభ్యంతర
గృహంబునకుం దోడ్కొని పోవునప్పు డప్పుడమితోc
డెడనెడం బుణ్యాంగన లొసంగు నీరాజనోపచారమ్ము
లాదరించుచుc గక్క్యాంతర ద్వారదేశంబుల
మంగళార్థంబుగా నిడిన పూర్ణకలశముకురాది
పదార్థంబులc గనుంగొనుచుc దోరణస్తంభాయమాన
రంభాతరుకిసలయొత్తల తాళవృంతానిలంబులc
గుంతలంబులు చలియింప మంథరగతిc
గింపురుషవృషభం డగు గంధర్వరాజప్రధానుం
డొసంగు కైదండ గొని యల్లనల్లన నడచి
పురోహితబ్రాహ్మణబంధుపురంధ్రీసందోహనీరంధ్రం
బయి వైవాహిక క్రియారంభసంభార సంభ్రమద్రంభాది
మరుద్రంభోరువుల కలికి నునుసోగపలుకుల
కలకలంబునం గొలగొల మను కొతుకాగారంబు సొత్తెంచి.

౭౬

చ ప్రభలు నభోవిటంకమున
భానుమరీచులంc బ్రోదిసేయంగా
స్తుభనిభ నూత్నరత్నపరి
శోభిత మై గరుడాశ్మవేది రు
గ్యీభవము పొల్పుగుం జవిక
విద్రుమపాద సువర్ణపీఠిపైc
బ్రభుత దలిర్ప మామ పను
పన్ వసియించె నుదంచితస్థితిన్.

75

as Vedic chants filled the sky. The prince received the lights waved in offering by lucky women and looked happily at the water pots brimming over and the mirrors placed as a blessing in the gateways leading inward. The breeze coming from the wide, tender leaves of banana plants set in place as pillars to prop up an arch made of garlands played with the curls on his forehead. Walking with dignity, he took the hand of the chief minister to the gandharva king—a member of a godly clan*—and entered the wedding pavilion, which was packed with priests, Brahmans, relatives, and auspicious women and humming with the sweet drawn-out words of girls from heaven, like Rambha, who were getting more and more excited by all the wedding paraphernalia.

76

Lights were dancing in the sky, enhancing
the brilliance of the sun, and the dais made of emeralds
was studded with new gems equal to the *kaustubha*
that Vishnu wears, and there was a seat for the groom
fashioned from coral and gold. At a sign from his father-
    in-law,
he took his seat, like a king.

---

* Kimpurusha.

౯౭

క విధియుతముగ ఖచరుండవ
న్యధినాథున కొసంగెం బసిండిహరివాణమునన్
మధురమఖభుగ్గవీ దధి
మధురస సంపర్క మయిన మధుపర్కంబున్.

౯౮

తే అంచితాకృతి సాక్షాత్కరించినట్టి
రమకుం బ్రతివచ్చు సురమనోరమ మనోర
మ యనుదాని ననుంగుజామాతం గైట
భారి సరింగాగ నర్చించి దారవోసె.

౯౯

క తదనంతరంబ హర్షము
పొదలు మదిన్ మెట్టుం బ్రాల పుట్టికలయెడం
గదియం బట్టిన పెండెరం
గదియించిరి బంధుజనులు కన్యావరులన్.

77

The king of the sky gave that king over all the earth
the *madhuparka* mix of honey and curds
from the milk of the Wishing Cow
in a vessel of gold, as the rite prescribes.[22]

78

Then he worshiped his beloved son-in-law
as Lord Vishnu[23] and poured water into his hands
as he gave him the gift of his daughter,
Manorama, the very image of the goddess Rama*
who brings joy to the hearts of the gods.

79

Next to baskets of "foot rice"[24] the relatives
draped a curtain between bride and groom
with a particular joy.

─────

* Ramā, that is, Lakshmi.

౮౦

ఉ అప్పుడు తూర్యముల్మొరయ
నమ్మిథనమ్ము విలోకనస్పృహం
దెప్పలcదేల వంపcబడు
తెల్లని చీరతెరం గ్రమంబునం
గొప్పు మొగంబు నట్టిం జనుం
గొండలుc దేcప లతాంగిపోలెc జె
ల్వప్పతిలన్ సుధారసప
యోనిధి పెందెరc బుట్టు నిందిరన్.

౮౧

చ కటకరవంబు బోరుకలం
గన్ రమణుల్తెరచీర వంచినం
దటుకున రాజుమొ మెదుటం
దారసమైన లతాంగి నేత్రముల్
చటులత లజ్జc దల్లడిలె
జాలరి చేవలం బాసి ధాత్రిపై
నటు నిటు మిట్టిమిట్టి పడు
నంబుచరంబులం బోలె నత్తటిన్.

454

80

Bride and groom could hardly wait to see each other
as, with a flourish of trumpets, the curtain
was slowly, very slowly, lowered. Now she appeared—
first her hair, then her face, her neck, and her full
breasts, like Lakshmi emerging, exquisite,
on a wave in the ocean of milk.

81

When the women lowered the curtain with a jingling
of bangles, the groom's face appeared right before
his bride's eyes, which quivered in shyness
like fish leaping from water.

౭౨

మ అవనీశత్రిదశేంద్రు చూపుబరి క
న్యాగండపాళిద్వయా
నవలావణ్యరసంబుఁ గొల్లగొని యం
తం జెంత ఫాలంపురా
జు విలోకించి చలించి కై కొనిన యా
సొమ్మెల్ల ఘర్మంబుకై
తవ మొప్పన్ వెస డించి తూఁటఁ గబరీ
తాపించ కుంజాతమున్.

౭3

ఆ రాజుచూడ్కి కప్పుడు రాజీవముఖిచూడ్కి
లెదురుకొనియె లజ్జ గదికి కొదికి
జడిసి జడిసి జహ్న్నసంభవాంభోవేణి
కెదురు లెక్కు మీల కొదమ లనఁగ.

౭ఓ

మ తనుమధ్యత్రివళుల్నటింప నిలమీఁ
దన్ మట్టియల్మోవఁగాఁ
గనుపాపల్పయితెప్పలం గదియ ను
త్కంఠాగ్రయై నిక్కి నా
ఘనిమౌళిం దలఁ బ్రాలు వోసె నవలా
దోర్ములకూలంకష
స్తనవిస్ఫూర్తికి సందిదండల ధళల్
సాహోసినాదం బిడన్.

82

Like a thief, the bridegroom stole
the beauty of her cheeks with his eyes. Then he turned
his gaze to her forehead that was like the moon.
But the moon is a king, so, afraid of being punished,
the groom gave back what had been taken, and that
became gleaming drops of sweat on her face,
while his glance hid in the forest
of her dark hair.

83

The bride's eyes encountered the gaze
of the prince and shyly withdrew, then looked
again, like fish struggling to swim upstream.

84

The three folds on her thin belly were quivering and her
    toe-rings
dug into the ground and the pupils of her eyes reached for
her eyelids and she stretched her neck and her breasts
rubbed against her raised arms and her golden armlets
cheered her on as she poured the wedding rice
over the groom's head.

౮౩

చ ముదివడు కంకణప్రభల
ముత్తెపుసేసలు దోయిలించి యె
త్తెదుతతీ బాహుమూలకుచ
దీప్తులపైఁ బతిదృష్టి పర్వినం
బోడమిన లజ్జఁ బాణియుగ
మున్ వెస వంచియ మౌళిమీఁదికై
పొడువునఁ జల్లె లేనగవు
పొల్తుక తెప్పల నప్పళించుచున్.

౮౪

క సకలక్ష్మాపతి యిడఁ గొ
మ్మకచంబులనుండి రాలె మౌక్తికములు సా
త్త్విక జనిత గండ ఘర్మం
బుకదంబాసార గరిమఁ బునరుక్తములై.

౮౫

క పతి సతిపై నిడు ముక్తా
వితతి పడం దొడఁగె వడి భవిష్యత్పురుషా
యిత నిర్ధయరతిరభస
చ్యుత సితకబరీప్రసూన సూచక మగుచున్.

85

While she was lifting her arms to pour the pearls of rice,
their white mixing with golden light from her bracelets,
the prince fixed his eyes on her radiant breasts
that had come into view. She sensed this and, overcome
by shyness, lowered her arms and tossed the rice
on his head from a slight distance, hiding her smile
with her eyelids.

86

Now the prince of all the earth poured rice on *her* head,
and the grains rolled down from her hair
while beads of sweat poured from her cheeks
to reveal her desire,[25] pearls
matching pearls.

87

The white pearls he was pouring
fell rapidly from her hair as if to show
how in the not-so-distant future
flowers would fall from her hair
as she lay on top of him, fiercely making love.

౮౭

శా కట్టెన్ మంగళసూత్రమున్ శరధి శం
ఖశ్రీలకున్ బొమ్మలం
గట్టం జాలెడు కంఠపీఠి నిఖిల
క్ష్మాభర్త శోణద్యుతుల్
దట్టంబై నఖకోరకోత్కరము త
ద్దైవేయ హైమస్ఫుర
త్పట్టస్థాపిత పద్మరాగముల పం
తంబుల్విడంబింపఁగాన్.

౮౯

క అట్టియెడఁ బెండ్లిపనులన్
దిట్ట లగు పురంధ్రు లచట నిలిపిరి వహ్నిం
బెట్టిరి మణిపీఠి సురీ
పట్టముపై బఱచి రందుఁ బతియును సతియున్.

౯౦

క ఆశుద్విజహుత హరితశ
మీ శాఖాశకల నినద మేదుర విశదా
భీశుజ్వాలాజాల హు
తాశక్రోడమున వేల్చి రాహుతు లెలమిన్.

88

Then he tied the wedding string around her neck,[26]
which surpassed any conch from the sea
in its beauty, and as he did so he bent his bright
red fingernails that couldn't quite compete
with the rubies glittering
on her golden necklace.[27]

89

Women skilled in the details of the ritual
brought fire and prepared a seat studded with jewels,
covered with silk cloth from Surat, for the bride
    and groom.

90

The young couple made offerings to the fire
that was quickly ignited by Brahmans with twigs
of the green *śamī* tree
sizzling with bright flames.

౯౧

తే   తోయజామొద లాజలు దోయిలించి
     ప్రమదమున వేల్వ నొకకొన్ని చెమటనంట
     వ్రేళ్ళు గనుపట్టె గెంజాయ వీతిహొత్రు
     నాలుకలు సాటిరాకున్న నవ్వెననగ.

౯౨

తే   స్తనగుళుచ్చ వధూ దేహదాడిమీ ల
     తామతల్లికపై హోమ ధూమ మడరె
     భర్త కభిమత రతిమహో ఫలవిపాక
     మగుటంగోరి ఘటించుదోహద మనంగ.

౯౩

మ   జగతీనాథవతంస మానతశిర
     స్సుమ్మేళనన్ నెయ్యపుం
     జగడంబుల్ప్రియమొప్ప మాన్పెడుతటిం
     జంచత్కిరీటాగ్ర ర
     త్నగణస్పర్శసహంబు గావలసియో
     నాం గోర్కి దైవాఆ న
     మ్ముగువం బాదతలంబు వట్టి సనెకల్
     మట్టించె మోదంబునన్.

91

The bride, fragrant as the lotus, picked up a handful
of puffed rice and happily offered it to the fire.
A few grains stuck to her bright red fingers, damp
with sweat, and it seemed that these fingers
were laughing and showing white teeth,
mocking the fire whose flames
paled in contrast.

92

Smoke, they say, makes the pomegranate tree burst
into fruit. Smoke now swirled around the bride's body
with its flowering breasts to yield fruit
in the form of passion that would soon
please her husband.

93

As if to get her used to the feel of the jewels in his crown
touching her feet when he would bow to her to win her
    over
when she'd be upset with him someday,
he took her foot in his hands and placed it
with care and joy on the grinding stone.[28]

೯౪

క కడునవ్వించుచుc జెఅంగులు
ముడివెట్టం బేరంతాండ్రు ముదిత కనుబొమల్
ముడివెట్టె నాలిసిగ్గున
ముడివెట్టైన్ నారి చెఅకు మోసున మరుcడున్.

౯౫

సీ పరిణమించిరి ధరామరపురంధ్రీహస్త
ఘటిత చేలాంచల గ్రంథికలనc
బరిపూర్ణనిష్ఠ గొల్చిరి ప్రదక్షిణపూర్వ
వినతి నాలుకలార్చు వేడివేల్పు
వీక్షించి రుడువీథి నక్షీణ సుస్థితి
స్థాయిc దీషిత రమాధవుని ధ్రువునిc
బరిణయప్రాప్త సప్తర్షి ప్రియాప్రేక్ష్య
సాక్షాదరుంధతీ సతి కెరంగిరి

తే సకల సంయమిగణ నమస్కరణ కృత్య
మాచరించి తదీయ హస్తాభిమంత్రి
తాక్షతలు మౌళిc దాల్చి రత్యాదరమున
దంపతులు బంధుకోటి కుత్సవ మెలర్ప.

94

Gleefully, the women tied together the edges of the
    clothes
the bride and groom were wearing. She knitted her
    eyebrows
in a pretence of shyness as the love god tied the string
to his sugarcane bow.

95

The young couple were happy when the Brahman women
tied their clothes together.
They circled the fire god and worshiped his flames
with pure attention.
They looked at Dhruva, the stable star in the sky*
who had pleased Rama's husband, Vishnu.
They bowed to Arundhati, most worthy
of honor among the wives of the Seven Sages
who had come to the wedding.
Then bride and groom gratefully received on their heads
grains of rice blessed by ascetics,
while all the relatives were overjoyed.

* The Pole Star.

೯౬

ఉ కూరిమి మంత్రితోడ నల
కూబరుఁ డేకత మాడి పెద్దబం
గారపుఁ గోరఁ గల్పవని
కాజనికాంతములైన చీరలున్
హార విభూషణావళియు
నమ్మిధనంబునకుం ప్రియంబుతో
నారదమౌనిచేత నద
నం జదివించెఁ గుబేరుపేరుగాన్.

೯౭

క కలిమి మొఅయంగ మఱియుం
గల బాంధవులోసఁగి రపుడు కాంచనమణిభూ
షలుఁ జీరలు నరపతికిం
బొలఁతికి నుడుగరలు ముదము పొదలఁగ నంతన్.

466

96

Nalakubara consulted his favorite adviser
and then asked Narada to announce, at the right moment,
in the name of Kubera,* the gifts
presented to the couple on a golden plate—
saris born fresh from the Wishing Tree and many fine
necklaces and jewels.

97

After that, other relatives came forward
to give their gifts—precious clothes and
many ornaments of gold.

* Kubera is the gods' banker and father of Nalakubara.

౯౮

సీ పొగడపూవంటి కంపుల మదాంబువులును
మధువర్ణ దంతశంబములు మెఅియ
భీకర స్వర చారు బృంహితంబులు ఘనాం
గారకగ్రహ కాంతి కన్నులమర
నిలఁ జుట్టువడు తొండముల మించు పూర్వాంగ
మెత్తరంబై పిఱుం దత్తమిల్లఁ
గటము లుత్కటములై నిటలముల్బటువులై
సిబ్బెంపు మొగముల నుబ్బుమీఅ

తే స్వర్ణ కక్ష్యాంకుశప్రాస శరధి శార్ఙ్గ
ఖేట కుథ ఘంటికాద్యలంకృతులఁ జెలువ
మెసఁగు గంభీరవేది భద్రేభశతము
నల్లునకు నిచ్చె గంధర్వ వల్లభుండు.

౯౯

శా ఉర్వీజానికి మామ యిచ్చె శిఖిపిం
ఛోద్భాసివర్ణంబుచే
నర్వాచీనఘనాళి రోహితసహ
ప్రాకీర్ణగా మింటఁ బూ
షార్వస్తోమముఁ జిత్రయానముల నూ
టాడించు గాంధర్వగం
ధర్వవ్యూహము దీప్తిచండమణికాం
డస్వర్ణసన్నాహమున్.

468

98

The gandharva king gave his son-in-law
a hundred regal elephants redolent
of *pŏgaḍa* flowers, their tusks hard as diamond
and colored like honey, their eyes red
like the planet Mars, their trumpeting
frightening yet pleasing to hear, their trunks so long
they folded inward so as not to touch the ground,
the front of their bodies raised high and the back
sloping low, with wide temples and round foreheads
and rose-colored spots on their faces, and hanging
from the golden belts around their waists there were
goads, spears, quivers of arrows, bows, shields,
with lovely blankets round their spine.

99

The father-in-law gave to his son-in-law many fine
    gandharva horses
in all the colors of the rainbow that runs straight
through monsoon clouds or the colors in a peacock's tail,
more versatile in their movements than the horses
that carry the sun, girded with saddles of gold
that were studded with precious gems.

౧౦౦

క తళతళని తరణీ మొఱుంగులం
దలతల మను మణుల మొఆసి తలంచినచోటన్
నిలుచు విమానము భీచర
కులతిలకుండు కూర్మి పెండ్లికొడుకున కొసంగెన్.

౧౦౧

వ మఱియు రజత మహారజత శయ్యాసనభాజన
డోలాకలాచికాఘటకటాహవీటికాపేటికాది
గృహోపకరణంబులును, మరకత కురువింద
పురుషరత్న పురందరమణీ మౌక్తికాది మహారత్న ఘటిత
కటకతులాకోటికంఠికాంగదైకావళీ కాంచికోర్మికాదికలాప
కలాపంబులును, విచిత్ర నేత్ర పేశల కౌశేయ చీనాంశుక
ధట్టంబులం బెట్టినట్టి పెట్టియలును, అమూల్యాగరు
మృగమద సంకుమద కుంకుమ పటీర కర్పూర
హిమాంబుపూరంబులు దట్టుపునంగునగలుసత్తును
మంచిగందవొడి చాం దుదయ భాస్కరంబు లోనుగాంగల
పరిమళద్రవ్యసంభారపరంపరలును, జవ్వనంపు గ్రొవ్వన
నివ్వటిల్లి మువ్వంపువాతెఱలు విశ్వ నవ్వు నునుసోగ
వెన్నెలలం గలసి పిసాళించు చంచల దృగంచల ప్రభలం
బచారించి, మొఱుంగు జన్నులం గన్నెతమ్మిమొగ్గల వన్నె
నటమటించి, పెన్నెఱుల మొఱుంగుదుమ్మొదవన్నెం
దటమటించి, నెన్నడుముల విన్నువెన్నుదన్ని,
బటువుమిగిలి విటనికాయంబు రాయిడింబడి
పుటపుటనైన కూలంకషచాటువులమాటకారితనంబు
మొఆసి, నాగరికపుం బనుల గరగరికల
గళరవచ్చులాలాపాచరణంబుల రవణంబుల

100

And one more gift: a chariot that could fly through the sky
and stop wherever its rider desired, and that was
covered in gems so bright they could order the sun's rays
to move out of their way.

101

And still more: household goods like beds and cushions
and plates and swings and spittoons and water pots and
boxes for betel leaves, all made of silver and gold; brace-
lets, anklets, neck-rings, armlets, single-string necklaces
of pearls, belts, and rings, all inset with emeralds, rubies,
diamonds, sapphires, and pearls (to name but a few); boxes
packed with colorful saris and Chinese silks; first-class
perfumes made from priceless aloe, musk, civet in two vari-
eties, saffron, sandal, camphor, cool rose water, essence of
aloe, finely ground sandal powder, black *cādu* for the fore-
head dot, and the rare Sunrise Scent. And there were also a
thousand maidservants in the full flush of youth, bedecked
with jewels: when they opened their lips, their smiles mixed
with the moonbeams shining from their darting eyes; their
breasts were smoother than fresh lotus buds, their black hair
darker than bees, their waists leaner than empty space but
still strong, their words honed by flirting and punning with
men who chased after them. They were capable of uttering
the sweet sounds of love, and with double meanings, as they
moved gracefully from task to cultivated task. Needless to

మిసమిసలంబస గలిగి మేలిమైన కులుకుల
రసికజనంబుల మనంబుల మరులుకొలుపం జాలి
సురుచిరాభరణ భూషితంబగు పరిచారికాసహస్రంబును
గూఁతునకు నరణంబుగా నిచ్చి మటీయును.

౧౦౭

సీ   అవనతాంగుష్ఠాగ్ర హర్యనిర్యద్రత్న
        ఖని ఘనాంతరిత శృంగాటకములు
      మద ముదావహదివ్య మైరేయ ధౌరేయ
        గోత్రభిద్వీటపి నిష్కుటయుతములు
      మహిళాకదంబ డింభగ్రాహ్య గృహచర
        న్మృగనాభి సౌరభ్య నిర్భరములు
      ప్రఖరాఖు నఖర ధారావిదీర్ణేర్ధ్ధీర్ణ
        సౌవర్ణమృత్కర్ద జాంగలములు

తే   కోక కలహంస ముఖరితాబ్జాకరములు
      సిద్ధచారణగంధర్వ సేవితములు
      మందరద్రోణిఁ గొన్ని గ్రామములు గూర్మి
      తనయ పసుపున కొసఁగె గంధర్వవిభుఁడు.

say, they ran circles around even the most expert lovers. All
these were given as bride gifts to the bride.

102

If you merely scratch the earth at the crossroads with your
    big toe,
precious stones emerge from the mines underneath.
In the gardens there are wishing trees that yield wine
to make you happy.
Here even women and children collect musk from the
    musk deer
roaming outside the fragrant houses.
There's so much gold in the soil just beyond the villages
that even rodents scratching with their sharp nails
find it everywhere.
Lotus ponds echo with the sounds of geese and
    cakravākas.
Perfect beings and musicians and messengers from the
    skies
come to visit the valley of Mount Mandara, where
the gandharva king gifted his daughter a few villages—
toward the cost of turmeric.

౧౦3

తే పౌరయాత్రిక సుర సిద్ధ చార ణాహి
యక్ష గంధర్వ సాధ్య విద్యాధరులను
నిజపురంబుల కనిచె నిందీవరాక్షుం
డుడుగర లొసంగి విభవంబు గడలుకొనగ.

౧౦౪

వ అనిన విని జైమినిమునీంద్రుండు మీదటి వృత్తాంతం
బానతీయవలయు నని యడుగుట యును.

౧౦౫

మ అతులక్షాంతిగభీర ధీరహితచి
త్తాంభోజ భోజక్రమా
పతివిద్యాపరిపాక పాకరిపుఖం
భద్బేగ భోగాశిప
త్రితరస్నూర్యనుభావ భావభరిత
శ్రీకాంత కాంతారపా
తితకాళింగకులేశ లేశతరవ్ప
త్రిక్షీణవైరివ్రజా.

103

King Indivaraksha sent off all who had come for the
    wedding
and were now ready to go home—gods, siddhas, cāraṇas,
snakes, yakshas, gandharvas, sādhyas, and vidyādharas—
and loaded them down with gifts, to his greater glory.

104

Thus the birds left off speaking, and Jaimini had to ask them
to tell him the rest of the story.

105

Listen, great king: Your tolerance is unfathomable.
Your mind knows no fear. You are a mature scholar,
like King Bhoja. You enjoy life, like Indra. You're swift
as the great eagle, and full of force. Lord Vishnu
is always in your thoughts. You drove the Kalinga king
into the jungle. Your enemies stand no chance.

౧౦౬

క నాగాంబాసుత జితకద
   నాగత మదనాగ సంగమానూప గృహ
   భోగా భోగపురందర
   భోగీంద్రశయాన పురుష పూజాప్రవణా.

౧౦౭

మాలిని.
   సరభస జయధాటీ చండవేదండకోటీ
   కరవమధు హిమానీ కంపితాశావధాటీ
   పరమహిత హసంతీభావభాగ్బ్బారితేజః
   పరుష దహనకీలా ప్రస్ఫురచ్చక్రవాళా.

106

Son of Nagamba! Elephants you conquered
in battle crowd your stables, soaked with must.
Living in luxury like Indra, you most enjoy
worshiping the god who sleeps on the great snake. *

107

The elephants you captured on the battlefield
are spraying such heavy mist from their trunks
that space itself would be shivering
but for the flames of your valor that warms
the whole world, like a burning brazier, all the way
up to the towering mountains at the edge of the earth.

---

* Vishnu.

గద్యము.

    ఇది శ్రీమదాంధ్ర కవితాపితామహ సర్వతోముఖాంక
పంకజాక్ష పాదాంబుజాధీన మానసేందిందిర
నందవరపుర వంశోత్తంస శఠకోపతాపస ప్రసాదాసాదిత
చతుర్విధ కవితామతల్లి కాల్లసాని చొక్కయామాత్యపుత్త
పెద్దనార్య ప్రణీతంబైన స్వారోచిషమనుసంభవం బను
మహాప్రబంధంబునందుఁ బంచమాశ్వాసము.

The great poem called "The Birth of Svarochisha Manu" was written by Allasani Cokkayamatya's son Peddanarya, known to all as the "Creator God of Telugu Poetry," who comes from a family of Nandavara Brahmans, whose mind hovers like a bee around the lotuslike feet of lotus-eyed Vishnu, and who was blessed by his guru Shathakopa with the ability to compose all four kinds of fine poetry. Chapter 5 ends here.

షష్ఠాశ్వాసము

క శ్రీకృష్ణరాయ మనుజేం
ద్రా కాంతాపంచబాణ నరసింహ ధరి
త్రీకాంతగర్భవార్నిధి
రాకాహిమధామ కర్పురదళవిరామా.

వ అవధరింపుము శకుంతంబు లబ్బాదరాయణాంతేవాసి
కిట్లనియె నంత నొక్కనాఁడు.

480

Chapter 6

1

King Krishnaraya! You're like the love god
to women, the brightest light in the dynasty
of King Narasimha, and death
to your enemies.

2

Listen to how the birds went on speaking to Jaimini,
Vyasa's student.

3

సీ పాండురప్రభఁ గ్రిందువడిన చీఁకటివోలె
జిగి నొప్పు నీలంపు జగతి మెఆసి
యొస్నత్యమున మ్రింగినట్టి నింగులు గ్రక్కు
కరణి ధూపము గవాక్షముల వెడల
ధారుణీసతి సుగంధద్రవ్యములు దాఁచు
నరలపేటికవోలెఁ బరిమళముల
నెలవు లై చెలువారు నిలువుల విలసిల్లి
కొఁణీగఁ బారావత కులము వదరఁ

తే బసిఁడినీట లిఖించిన ప్రతిమ లమర
నీఁగ వాలిన నందంద యెలుఁగు లొసఁగు
నట్టి సకినలమంచము లాదిగాఁగ
మెఆయు పరికరముల నొప్పు మేడమీఁద.

౪

క రమణునికడ కనుప మనో
రమకున్ మజ్జనము దీర్చి రవరవ కచపిం
చమునకుఁ గాలాగురుధూ
పము వెట్టి జవాది నంటు వాపి నిపుణతన్.

3

At that time, in the upper level of the palace,
where the floor studded with blue sapphires
looked like darkness beaten down by white light,
and incense poured from the windows as if the tall
    building
had swallowed up the sky and was now spitting it out,
and each level was filled with fragrance as if the whole
    palace
were a box with many drawers where the earth goddess
kept her perfumes, and pigeons were cooing in the eaves,
and there were dolls painted with liquid gold and toy birds
on the beds that squeaked if even a fly happened to light
    on them,
and other such devices,

4

Manorama's friends prepared her to go to her husband.
First they bathed her and dried her hair, thick as a
    peacock's tail,
with incense of black aloe, then they straightened it out
with civet.

౫

సీ చెంగల్వపూదండ సేర్చి పెందుఱుముపై
ఘనసారమున సూసకము ఘటించి
పన్నీటితోఁ గదంబము చేసి మృగనాభిఁ
బూసి కుంకుమ సేసబొట్టు తీర్చి
విశదముక్తాదామ రశనఁ జందురకావి
వలిపప్పు వలువపై నలవరించి
యఱుత వెన్నెలగాయు హార మొక్కటి పెట్టి
మణుల సొమ్ములు మేన మట్టుపఱిచి

తే కన్నుఁగవ గెల్చి డాకాలఁ గట్టె ననఁగ
ఘల్లుఘల్లునఁ బెండెంబు గండుమీలు
గదల నల్లన నడపించి పాదివి తెచ్చె
నెచ్చెలులపిండు యువతి నా నృపతికడకు.

౬

క తెచ్చుటయుఁ గేళిభవనముఁ
జొచ్చెనొ చొరదో యనంగ సుదతుల నీడం
జొచ్చి పయిఁ గొప్పు దోఁపఁగ
నచ్చేడియ తలుపుదండ నల్లన నిలిచెన్.

౭

క తదనంతరంబ బోటులు
చదురుల నగవులను బ్రొద్దు జరిగినఁ గేళీ
సదనము నొక్కొక పని నెప
మొదవఁగ వెడలుటయుఁ జిత్త ముప్విళ్ళూరన్.

5

They tied bright red flowers in her hair and fixed
with fresh camphor her forehead ornament
running through the part. They mixed musk with rose
    water
and sprayed it over her body, and now they added a
    forehead dot
made from vermilion and rice and fastened a belt of pearls
around her fine red skirt and another string of pearls
    bright as moonlight
around her neck. They decorated her with still more gems,
and then they brought her, walking slowly,
while the images of fish on her left anklet were jingling
as if proud to have conquered all other women's eyes.[1]

6

When they arrived, she stood in the shadow
of her friends at the doorway, as if she had entered
and yet not entered, only the top of her head
showing inside.

7

For a while her friends teased her and made jokes.
Then they left, each making one excuse
or another. As her mind[2] was stirred
in anticipation,

౮

సీ దట్టంబు నీ కట్టినట్టి చెంగావికి
బాగు గా దని కేలఁ బయఁట నిమిరె
గోరంటొ గోళ్ళనిక్కువపుఁగెంపో యని
చెయి పట్టి నయమున సెజ్జ సేర్చె
నగరుధూపముచేత నయ్యో తనూవల్లి
సెక సోఁకెనని యెదఁ జెయ్యివెట్టె
మృగనాభికా మకరికలఁ గప్రము మించె
నని మూరుకొనుచుఁ జుంబన మొనర్చె

తే హారమణు లిటు సూపు నా యఱుత నున్న
హారమణులకుఁ గాంతి నీ డౌనొ కావొ
యనుచు నక్కునఁ గదియించు నా నెపమునఁ
గంపమును బొందు సతిమేను గౌఁగిలించె.

౯

వ అట్లు కవియం దమకించి త్రస్తరులఁ గుస్తరింప నింపు
గలిగియు మునుమున్న మనంబునం బొడమి యుండు
నడలప్పుడు తలంపునం బాఱిన సమర్థుండగు నతనిచే
నది తీర్పించుకొనం గలయదియై నవోఢ గావున మాటలం
దేటపడం జెప్ప శంకించి స్త్రీ స్వభావంబునం దొరఁగు
కన్నీరు కంకణక్రేంకృతులు మీఱ గోరఁబాఱ మీటుచు
నూరకయున్నం గనుంగొని యవనిపతి పుంగవుం
డంతరంగంబునం జెంగలించు కౌతుకాంకురంబు
కరఁగుపడ వెఱఁగుపడి యుద్వేగ సమన్వితుండై
సంభ్రమించుచుఁ జెక్కుటద్దంబులు నొక్కి కురులు చక్కం
ద్రోయుచుం 'దోయజాక్షి యక్షయానందసంధాయకం
బగు నిట్టి క్రీడాసమయంబున వగపునకుం గారణంబేమి

8

Svarochi stroked the top of her sash and said:
"This doesn't go well with your red skirt."
He took her hand and said, "Is this from *goraṇṭa* leaf or
the real color of your fingernails?"[3] He pulled her
toward the bed. "Your delicate skin
is parched by aloe smoke," he said,
laying his hand on her heart. "And these little
crocodiles painted on your face—there's too much
camphor in them." As if trying to smell them,
he kissed her. "Let me have a look at your necklace.
Is it as white as the one I'm wearing?" As she trembled,
he brought her close.

9

He was eager to bring her still closer. She was pleased by his
loving, teasing words, but she also was mindful of her earlier
sadness. She wanted her husband to clear it away, and she
believed he could do it. But being a shy new bride, she hesi-
tated to speak openly to him; so, like a woman, she started
to cry, flicking away her tears with her fingernails while her
bangles jingled. She sat there, saying nothing. He looked at
her, and the joy that was surging in his heart melted away. He
felt both alarmed and surprised. He held her cheeks, brush-
ing away her loose curls, and asked her, "Why are you sad
at a moment when we should be playing, happy and wild?
Have I done anything wrong? Did anybody else do anything

నా యెడం గల్ల యేమేనియుం బాటిల్లదుగదా యొవ్వరే
మప్రియంబు గావించి రెఱింగింపు వారిన్ దండించెద
నేమి సాధింపవలయుఁ జెప్పు మది వేధ చేసున్న
సాధించెద మదీయంబులగు నర్ధజీవితంబులు
భవదధీనంబు లుమ్మలిక యింత యేటి' కనుటయు
నబ్బోటి గ్రేటుచు నిట్లనియె.

౧౦

ఉ   అక్కట నా యెడన్ మిగుల
నక్కఅ గల్గి చరించు నెచ్చెలుల్
చిక్కి మునీంద్ర శాపహతిఁ
జెందిన దుర్ధమరోగబాధలం
బొక్కుచు నున్నవారు వన
ఘూములఁ దద్దశ మాన్పవేని నా
కెక్కడి సౌఖ్య మన్నఁ దర
ళేక్షణఁ జూచి స్వరోచి యిట్లనున్.

౧౧

క   పరితాప మింక నేటికి
హరిణాక్షి మదీయ సంచితాయుర్వేద
స్ఫురణమునఁ బరిహరించెద
నరు దనఁగ భవత్సఖీజనామయభరమున్.

to hurt you? Tell me, and I'll punish them. Tell me if there's something you want. I'll get it for you, even if it's in the hands of God himself. My life, everything I have—they're yours. Why are you crying?" She cleared her throat and said:

10
"My best friends, who dearly care for me,
are suffering an incurable disease
because a sage cursed them. They're still
in the wilderness with no one
to help them. If you can't cure them,
how can I be happy?" Svarochi looked at her and said:

11
"There's no need to worry, my girl with lovely eyes.
I know the cure. I'm trained
in medicine. I'll heal your friends.
You'll be surprised.

౧౨

క   నా వెనుక రమ్ము నీ సఖు
లే వనమున నున్నవార లిపుడ చికిత్సం
గావింతు ననుచు రయమున
నా వనితయు దాను నచటి కరిగి యొకయెడన్.

౧౩

ఉ   ఆ రజనీశబింబ రుచి
రాస్యలఁ గాంచి తదామయవ్యథా
భారము మాన్పఁగాఁ దమి న్న
పాలుఁడు తత్కలధౌతగేత్రకాం
తారపదంబునం దుపచి
తం బగు మందును దత్క్రియోచితా
హారము నెమ్మి నిచ్చుచు న
నామయధన్యలఁ జేసె వన్నెగాన్.

౧౪

శా   ఆ దివ్యౌషధరాజిచేఁ దమమహో
వ్యాధివ్యథల్దీటినన్
మోదంబంది లతాంగు లంబుజకులం
బున్ నవ్వకందేయితో
సౌదామిన్యభిరామ దేహరుచితో
సంపూర్ణచంద్రానన
శ్రీదర్ప్పోన్నతితోఁ జెలంగి సురనా
రీసూను గీర్తించుచున్.

12

Show me where they are.
I'll start the cure right now."
He and his bride hurried off
to the wilderness, where

13

he saw the young beauties and quickly,
eager to heal them, looked for the herbs
that grow on that Silver Mountain.
He gave them food to go with that medicine
and cared for them, gradually freeing them
from their sickness.

14

When the powerful herbs had vanquished
the agony of illness, the young girls brightened up,
their eyes shining like a whole pond
of lotus flowers, their skin luminous as lightning,
their faces proud as the moon. They sang his praises
in voices flooded with joy.

౧౫

క మా కుపకార మొనర్చితి
నీకుం బ్రతిసేయ నెట్లు నేరుతు మైనన్
లోకోత్తర మా వలనను
జేకొనుకార్యములుఁ గలవు చెప్పెద మెలమిన్.

౧౬

క మును మాదగు వృత్తాంతము
వినిపింపఁగ వలయు నీకు విస్తృతముగ భూ
వినుత విను మనుచు నం దొక
వనజేక్షణ పలికె మధుర వాగ్జితశుకియై.

౧౭

తే అనఘ మందార విద్యాధరాత్మభవను
నను విభావసి యంద్రు గంధర్వవరులు
తెలిసియుందుదు నిమ్మహీతలమునందుఁ
బరఁగు మృగపక్షిజాతుల భాషలెల్ల.

౧౮

క అమ్మేటివిద్య నాచే
నిమ్మగ నంతయు నెఱింగి నృప నన్ను వివా
హమ్మగు మనవుడు రెండవ
కొమ్మ మదిం బ్రేమ గడలుకొన నిట్లనియెన్.

15

"You have saved us. How can we repay
our debt? But still, there may be things
we can do for you, you marvelous young man.
We'll explain.

16

First we should tell you who we are.
Listen." Now one girl began speaking,
her voice sweeter than any parrot's.

17

"I'm the daughter of the vidyadhara called
Mandara. The gandharvas call me Vibhavasi.
I happen to know the languages of all beasts
and birds on this earth.

18

I'll teach you all those languages.
Marry me, my prince." Now the second girl
took over, her heart in flood
with love.

౧౯

ఆ పారుఁ డనఁగఁ బరఁగు బ్రహ్మర్షి మా తండ్రి
యతఁడు విద్య లెల్ల నభ్యసించి
తపము నిచ్చఁ జేయఁ దలపోసి కీరభ్యం
గాలిరమ్యమైన యాశ్రమమున.

౨౦

మ ఫలమూలచ్చుదనాంబు భుక్తిఁ బవనా
భ్యాసక్రియాయుక్తిని
ర్ధళితాంతర్గత శాత్రవప్రకర జా
గ్రద్ధర్వసర్వస్వుఁడై
చలికిన్ వానకు నెండకున్ మన మను
త్సాహంబు గానీక కం
దళితానందమునన్ ముకుందచరణ
ధ్యానావధానంబునన్.

౨౧

క అంగుష్ఠము నిల మోపి ప
తంగునిపైఁ జూపు సాఁచి ధగధగ లర్చి
స్తుంగత నింగులు నాకెడు
నింగలములు నాల్గుదెసల నిడుకొని కడఁకన్.

19

"My father is a supreme sage named Para.
He's studied everything that is there
to learn. He decided to take on
a burning penance in a hermitage
humming with parrots and bees.

20

He lived on fruit, roots, leaves, and water.
He controlled his breath. He conquered
all the enemies he felt inside, including pride.
He never wavered, even in the cold,
or rain, or burning heat. He kept his mind
focused, with ever-increasing joy,
on Vishnu's feet.

21

He stood on his big toe and kept his eyes
fixed on the sun, with fires blazing
on all four sides, their flames reaching
up to the sky.

౨౨

క సుర గరుడ యక్ష రాక్షస
నర కిన్నర సిద్ధ సాధ్య నాగోత్కర మి
ట్లరు దనంగం దపమొనర్చెం
బురుహూతుండు దాననాత్మం బొడమిన భీతిన్.

౨3

క తనయొద్దం బుంజికస్థల
యను నచ్చర లేమ యున్న నమ్ముని కడకుం
జనుమని యనిపినం బతి శా
సనమున వని కేంగుదెంచె సంభ్రమలీలన్.

౨౪

చ చిలుకలు ముద్దుంబల్కులకుం
జేరంగ రా నెటివేణికాంతికిన్
మలయుచుం బై పయిన్ మధుప
మాలిక వాయక సంచరింపంగా
నలస విలాసయానమున
నమ్మునిపాలికి వచ్చె వేల్పుండి
య్యలి నునుసానం బట్టిన య
నంగుని మోహనబాణమో యనన్.

౨౫

వ ఆ సమయంబున.

496

22

Everyone—gods, antigods, *garuḍas, yakshas,*
kinnaras, siddhas, sādhyas, nāgas, and humans—
said his penance was simply impossible.
Indra began to worry.

23

He ordered a fine apsaras girl named
Punjikasthala to go to that sage. So off she went,
in a flurry.

24

Parrots followed her when they heard her voice.
Bees, drawn by her dark hair, hovered around her
like a garland. Walking with ravishing languor,
she arrived like an arrow from the love god,
specially sharpened for this mission.

25

Then

౨౬

చ అనువగు సుళ్ళ నొప్పు మల
యానిలవాహము నెక్కి తేంట్ల న
ల్లిన నిడువాగెఁ బూని లవ
లీ నవవల్లిక లెమ్మెసొమ్ములై
పనుపడఁ జెట్లు వట్టి మను
ప్రాఁతదళమ్ములతోడఁ దోలె నా
మనిదేర మంచురాజు మడి
మంచగఁ గోయిలగంట మ్రోయఁగన్.

౨౭

సీ సొన దేటి పాటమరించి నెఱవాసినయట్టి
యాకురాలుపు గండ్లయందుఁ దొఱఁగి
యతిబాలకీరచ్ఛదాంకురాకృతిఁ బొల్చి
కరవీర కోరక గతిఁ గ్రమమున
నరుణంపు మొగ్గలై యరవిచ్చి పికిలియాఁ
గలదండలట్లు గుంపు లయి పిదప
రేఖ లేర్పడఁగ వర్ధిలి వెడల్పయి రెమ్మ
పసరువాఱుచు నిక్కఁ బసరు కప్పు

తే పూఁటఁపూఁటకు నెక్కఁ గప్పునకును దగిన
మెఱుఁగు నానాఁటికిని మీఁద గిటిగొనంగ
సోగయై యాకు వాలంగ జొంప మగుచుఁ
జిగురు దళుకొత్తెఁ దరులతా శ్రేణులందు.

26

Spring arrived like a king, riding
the south wind like a horse with auspicious
slight ringlets. In his hand he held long reins
woven from bees, and he wore ornaments
of blossoming vines. He drove off his enemy,
winter, together with the old leaves lingering
on the trees as cuckoos sounded
the clarion call of victory.

27

Wherever a dry leaf falls, in the little hollow
it leaves behind, a drop of sap appears,
hardens, and then falls off. Then,
a tiny bud emerges, light green like a baby
parrot's wing. Slowly it opens just a little,
reddish like the buds of the *karavīra* tree.
Soon there are many of them, like garlands
woven from the red down of the bulbul,
and as they grow and widen, veins develop,
and the stems turn green and stand up.
Gradually the shades of green thicken
and a sheen appears, brighter day by day,
until there are leaves hanging down—
a whole crowd, beautiful to the eyes.
It happened then, on every tree and vine.

౨౮

క హిందేళంబునఁ బాడిరి
బృందారకసతులు విరహి బృందార్తిగఁ ద్రేఁ
చెం దేఁటులు వాసంతిక
విందునఁ బికళిషవు దాది వెడలం దోలెన్.

౨౯

సీ చలిగాలి బొందుమల్లెల పరాగము రేఁచి
నిబిడంబు సేసె వెన్నెలరసంబు
వెన్నెలరస ముబ్బి వెడలించె దీర్ఘికా
మంద సౌగంధిక మధునదంబు
మధునదం బెగఁబోసె మాకందమాలికా
క్రీడానుషంగి భృంగీరవంబు
భృంగీరవం బహంకృతిఁ దీఁగె సాగించెఁ
బ్రోషితభర్తృకా రోదనముల

తే విపినవీధుల వీతెంచెఁ గుపిత మదన
సమదభుజనత సుమధనుష్టాంకృతములు
సరస మధుపాన నిధువనోత్సవవిలీన
యువతి యువకోటి కోరికల్ చివురు లొత్త.

28

The godly women were singing Hindola raga,
an agony for separated lovers. Bees drank
their fill of honey from the *vāsantika* vines.
Crow mothers drove the baby cuckoos
from the nest.[4]

29

White-jasmine pollen carried by a cool wind
thickened the moonlight,
and the moonlight, in turn, released
rivers of honey from red lotuses
blooming in the pools, and the rivers
of honey heightened the music of bees
playing on the mango trees, and the heedless
bee music doubled the wailing of women
whose husbands were far away. All over
the forest you could hear the fierce twanging
of the love god's bow fanning the flames at wild parties
of young men and women, drinking and making love.[5]

30

క అత్తటి మురిపపుసడఁ జెలి
కత్తియగమి గొలువ మృదుల కలభాషలఁ ద
క్ఫొత్తెడు వెదనగవులతోఁ
జిత్తభవుం దార్వ ననలు చిదుము నెపమునన్.

3౧

చ అలకని జీబులోఁ గుసుమ
మద్ధినపావడ దేఁపఁ గొప్పు చెం
గలువలవల్పుఁ జన్నుగవ
కస్తురితావియుఁ ద్రస్తరింప నం
దెలరెద మీఅఁ బెన్నిధిగ
తిన్ వ్రతికిం బొడకట్టె వేల్పుఁడె
య్యలి చిఅుసానఁ బట్టిన య
నంగుని మోహనబాణమో యనన్.

3౽

తే అత్తఅంగున నదిరిపా టారజంపు
వన్నెఁ బొడకట్టి తాఁ బాడు సన్నరవళి
పాట లలిర్ఘుంకృతిశ్రుతిఁ బాడుకొనఁగఁ
జూడకయ చూచు చూపుతో సుడియుటయును.

30

At that time Punjikasthala came with a group
of her friends, all of them sweet-spoken,
smiling seductively, alluring as they moved,
on the pretext of picking flowers—and the love god
was ready and waiting.

31

She was wearing a red skirt that showed through
her transparent sash, and red lotuses
in her hair and the musk on her breasts were
casting fragrance, and her anklets were jingling.
The sage saw her—like a gift of the gods.
She was an arrow sharpened on a whetstone
by the love god.

32

He saw her in all her beauty.
The gentle song she was singing melted into
the humming of the bees as she looked
without quite looking at the sage.

33

చ   తలకొని దాని తమ్ములపు(
దావియు మోవియు(గొను మేను న
గ్గలపుమెఱుంగు లీను తెలి
గన్నులు(జన్నులు భృంగమాలిక
నెలిచిన యారుతీరు(దగు
నెన్నడలుం దొడలున్ వివేకముం
గల(ప(గ(గాంచి పంచశర
కాండ విఖండిత ధైర్యసారు(డై.

34

క   మేను గరుపాఅ(దమి న
మ్మొని జపము(దపము(దన్ను మఅిచి యనంగ
గ్లాని(బడి కదిసి వడ(కుచు
హీనస్వర మొస(గ(బ్రోవవే నన్నునుచున్.

35

తే   చెయ్య పట్టినమాత్రాన శిరసు వంచి
యవశచందాన(బై్రాలు నవ్వధూటి(
బర్ణశాలాంతరము(జేర్చి బ్రాహ్మణుండు
కెరలు కోర్కుల(గంధర్పకేళి(దేల.

33

The fragrance wafting from her mouth,
the shape of her lips, her waist, her whole body,
the light flashing from her eyes, her breasts,
the line of hair down below, darker
than any bees, her way of moving, her thighs—
all these shook his composure. Desire
breached his defenses.

34

His body bristled. He forgot
his penance, his prayers,
and himself. Tortured
by love, and trembling, in a faint voice
he begged her: 'Help me.'

35

The moment he took her hand in his,
she bent her head and fell into his arms,
giving herself to him. The Brahman
took her into his hut of leaves and made love
to her in rising waves of desire.

౩౬

క తప మంతయుc బొలివేఁగ
నప్పు డన్నియు నుజ్జగించి యయ్యంగనతోc
దపసి మనోజక్రీడా
విపులైశ్వర్యంబు లనుభవించుచు నుండెన్.౧

౩౭

క ఈ రీతిc గొంతకాలం
బారామ మహా మహీధరారణ్యములం
దా రామ వలలc దగిలి వి
హారము సలుపంగ గర్భమై తఱి యగుడున్.

౩౮

క అంత ననుఁగాంచి యది విపి
నాంతరమునc బాఱవైచి యరిగెc గృపార్థి
స్వాంతుc డగు సంయమీంద్రుఁడు
జింతింపకపోయె నేమి చెప్పుదు నధిపా.

506

36

His penance was left in ruins. He gave
everything up and lived only for the luxury
of loving that woman.

37

Caught in the snare of love, he played with her
in groves and hills and forests. After some time
she became pregnant. When it was time for her delivery—

38

she gave birth to me, cast me
into the depths of the forest, and went away.
As for him—though he was a kind man at heart—
he didn't give me a thought. What more can
I say, my king?

౩౯

వ అట్లు వైచి చనుటయు నా(కటం గటకటం
బడుచుండి తీంద్రించు శశిమండలంబున వెడలు
శిశిరకిరణప్రణాళికామిళదమృతరసగ్రాసంబునం జేసి
కొన్ని పూఁటలం బుటపుటనైన నన్నుం గనుంగొని
మునీంద్రుండు ప్రియం బంది నిజాశ్రమంబునకుం గొని
చని శశికళాసంవర్ధిత నగుటంజేసి నాకుం గళావతి యను
నామం బిడి పెనుచుచుండ నేనును జనక సేవాపరతం
బ్రవర్తిల్లు చుండునంత.౼

౪౦

క ఎవ్వరు చూచినఁ జూపుల
చివ్వకుఁ బద నడఁగి నడచు సిగ్గున నొఱపై
రవ్వకు మొదలగు పాపపు
జవ్వన మెదిరించె జిగి యొసంగ నా మేనన్.

౪౧

శా ఆ వేళం బొడగాంచి భూచరుఁ డికం
దాసక్తి దేవాపి సం
జ్ఞావంతుండు సబాంధవ్యం దగుచు ని
శ్యంకన్ నను న్వేఁడువాఁ
డై వాచంయముఁ దగ్ని కార్యనిరతుం
డై యున్నచో బర్లశా
లావాసంబున కేగుదెంచి నిజభా
వాకాంక్ష సూచించినన్.

39

After they had left, I lay there crying. I survived by swallowing cool, life-giving moonbeams. After a few days, I grew healthy. My father found me and felt a twinge, and took me to his hermitage. He called me Kalavati, Moon Girl, because I was nurtured on moonbeams. He raised me, and I grew up, devoted to my father.[6]

40

I grew into a woman. When men would look at me,
I'd feel shy and try to cover my body—and that only
made me more attractive. I hated being beautiful,
but it was all over me.

41

Then a gandharva named Devapi saw me
and wanted me. Together with his relatives
he went to my father's hut when he was busy
at his fire rituals and boldly expressed his wish.

౪౨

సీ. శిఖిపించదళపరిష్కృతములై సేమంతి
విరుల తీరగు శిరో వేష్టనములు
నెఅగంటిచూడ్కిం దాయెతుల బాహులు వంచి
నారాజు లల్లార్చు నారజములుం
గాదంబరీ గంధగర్భంబులై వచ్చు
ఘనసారమిళదాస్య గంధములును
దరహాసములం దేంచు తాంబూల సేవాంధ
కారితాధర రద క్షతుల యొఅపుం

తే. జితులుగందంపుం బూంతలు జిహ్వకలకు
నసుపు నెఅవాది బంటు పంతపుం బదరులు
ఘన మగు జుగుప్స వెనుప నజ్జనముం జూచి
ఋషి మనంబునం గడు నసహ్యించుకొనుచు.

౪3

శా. ఆహో ధన్యుడ నైతి మద్విమలవం
శాచార విద్యా తప
శ్శ్రీహోమాదులు నేండుగా తుది ఫలిం
చెన్ నాగవాసంబు మ
ద్దేహక్షోణికి బిడ్డ వేండుటకు నే
తేం గాంచుటన్ బ్రాహ్మ్య మిం
కోహో చాలుం బొకాలిపోయెదరో పో
రే నోటి క్రొవ్వేటికిన్.

510

42

They were all wearing headdresses like chrysanthemums
and lined with peacock feathers, and when they moved
their arms flashing with amulets, the swords
tied to their waists reflected the redness
of their drunken eyes. From their mouths came
a strong smell of liquor mixed with camphor, and the bite
marks on their lower lips that were hidden by constant
chewing of betel showed through whenever they laughed.
There were streaks of dry sandal paste all over their
  bodies,
and proud boasts of valor came flowing from their
  tongues.
All this produced in my father a deep disgust. The sage
simply hated them.

43

'Finally, I got lucky. Today my family's pure tradition
of learning, prayer, and fire rituals has borne fruit.
I see a family of whores has come to my house
to ask for my daughter's hand. Enough of being
a Brahman. Get out of here! Stop blabbering.

౪౪

క మీ తరమువార లేతటి
నేతరితనమునఁ దపస్వీ గృహకన్యకలన్
వీతభయవృత్తి వేఁడిరొ
కో తముఁ దర్కింప కౌర క్రొవ్వ లటంచున్.

౪౫

క వసుధేశ ముక్కు దుస్సిన
పసరము క్రియఁ గెరలి తిట్టెఁ బక్కున ఋషి వా
రుసురు మని వెడలిపోయిరి
ముసలి గదా పుట్టినిల్లు ముఖ్యోష్ణతకున్.

౪౬

వ అట్టి యొదం దన మనోరథంబు విఫలం బగుటకుఁ
గ్రేధాంధుండై నన్నభిలషించు గంధర్వం డిట్లనియె.

44

Has anyone in your family, in any generation,
ever had the guts to ask
for a Brahman girl? You're swollen
with pride.'

45

Then, oh my king, the sage, angry as a bull
when the halter through its nose is let loose,
cursed them again and again. They left,
deeply humiliated. That's how old men are.
Only their tongues have any strength.

46

His desire blocked in this way, the gandharva who wanted
me went blind with anger and said:

৪౨

శా నీ వైశిష్ట్యము తిట్టులన్ మెఱయునే
నీకంటె నేఁ దక్కువే
యావే కన్యక నీవు గాక మటి మ
ద్వృత్తాన్వయాచారముల్
నీవా పేర్కొనుపాటివాఁడ విలఁ గాఁ
నీ నిల్తుగా కేమి పో
పో విప్రాధమ నిన్నుఁ బోల నిఁకఁ న
ల్పుల్లేరు దంభప్రతా.

৪౬

తే అనుచుఁ బగచాటి పోయి నాఁడర్ధరాత్ర
సమయమున శస్త్రనిహతి మజ్జనకుఁ జంపె
నట్ల యగుఁ గాక పుడమి గామాంధచిత్తఁ
డెవ్వరి వధింపఁ డెటు సేయఁ డేమి గాఁడు.

৪౯

తే అపుడు మెడఁగోయ ముని రేఁజు టాలకించి
మేలుకొని దివ్వె యిడి సంభ్రమించి యేడ్చు
నన్నుఁ బొదివిరి పొరుగింట్ల నున్న తపసు
లా దురాచారుఁడును బాఱ నటకు మునుప.

47

'The language you've used shows your status.
Am I inferior to you in any way? You don't want
to give me your daughter. Fine. But why insult
my family and our ways? I'll see the end of you.
Go to hell, you stupid Brahman. There's nothing worse
than a phony sage.'

48

He made no secret of his hatred, and that very night
he killed my father with a knife. That's how it is.
A man blinded by lust will do anything, will kill
anyone, will stoop to any level.

49

I heard my father gasping for breath; his neck
was cut. I lit a lamp. I was shaken. I began to cry. Sages
who were nearby embraced me and comforted me.
The killer ran away.

৯౦

వ అంతం దెలతెల వేగుటయుc బ్రభాతసమయంబున.

৯౧

క ధారాళక్షతజోక్షిత
ఘోర జరాధవళితోరుకూర్పుముగc గరా
చూరిని మెడ దెగియుట జా
గారంబునc బడిన మూcడుగాళ్ళ ముసలికిన్.

৯౨

ఆ అగ్ని యిచ్చి యకట యాబాల్యముగ నన్నుc
బెనిచెc దల్లి వైచి చనిన పిదపc
దానె తల్లిమాౘునై నెమ్మి నట్టి మ
జ్జనకుc డీల్గె నేటి మనికి యనుచు.

৯3

క వందురి వగలన్ దేహము
పొం దెడలcగc జూచు నన్నుc బొడగని దివిc దా
నెందుల కేcగుచునో గిరి
నందన దిగి వచ్చి కరుణ నా కిట్లనియెన్.

516

50–51

Blood surging from his neck and soaking his white beard,
that old man fell dead right there, in the forest hut.
When morning came,

52

I cremated him and mourned him:
'After my real mother deserted me
when I was a baby, he took care of me
like a loving mother. That father of mine is dead.
Why should I go on living?'

53

In my grief, I was about to kill myself.
Just then Parvati, who was going somewhere
in the sky, saw me and came down. She spoke
to me in kindness.

౫౪

మ   అతిసౌందర్యనిశాంత మీతను వల
భ్యం బిట్లు శోకాతురా
న్విత వై దీనిc దొఅంగcగాc దగునె త
న్వీ చాలు నీసాహసం
బతిలోకుండు స్వరోచి నీకుc బతి యౌ
నారాజుc జేపట్టి య
ప్రతిమశ్రీవిభవంబుc గాంచెదవు నా
పల్కొండుగా నేర్చునే.

౫౫

క   వినu మదియుంc గాక పద్మిని
యనc బరcగిన విద్య నేc బ్రియంబున నిత్తం
గొను నీవు తత్ప్రసాదం
బున నీకు నభీష్టసౌఖ్యములు సిద్ధించున్.

౫౬

వ   అని రహస్యంబుగా నవ్విద్య నాకు నుపదేశించి
ముక్కంటివాల్గంటి మింటిచొప్పునం జనియె నేనును
దద్వచనామృతాస్వాదనంబ యూ◌ాతగాc బ్రాణంబులు
వట్టుకొని యున్నదాన నా స్వరోచి నీవ కాc దలంచెద
వంచనాలాపంబు లుడిగి య ప్పుడ్మినీ విద్యారత్నంబుతోc
గూడ నన్నుc బరిగ్రహింపు మనిన నంగీకరించి య
మ్మహీవిభుండు.

518

54

'You have a body of extreme beauty
like no one else. Do you want to throw it away
in your sorrow? Stop this desperate act.
Handsome Svarochi, a man out of this world,
will be your husband. In his company
you'll find unparalleled happiness.
My word never fails.

55

One thing more. I'll teach you a mantra
called Padmini—and with that
you'll get any pleasure you may want.'

56

Shiva's wife secretly instructed me in that mantra and flew
away. I kept myself alive by remembering her sweet words.
You must be that Svarochi. Let's not waste time talking. Take
me along with my Padmini."

ఇ౭

క ఏకాగ్రత నవ్విద్యలు
గైకొని పుణ్యాహపూర్వకంబుగ గుణర
త్నాకరుం డయ్యెద్దఅ న
స్తోకోన్నతిం బెండ్లియయ్యె సుముహూర్తమునన్.

ఇరా

ఉ ఆ సమయంబునన్ మొరసె
నభ్రపథంబున దేవదుందుభుల్
సేసలు చల్లి రచ్చరలు
సిద్ధనికాయము చేరి సన్నుతుల్
సేసెం బ్రసూనవృష్టి గురి
సెన్ జనరంజనకారివాసనో
ల్లాసములై చెలంగె శుభ
లక్షణ దక్షిణగంధవాహముల్.

ఇ౯

క ఈ విధమున నుద్వాహం
బై వేలుపువెలందిపట్టి యంచితమతి న
ప్పూపుంబోడులు మూపుర
తో వివిధ విహారసంగతులం దత్పరుండై.

57

The king agreed. He focused his mind and learned
what the girls had to teach him. Then, at a good
moment, he married them both to the sound
of chants declaring a good day.

58

Gods celebrated in the sky, beating drums.
Their women sprinkled rice for good luck.
Siddhas sang choruses of praise. Flowers
rained down. A fragrant breeze blew
from the south, bringing joy.

59

Varuthini's son, married to all three women,
spent his time playing inventive games.

౬౦

సీ   గంగాతరంగిణీ రంగత్తరంగ శీ
         కర శీత సైకతోత్కరములందు
         మందార మాకంద మకరంద తుందిలేం
         దిందిరానందక్రుస్నందనమలం
         గాంత నిశాకాంతకాంతవిత్తర్ధికా
         క్రాంత భూభృద్బృంద కందరముల
         మస్రుణ బిసాహార మాంసల హంసికా
         సంపదాసార కాసార తటులం

తే   దమక తమక ప్రియుం డని తమక మెసంగం
         బడంతు లుప్పొంగం గ్రీడించెం బద్మినీ ప్ర
         భావ ఘటితాన్నపానభూషావిశేష
         మాల్యవస్త్రానులేపసామగ్రిం జెంది.

౬౧

మ   అరవిందాక్షులం దాను నిట్లభిమత
         వ్యాపారముల్సల్పుచున్
         ధరణీశం డొకచోటం గాంచె లఘు శీ
         తస్వచ్ఛ వాఃపూరమున్
         వర కీరవ్రజ చంచుపాటిత తట
         వ్యాకీర్ణ మందార కే
         సర మాకంద వినిస్సరత్థల రసా
         సారంబుం గాసారమున్.

60

On beaches cooled by spray from the waves
of the Ganges and in pleasure groves where nectar
of mango and *mandāra* drove the bees mad with delight
and on moonstone beds in mountain caves and on the
    shores
of lakes thick with geese grown fat on lotus stems
he made love to them, and each of the women was sure
that he loved her most. The Padmini provided everything
they needed—food, drink, garlands, clothes, jewels,
and perfumes.

61

While he and his beautiful wives were enjoying
    themselves,
the king noticed a pool of cool, limpid water with
mandāra, kesara, and mango trees on its banks. Parrots
were pecking at the fruits, and sap was flowing
into the water and making it sweet.[7]

౬౨

క కని తత్తటస్థలంబున
ననుమతి విహరించె సవిధ హరిహయవర నం
దన నందన హరిచందన
వన పవనార్భక వినోద వశగతుఁ డగుచున్.

౬౩

ఉ అందొక యంచలేమ గహ
నానిల సంచలదూర్మి మాలికా
మంద విహార సౌఖ్యమున
మత్తిలి దవ్వుల నున్నచక్రవా
కిం దగఁ జేరఁ బిల్చి పరి
కించితె యొంతతపం బొనర్చి రీ
యిందునిభాస్యలుం బతియు
నేకమతిం గవగూడి యుండఁగాన్.

౬౪

క మెలఁతకుఁ బతిపై నైనను
మెలఁతుకపైఁ బతికి నైన మేలగు ఇెందుం
గలయది మెలఁతకుఁ బతికిన్
వలపు సమం బగుట జన్మవాసన చెలియా.

62

He went on playing there as he pleased, losing himself
in the sweet breeze blowing through the sandalwood
trees nearby, in a garden that was like an offshoot
of Indra's garden in the sky.

63

A goose in that lake, a little drunk from happiness
as she rode the waves touched by the breeze
from the garden, hailed a ruddy goose
in the distance and said to her: "Can you see?
How lucky are these beautiful women
and their husband! They're of one mind.

64

Normally you see that a woman likes her husband
more than he likes her, or the man loves his wife
more than she loves him. If man and wife love
each other equally, it's a matter of luck
from a former life.

౬౫

ఉ కావున వీరియందు నధి
కం బగు కూరిమి గల్గియుండు నీ
భూవలయాధినాథునకుఁ
బొల్పుగ నీవిఘనందు నగ్గలం
బీ వనజాయతాక్షులకు
నిచ్చుఁ బ్రియం బది గానఁ బూవునుం
దావియుఁ బోలెఁ జాలఁ బ్రమ
దం బొనరించిరి నాకు నెచ్చెలీ.

౬౬

వ అని పలుకు నమ్మరాళలోలనయన పలుకు లాలంబుచేసి
చక్రవాకి యిట్లనియె.

౬౭

చ ముదమున నిమ్మహీశుఁ డొక
ముద్దియ చూడఁగ నొక్కకాంతతో
సదమదమై కడంగి రతి
సల్పుట తెల్లమిగా నెఱింగియున్
మది వివరించి రేయ కఖి
మానము దక్కిన వీరి కూరుముల్
వదలక పెద్ద సేసెదవు
వందిగతిం దగ వీ విచారముల్.

526

65

This king loves his wives intensely, and they,
in turn, love him just as much. They're united
like a flower with its fragrance, and this
makes me happy, my friend."

66

The ruddy goose dismissed her words and said:

67

"You've seen with your own eyes how this king
makes love to one woman while the others
are watching. Aren't you disgusted?
You call that love? And then you praise them
like a court poet. It's not right.

౬౮

చ పలువురయందు నొక్కనికి
బ్రాఁతియు నొక్కనియందుఁ జూడ న
గ్గల మగు ప్రేమ పల్వురకుఁ
గల్గుట యద్భుత మట్టులుగాన యి
వ్వేలఁదులయందుఁ గూర్మి పస
వీనికి నేమియు లేదు వీనియం
దలవడఁ గల్గదీ జలరు
హొక్కులకుం బ్రియ మెవ్విధంబునన్.

౬౯

క మనుజేశుఁడు కొలిచిన పరి
జనములతో నిష్టగోష్ఠి సలిపెడిచో నె
ట్లనురాగ మట్ల కూరిమి
వనితలు పెక్కంద్రయం దవశ్యము పతికిన్.

౭౦

క ఈ నెలఁత లీమహీశు న
హీనగతిం దగిలిరేని నితఁ డిక లేమం
దా నెలమిఁ గూడునెడ నే
మానిని ప్రాణేశుమీఁది మమత మెలంగున్.

68

It's impossible for one man to love many women
or for many women to love one man. There's no
real love here. He does not love them, and there's no way
they could love him.

69

Kings always play games
with their servant girls, and you can be sure
that's the kind of love they show
their many wives.

70

Let's say these women are deeply in love
with this king. But how could any woman
keep that feeling alive if she knew
that her man was making love to another?

౯౧

క కావున దాసీనికరము
కైవసమై సంచరించు క్రమమున విద్యా
ప్రావీణ్యవైభవోన్నతి
చే వచ్చిన వారి వీరిఁ జెప్పకు మింకన్.

౯౨

ఆ తగులు నెవ్వఁడెక్క తరుణికి నొకనికి
మెలంత వలచు నదియ మే లనంగ
వచ్చుఁ గాని పెక్కు వనితలపైఁ గూర్మి
గలుగు ననుట బొంకు గాదె తరుణి.

౯౩

చ పలుకులు వేయు నేమిటికి
భాగ్య సమన్విత నేన మద్విభుం
డీలఁ గలధన్యఁడంచు నెలుఁ
గెత్తి వరూథినిపట్టి ముందటం
బలుకు రథాంగమానవతి
పల్కు లతం డీల జంతుమండలీ
విలస దశేషభాషలఁ బ్ర
వీణుఁడు గాన యొటీంగి సిగ్గునన్.

71

These women were drawn to him
by his skills, his wealth, and his power.
They obey his commands
like servant girls. Don't say more about them.

72

If a man is attached to one woman,
and a woman loves one man,
that, one can say, is a good thing.
But a man loving more than one woman
is a lie.

73

Why so many words? I'm the luckiest woman
in the world. And my husband is the luckiest man."
That's what the ruddy goose said in a loud voice
while Varuthini's son was listening. He happened
to know the languages of all birds and beasts,
so he understood and was ashamed.

౯౪

క తలవాంచి యుస్సురని మది◌
దలపోయుచు మానరాని తమకంబున నా
నెల◌తలతో నూతే◌డులు
విలసితగతి సౌఖ్య మనుభవించుచు నెలమిన్.

౯౫

శా కాంచెన్ భూవిభు◌ డెక్కనా◌డు కనకా
ఖర్వప్రభామంజులా
స్యాంచన్ మేచకరత్నవిభ్రమ సనా
థానూన దృగ్రోచులన్
మించుం బ్రాయపు లేటిపిండు తను◌ గూ
ర్కిం జుట్టిరా◌ దద్వనో
దంచదుద్ఘామి◌ జరించు నొక్కహరిణీ
త్తంసంబు నింపార◌గాన్.

౯౬

క కని సతులకు◌ జూపెడు తటీ
ఘనముగ◌ దమచెవుల వాలు◌ గన్నులు సోలన్
మొనసెలవి యెత్తి ప్రియునా
ననమున్ మూర్కొనుచు నట్టి నాకెడువేళన్.

74

He bent his head low, sighing,
thinking about things. But since he couldn't
give up his desire for those women, he went on
making love to them for a hundred years more.

75

Then one day he saw a stag surrounded by deer,
their faces shining like gold and their eyes
dark as blue sapphire. They were moving
through that wilderness.

76

The eyes of the does reached all the way
to their ears. They were sniffing
the stag's face, lifting the edges of their lips
and licking his neck. Svarochi wanted to show them
to his wives.

౨౨

శా హుంకారం బొనరించి వే తలఁగుఁ డో
హో నేను స్యారేచినే
పంకేజాక్షులతోడ నెల్లపుడు ద
ర్పస్ఫూర్తిఁ గ్రీడింప ల
జ్ఞాంకూరం బడఁగించినారు తలపో
యన్ నాకు రేఁతయ్యె మీ
రింకం బోయి వరింపుఁ డెక్కరుని భో
గేచ్ఛన్ నివారించితిన్.

౨రా

చ బరువన కింతులం దనకుఁ
బల్వుర గూర్చుట భోగవాంఛఁ గా
కరయఁగ నొండు గాదు ధన
మన్న ధ్రువంబుగ నంగనాజనో
త్కరసముపార్జితం బటులు
గావున వీనికి లే దిహంబునుం
బరమును నన్ను నట్ల పఱు
పం బనిలే దిది చెప్ప నేటికిన్.

౨౯

క వీని విధంబున వనితా
ధీనుఁడ నై పెంపు దక్కి తిరుగుచు నుండం
గా నే వెట్టినె తమకము
మాని చనుం దన్న నవియు మసలక చనియెన్.

77

Suddenly the stag grunted and said to the does:
"Get away from me! Do you think I'm Svarochi,[8] who
    makes love
to women all the time, proud of his vigor? It seems
you've given up all shame. I've lost my taste for this.
Go find some other stag. I've put an end
to my desire.

78

This man has easily gathered women around him.
It's nothing but an excess of lust. As for his wealth,
he got it from the women. So he has no honor in this world
nor a place in the next. Don't let me become
like him.

79

I'm no fool, to live like him, enslaved
to women, without pride. Just go away."
And they left.

౮౦

క ఈ కరణి దూఆనాడిన
యా కృష్ణమృగంబు పల్కు లట మున్నుగ న
క్కొకసతి యన్న మాటలు
నేకంబై తన మనంబు నెరియం జేయన్.

౮౧

ఉ ఆరయ నిట్టిరోఁతలకు
నాలయముల్జలజాక్షు లేటికిన్
వీరలతోడిసంగ మీఁక
వీడెద నంచుఁ దలంచి తోన దు
ర్వారములైన కోరికల
వంక వివేకము చొప్పు దక్కి యిం
పారఁగ నాఱునూఱు సుర
హాయనముల్చరియించెఁ గ్రమ్మఱిన్.

80

The stag spoke in these harsh tones, condemning him,
and his words fused with those spoken before
by the ruddy goose, burning the king's mind.

81

He thought: "Why should I spend my time
with these disgusting women? I'll give up
all contact with them." But no sooner
did he think the thought than lust overtook him
again, and he spent six hundred more years of the gods
with them, with no second thoughts.

౮౨

వ   తదనంతరంబ క్రమక్రమంబున మనోరమయందు
విజయుండును విభావసియందు మేరునందనుండును
కళావతియందు విభావసుండును నను నందనులం
గాంచి పద్మినీ విద్యాప్రభావంబునం బాకశాసన
దిశాముఖంబున విజయునకు విజయాఖ్యపురంబును
గిన్నరేశ్వరహరిదంతంబున మేరునందనునకు గంధవతి
యను పుటభేదనంబునను దక్షిణంబున విభావసునకు
ధారాహ్వయోదార మహానగరంబునుం గల్పించి యనల్ప
విభవంబున నక్కుమారుల నప్పట్టణంబులకుం
బట్టంబుగట్టి కృతార్థుండై యొక్కనాఁడు.

౮౩

ఉ   శాసితశత్రుఁ డాన్నృపతి
చంద్రుఁడు తూణధరుండు సజ్య బా
ణాసన పాణిపంకజుఁడు
నై మృగసంఘములెల్లఁ బెల్లు సం
త్రాసము నొందఁ గూరత న
రణ్యమునన్ మృగయా కుతూహలో
ల్లాసమునం జరించెఁ జల
లక్యవిభేద విధావధానుఁడై.

82

In the course of time, Manorama gave birth to a son named
Vijaya; Vibhavasi gave birth to a son called Merunandana;
and Kalavati gave birth to a son called Vibhavasa. With the
power of that Padmini charm, he created in the east a city
called Vijayapuri for Vijaya, and in the north a city called
Gandhavati for Merunandana, and in the south a great city
called Dhara for Vibhavasa. He enthroned each of them in
his respective city with great glory. Now he felt fulfilled.
Then one day

83

the king, scourge of his enemies, went hunting
with his bow in hand and a quiver of arrows
on his back. He took a cruel pleasure in what he was doing,
terrifying all living creatures, shooting at anything
that moved.

౮౪

వ   ఆ సమయంబున.

౮౫

క   కుటిల కృశ సాంధ్యరజనీ
విట కోరక కోమలచ్చవిస్పుటదంష్ట్రో
ద్భట పోత్ర ఖనిత్రాగ్ర
స్ఫుటితవనీధాత్రి నొక్క పోత్రిం గనియెన్.

౮౬

సీ   జంభారిభిదుర సంరంభంబు వీక్షించి
జరుగు నంజన మహాశైల మనఁగ
ర్యుంర్యూప్రభంజనాస్ఫాలనంబున కుల్కి
యరుగు సంవర్త కాలాభ్ర మనఁగఁ
గఱిన కంఠేకాలకంఠమూలము వాసి
వెస వచ్చు నుజ్జ్వలక్ష్వేళ మనఁగఁ
గలుషధూర్వహఖలోత్కరముపైఁ బఅితెంచు
దండధరక్రూరదండ మనఁగ

తే   ఘుర్ఘురారావ సంఘాత ఘూర్ణమాన
సప్త పాథోధిపాథః ప్రచండ నక్ర
తిమి తిమింగిల మగుచు నభ్రమును మహియుఁ
గ్రమ్ముకొని వచ్చు నొక యేకలమ్ముఁ గనియె.

540

84–85

Then he saw a boar with tusks shining gently
like the crescent moon at twilight. It was cracking open
the ground with its fierce snout, tough as an iron bar.[9]

86

It was Black Mountain fleeing the fury
of Indra's diamond weapon,
the dark Doomsday Clouds
lashed by fierce winds,
deadly poison slipped away from its safe place
at the base of Shiva's tough, black throat,
the punishing club of death coming at those
who bear a burden of sin.
He saw it rushing, filling all space of earth and sky,
churning up crocodiles and whales and other fish
in all seven seas.

౮౽

మ   కని మౌర్వీనినదంబు సేయుచు భుజం
గక్రూర నారాచముం
దన దోర్దండకృతాంతదండనిభ కో
దండంబునం గూర్చి బో
రన నేయం దమకించుచుండ నొక సా
రంగాంగనారత్న మ
జ్జననాథాగ్రణిం జేరి పంచజన భా
షాప్రౌఢిమై నిట్లనున్.

౮౯

క   నృప యీ క్రోడము నీకే
యపకారము సేసె దీని కలుగగ నేలా
కృప మదిం జొనుపక నావై
నిపు డీ శర మేసి నిగ్రహించుట యొప్పున్.

౮౯

క   అని పలుక నతఁడు నీ వీ
తనువుపయిన్ రేయ నేల తద్దయు గృహమై
యునికియుం గాదు గదా చెప్పు
మనవుడు నా హరిణి పల్కె నవనీపతికిన్.

87

Twanging his bowstring, he fixed an arrow,
cruel as a serpent, on the bow that was like
death's very weapon and was about to release it
when a beautiful deer approached and spoke to him
in elegant human words.

88

"What harm has this boar done you,
my king? Why are you angry at him?
Shoot me instead. Don't feel
it's unkind. Go on, kill me now."

89

He said: "Why are you tired of living?
It's not because you're starving.
Tell me." The doe replied:

౯౦

ఆ	అన్యసతులయందు నాసక్తుం డగువానిం
దమక మొదవి కూడ దలంచుకంటె
మరణ మైన మేలు మది వితర్కింపంగ
ననుచుం బలుకుటయును నవనివిభుండు.

౯౧

క	తావకహృదయం బెవ్వని
పై వదలక నిలిచె నీదు భావము దెలియం
గా వలయుం జెప్పు మన్నఢ
రావల్లభుతోడ హరిణి క్రమ్మఱ ననియెన్.

౯౨

చ	చెదరక నామనంబు నృప
శేఖర నీ యెడ నిల్చి మన్మఢ
ప్రదర పరంపరానిహతి
పాల్పడి వ్రేంగెడు నట్లుగాన నా
యెద తడంగింపు మన్న హరి
ణాంగన వీవు నరుండ నే ముదం
బొదవంగ నీకు నాకు మిఢు
నోచితకృత్యము లెట్లు చేకుఱున్.

90

"Death is better than loving a man
who is attached to other women.
That's why I want to die."

91

"Who are you in love with? Tell me
about it, I want to know."

92

"It's you I'm in love with, great king.
My body is burning from the arrows
of desire. Take me in my passion."
He said: "You're a doe, and I'm
a man. How are we supposed to make love?"

౯౩

క నావుడు నను నాలింగన
మీ వనురాగమునఁ జేయు మింతియ చాలున్
భూవర యన్నఁ గృపార్ద్రుఁడు
గావున నా నృపతి హరిణిఁ గౌఁగిటఁ జేర్చెన్.

౯౪

సీ వల్లీమతల్లి లావణ్య సర్వస్వంబు
విమలాంగ రేఖ నావిర్భవింప
మంజుల మంజరీ మహిత సౌభాగ్యంబు
పరివృత్త కుచవృత్తిఁ బరిణమింపఁ
బల్లవచ్ఛద చారుభావానుభావంబు
మృదుహస్తలీల మూర్తీభవింపఁ
రమణీయ ముకుళ విభ్రమ భాగధేయంబు
కరరుహ స్ఫూర్తి సాక్షాత్కరింపఁ

తే జేసి మృగియై వహించు నక్షిద్వయంబు
భాసురంబుగఁ దన యంకపాళిలోన
మించు క్రొమ్మించు నుపమించు మెలఁత యగుచు
నిలుచు నవ్వనదేవత నృపతి సూచి.

93

"Just embrace me. That will be enough."
So the king, out of compassion,
took the doe in his arms.

94

The tender beauty of vines turned into
the curves of a woman's body.
Brilliant clusters of flowers
became her two full, rounded breasts.
New leaves in their loveliness
took the form of delicate hands.
The redness of buds entered into
her fingernails. Only the soft eyes of the doe
remained as they were on her face as,
in his embrace, the goddess of the forest
became a woman, a flash of lightning
come to earth.

౯౫

క   పూనిన విస్మయ రసమున
     మానిని మృగివై చరించి మటి యంగనవై
     కానంబడితివి చిత్రం
     బే నెన్నడు నెటుంగc జెప్పవే తెలియంగన్.

౯౬

సీ   నావుడు నమరకాంతాతనూభవుc జూచి
      యివ్వన దేవత నే నరేంద్ర
      సకల భూభువనరక్షాదక్షు మనువర్య
      నీ యందుc బడయు నెన్నిక సమస్త
      దివిజులు నన్నుc బ్రార్ధించిన వచ్చితి
      ననురాగవతి నైన నను వరించి
      పడయుము నాయం దపత్యంబు దీన నీ
      కగుc బుణ్యలోక సంప్రాప్తి యనిన

తే   నట్ల కా కని యయ్యంబుజాయతాక్షి
      నేకచిత్తంబుతోడ నంగీకరించె
      బాల యిట్లు సుఖాంబుధిc దేలుచుండి
      యంత గర్భిణియై శుభంబగు దినమున.

548

95

Mesmerized, he said to her:
"Up to now you were a doe.
Now I see you as a woman.
It's very strange. I've never known
anything like this. Tell your story."

96

She looked at Varuthini's son and said,
"My king, I'm the goddess of this forest.
All the gods begged me to have a child
by you, a Manu who would protect
the whole world. That's why I came here.
I love you. Marry me. Have a son
with me. You'll attain the supreme world."
He said: "Yes." He accepted her with
one thought in his mind. She was floating
on a wave of happiness. She became pregnant.
On a good day,

౯౨

శా కాంచెం బుత్తు విశాల నేత్రుc బృభువ
క్షీపీఠ విబ్రాజితం
బంచాస్యోద్భుట శౌర్యధుర్య ఘనశం
భద్బాహుc దేజోనిధిం
బంచాస్త్రప్రతిమాను మానఘను సా
మ్రాజ్యైకహేతుప్రభూ
తాంచల్లక్షణలక్షితున్ సుగుణర
త్నానీక రత్నాకరున్.

౯ఠ

క వేడుక నయ్యవసరమున
నాడిరి సురసతులు కిన్నరాంగన లర్థిం
బాడిరి గంధర్వులు గొని
యాడిరి సురతూర్యనినద మగ్గల మయ్యెన్.

౯౯

తే అట్లు జనియించి స్వారేచిషాఖ్య నతడు
శాంతి దాంతి దయా సత్య శౌచ నిరతుc
డై యకామతc జిరతపం బాచరించె
నచ్యుతునిcగూర్చి యంతc గృహార్థుంc డగుచు.

97

she gave birth to a son. He had wide eyes,
a broad chest, the courage of a lion, strong
and capable shoulders, an inner glow.
He was like the love god himself. He had dignity
and all the signs that would make him
a great king. He was good in every way.

98

The gods' women in the sky
danced, the *kinnara* women sang,
gandharvas praised him, and heaven
was filled with the sound of trumpets.

99

The boy was called Svarochisha.
He was naturally calm, controlled,
kind, pure, and truthful. For a long time
he meditated on Vishnu with no desire
in his mind. The god, moved by compassion,

౧౦౦

సీ నీలమేఘము డాలు డీలుసేయఁగఁ జాలు
మెఱుంగుం జామనచాయ మేనితోడ
నరవిందములకచ్చు లడంగించు జిగిహెచ్చు
నాయతం బగు కన్నుదోయితోడఁ
బులుంగురాయని చట్టుపల వన్నె నొరవెట్టు
హొంబట్టు జిలుంగు గెంఝెంబుతోడ
నుదయార్క్యబింబంబు నొఆపు విడంబంబుం
దొరలంగ నాడు కౌస్తుభముతోడ

తే జయజయధ్వని మౌళి నంజలులు సేర్చు
శర్వ శతధృతి శతమన్యు శమనశరధి
పాలకైలబిలాది దేవాళితోడ
నెదుటం బ్రత్యక్షమయ్యె లక్ష్మీశ్వరుండు.

౧౦౧

క ఈ తెఱంగునం దోఁచిన హరి
కాతండు సాష్టాంగ మెఱంగి యంగము పులకా
న్వీతంబుగ హర్షాశ్రువు
లేతెఱంగంగ జూచి భక్తి నిట్లని పొగడెన్.

100

appeared before him:
his body a luminous black, blacker
than the darkest clouds, his wide eyes
gleaming like a lotus flower, his shoulders
covered with a red silk shawl brighter
than the wings of his eagle, on his breast
the *kaustubha* gem that outshines the rising sun.
Shiva, Brahma, Indra, Yama, Varuna, Kubera,
and other gods were singing his praises,
their hands cupped over their heads.

101

Svarochisha bowed to Lakshmi's lord
as goose-bumps broke out on his body
and tears of joy welled up in his eyes.
He sang:

౧౦౨

కవిరాజవిరాజితము.

జయజయ దానవదారణకారణ
శార్ఙ్గరథాంగగదాసిధరా
జయజయ చంద్రదినేంద్రశతాయుత
సాంద్రశరీర మహః ప్రసరా
జయజయ తామరసోదరసోదర
చారుపదోజ్జిత గాంగర్ఝురా
జయజయ కేశవ కేశినిషూదన
శౌరి హరీ దురితాపహరా.

౧౦౩

సీ అవ్యయానంత విశ్వాత్మక విశ్వేశ
      బ్రహ్మవు నీవ కపర్ది వీవ
యింద్రుండ వీవ వహ్నివి యనిలుండ వీవ
      వరుణుండ వీవ భాస్కరుండ వీవ
యముడ వీవ వసూత్కరము నీవ రుద్రులు
      నీవ యాదిత్యులు నీవ విశ్వ
లీవ మరుత్తులు నీవ మంత్రములు నోం
      కృతి వషట్కృతి శ్రుతి స్మృతులు నీవ

తే వేద్య మీవ యావచ్చిన విబుధగణము
సర్వమును నీవ యొట్లన్న సర్వగతుండ
వగుట మటి నీవు గానివాఁడనఁగ నెవ్వఁ
డరయఁగను శేషభూతసమస్త శేషి.

554

102

"You smash demons with your bow, Lord,
and with your discus, mace, and sword.
Your body is brighter than moons and suns,
millions by millions. The Ganges flows
from your feet that are redder
than the petals of a lotus inside.
Keshava, killer of Keshi,*
Shauri, Hari—take away our faults.

103

You're endless, deathless, the life of the universe,
lord of everything, creator, destroyer,
king of all gods, fire, wind, water, sun,
god of justice, the eight Vasus put together
with all eleven Rudras and twelve suns
and ten All-Gods and forty-nine Maruts,
the chants, the syllable Om, the sound
in the offering, knowledge revealed and remembered,
the only one to be known. You're all the gods
who came with you. You're in everything,
and no one is not you. You are the overflow,
and we're what's left over.

---

* A horse demon who tried to kill the infant Krishna.

౧౦౪

మ పరతత్త్వం బగు నీకు మొడ్పుఁగరముల్
పద్మాక్ష కీర్తించెదం
బురుషార్థస్థితి నొప్ప నిన్నుఁ గరుణాం
భోధిన్ భవార్తున్ జడున్
శరణార్థిన్ ననుఁ గావఁగాఁ దగుఁ బ్రధా
నవ్యక్త కాలాత్మ యీ
శ్వర భూతంబుల కీవె కర్తవును బ్రో
వన్ భర్తవున్ హర్తవున్.

౧౦౫

చ విలయ తమిస్రవేళ నతి
వేల మహాంబుధి నూర్ధ్వలోక వా
సులు నతులై కనుంగొనెడు
చూడ్కుల కౌర్యహుతాశనక్రియా
కలితగతిన్ వెలుంగు ఘన
కాయవిజృంభణఁ జోతిమీన వై
కలయఁగఁ గ్రాలు నీ వెడఁద
కన్నులు ప్రోచు మమున్ మురాంతకా.

104

I bow to you. You are the truth.
I praise you. You are the goal
of all life, a flood of compassion.
I'm sick with the agony of existence.
I can't change. I need you. Save me.
You're the only one who is there.
You are time. You make and keep
and destroy all that is.

105

At the end of time, when everything was dark
and the ocean had swallowed everything,
your wide eyes burned like the fire under the sea*
as you became a huge shark, and all the gods
saw you glowing and bowed to you from the skies.
Killer of Mura: may those eyes look after me!

---

* *Aurva*, the fire burning as a mare's head under the ocean.

౧౦౬

చ   చటుల కృపీట సంస్థిత ర
      స్రాస్థలి ప్రీలక యుండ గార యి
      చ్చుటకునుబోలె శంఖమణి
      శుక్తికదంబము నుగ్గుగా విశం
      కట చరమాంగ మంథగిరి
      ఘట్టనఁజేసి ఘరట్టమై కృపా
      పటిమ జగంబుఁ బ్రోచు నల
      ప్రాక్కమఠంబు నినున్ భజించెదన్.

౧౦౭

చ   ఉరుతరవిగ్రహస్ఫురణ
      నుబ్బిన నీ రుపరిచ్ఛిదాముఖాం
      తరమునఁ దోరమై యొగయు
      ధార నజాండము గాజుకుప్పెతో
      సరి యనఁగాఁ దలాతల ర
      సాతలసీమలు సించి ధాత్రి ను
      ద్ధరణ మొనర్చినట్టి నిను
      నాదివరాహము నాశ్రయించెదన్.

106

When the earth was soaking in water for ages,
you made yourself into a tortoise and on your back
you took the grinding of Mount Mandara that crushed
conches and shells and precious stones into a paste
that you could smear as mortar to keep the earth
from crumbling.

107

With your huge body in the form of a boar, you plunged
into the ocean, and water surged up, flowing from
your jaws so that the universe looked like
a glass water jug tipped on its side while you
smashed through the layers of the netherworld
and lifted up the earth. I give myself
to you.

౧౦౮

మ కరుణించున్ మము నట్టి నీదు భుజయు
గ్మం బెద్ది పూనెన్ నభోం
తరసీమం దితిజాంత్రసక్త నఖ సం
తానంబుతో నో నృకే
సరి రాత్రించరభీతికై త్రిభువనా
స్థానీయవీథిన్ విక
స్వర శోణప్రగలంకృతక్రకచ భా
స్వత్తోరణస్తంభతన్.

౧౦౯

చ దనుజకులేంద్ర దత్త కర
తామరసస్థిత దానధారచే
ననిమిష దైన్య దుఃఖిత మ
హాముని మండల దృశ్య కశ్యపాం
గన నయనాంబువుల్గడిగి
కంజభవాండము మోవ లీల మైం
బెనిచిన దంభవామను ను
పేంద్రుని నిన్ను సమాశ్రయించెదన్.

108

Man-Lion: your arms, with the guts of the demon* stuck
to your claws, look like pillars adorned with red flowers
and shining with sharp saws standing in the assembly hall
in heaven—to scare off demons. May those arms
protect me.

109

You rose up to the Seven Sages† in the sky
and washed away the tears of Kashyapa's wife,‡ who was
        there,
grieving at the gods' pain, with the water
poured into your hand by Bali, the demon king.
Pseudo-Dwarf[10] that you were, you grew so tall
that your body rubbed against the edges
of the universe. You're the one
to help me.

---

* Hiranyakashipu.
† The constellation Ursa Major.
‡ Aditi, mother of the gods.

౧౧౦

చ తనదగు సంతతిం గనలి
తానె వధించిన పాపముల్చెడన్
మునిఁగెడు నాగుణోగ్రకిణ
ముల్మొనయంగ శమంతపంచక
మ్మునఁ బితృతర్పణచ్ఛలన
మున్కలువెట్టు భవద్భుజాయుగం
బున కిదె వందనంబు భృగు
పుంగవరూప విహంగవాహనా.

౧౧౧

మ పవిధారా పతనంబు గైకొనని య
ప్పౌలస్త్యు మై సప్తధా
తువులం దూఱు పరిశ్రమంబునకు ను
ద్యోగించె నా సప్తసా
ల విభేదం బొనరించి నిల్వక సలీ
లం జన్న యుష్మన్మరు
జ్జవనాస్త్రం బొసఁగున్ సిరుల్రఘుకుల
స్వామీ రమావల్లభా.

110

Assuming the form of a son of Bhrigu,
you, a warrior yourself, killed all other warriors,
who were *your* sons. To cleanse yourself of that sin,
you bathed in the pools of blood at Samantapanchaka,
as if making an offering to the dead. I worship your arms,
scarred by the bowstring.[11]

111

You shot your arrow, faster than the wind,
through seven *sal* trees and beyond,[12] as if
to show how you could pierce the seven elements[13]
that made up Ravana's body, which had resisted
even Indra's diamond weapon. King
of the Raghu family, husband of Lakshmi:
may your arrow give me all goodness.

౧౧౨

క పెరుఁగు ప్రలంబుని వీఁపునఁ
గరిపై హరివోలె విశదకాంతి నిలిచి త
త్కరణం బారాటముగాఁ
బరిమార్చిన నీదు బలిమిఁ బ్రణుతింతు హరీ.

౧౧౩

తే కొలుతుఁ దాదృగ్ఘవద్బాహు కులిశయష్టి
నెద్ది గిరివోలెఁ గడుపులో వృద్ధిఁబొందఁ
బగిలి రాకాసిదేహంబు మొగపు ముత్య
మయ్యె ముంగామురారి రంగై మురారి.

౧౧౪

క కృతయుగ మేతేర నలం
కృతికై కాశ్మీరపంక మిడి యలుకు క్రియన్
క్షితి యెల్ల మ్లేచ్చరక్త
ప్లుతముగఁ గావించు రౌతుఁ బొగడెద నిన్నున్.

112

As Balarama, you jumped on the giant Pralamba's
back, like a white lion on an elephant, and killed him.
I praise your power.

113

When you were Krishna,[14] you stuck your fist
through the demon Keshi's[15] mouth all the way
to his stomach. It grew into a mountain
inside him and broke him, shrinking his body
to the size of a pearl on your bracelet,[16]
Killer of Mura.

114

As a new Age of Beginnings arises, as if
preparing the ground by smearing it
with saffron paste, you will soak
the earth with the blood
of barbarians. I will praise you,
hero on horseback."[17]

౧౧౫

వ   అని ప్రస్తుతించినం బ్రసన్నుండయి పాంచజన్యధరుండు
వాత్సల్యంబున వత్సా వరంబు వేఁడు మనుటయుం
బ్రసాదం బని స్వారోచిషుం డిట్లనియె.

౧౧౬

క   దేవ భవద్దాస్యసుఖం
బే వేఁడెద దయకుఁ దగుదునే సాలోక్యం
బీవే యితరము లొల్లన్
నావుడు నాతనికిఁ బద్మనాభుం డనియెన్.

౧౧౭

క   సాలోక్యముఁ దుది నిచ్చెద
నేలు మిల ద్వితీయ మనువ వీవై నయధ
ర్మాలోలబుద్ధిఁ దిరముగ
వేలుపులకుఁ దపసులకును విధికిఁ బ్రియముగాన్.

566

115

Praised in this way, God, who bears the conch, was pleased
 and said: "My son,
ask whatever you want." Svarochisha said: "I am grateful.

116

I want to serve you. If you are pleased,
let me live in the same world
with you. I want nothing else."
Lord Vishnu Padmanabha said:

117

"I'll let you come into my world
in good time. Meanwhile, rule the earth
as the second king of men, with an unshaken
mind rooted in what is right and what is wise.
Make gods, sages, and the creator happy."

౧౧౭

చ అని మహిమన్ మనుత్వమున
కాతనిఁ బట్టము గట్టి పద్మలో
చనుఁడు విరించి శర్వముఖ
సర్వసుపర్వలతో నదృష్యుఁడై
చనియె నిజాలయంబునకు
శాస్త్రవినిశ్చయయుక్తి దండపా
లనముల నవ్విభుండుఁ బ్రజ
లం బ్రజలట్లరసెం గృపామతిన్.

౧౧౯

సీ వానలు సరవితో వర్ణించె సస్యముల్
వేళ్ళఁ గొల్చుగ విణ్టివీఁగి పండె
నారోగ్యపుత్రపౌత్రైశ్వర్యవంతులై
బ్రదికిరి నూతేండ్లుఁ బంచజనులు
పూవుఁబోఁడులు పతిదేవతలై రగ్ని
భయ తస్కరవ్యాధి భయము లడఁగె
ఫల పయఃకుసుమాది బహు పదార్థంబులు
రసగంధ సామగ్రి నెసక మెసఁగె

తే నీత్యుపద్రవ మృత్యురాహిత్యయుక్తి
ధరఁ బ్రజావృద్ధి తామర తంపమయ్యె
న్యాయపథమున స్వారోచిషాఖ్యమనువు
శ్రీలఁ బెంపొంది పాలించు కాలమునను.

118

Thus he crowned Svarochisha the king of men
and went home along with Brahma, Shiva,
and all the other gods. Svarochisha ruled
the people as if they were his children—
using his staff according to the rules of the books,
and with compassion.

119

Rains fell regularly. Crops grew in abundance
and yielded grain, even at the root.
Human beings lived a full life of one hundred years
in health and wealth, with children and grandchildren.
Women treated their husbands as if they were gods. The
    threat
of fire, thieves, and disease disappeared. There was plenty
of fruit, milk, and flowers; mercury and sulfur too.
Free from unexpected calamities and untimely death,
people multiplied like the lotus—when Manu Svarochisha
ruled the world.

౧౨౦

క కోరిక నీ స్వారోచిష
చారిత్రము వినిన వ్రాయ౦ జదివిన ధనధా
న్యారోగ్యపుత్రవంతులు
నై రూఢిగ౦ గంద్రు పిదప నమరత్వంబున్.

౧౨౧

తే అని మ్రుకండు తనూభవు౦ డను౦గు శిష్యు౦
డైన క్రోష్టికి వినిపించినట్టి యీ క
థా సుధాధార నించిరి దయ దలిర్ప
జైమినిశ్రుతిపుటముల శకునివరులు.

౧౨౨

శా వ్యాయామస్థిరసంధిబంధ కటకా
ధ్యక్షానుగక్లోణీ భ్ర
త్క్యయగ్రావభిదావిధాభిదురదోః
ఖడ్గాగ్ర యుగ్రాచల
జ్యాయఃకీర్తిభరప్రపంచ వరపం
చారామ రామామణీ
గేయామేయజయాంక పంకజదృగం
గీకార ధీరాకృతీ.

120

Anyone who listens intently to this story
of Svarochisha, or who copies or reads it, will live
in health and riches with children and grandchildren,
and in the end will surely reach the gods.

121

That's how the birds related the story to Jaimini,
as Markandeya had told it to Kroshti,
in a beautiful flow of words.

122

*You have a body firm from constant exercise. Your sword
broke the bodies of the kings who follow the Gajapati lord
of Kataka, just as Indra's diamond weapon shattered
mountains.*
*Your fame brightens the world more than the dazzling light
of Shiva's mountain. Women in the Five Garden Temples[18]
sing of your conquests. In fact, women with lotus eyes
always fall for your beauty.*

౧౨3

క కాంతా లతాంతశర యే
కాంతిక భక్తిప్రతోషితాంభోధిసుతా
కాంతా ప్రతాప రవిశశి
కాంతాయిత విమతన్నపతి కాంతాహృదయా.

౧౨౪

వనమయూరము.

రాజపరమేశ ఫణిరాజబల పుల్లాం
భోజముఖ భోజముఖ భూప విపులాంసో
త్రైజిత ధరాభరణ దీక్షితభుజా ని
ర్వ్యాజభయదాజివిజితారి నృపరాజీ.

గద్యము.

ఇది శ్రీమదాంధ్ర కవితాపితామహ సర్వతోముఖాంక
పంకజాక్ష పాదాంబుజాధీన మానసేందిందిర
నందవరపుర వంశోత్తంస శఠకోపతాపస ప్రసాదాసాదిత
చతుర్విధ కవితామతల్లి కాల్లసాని చొక్కయామాత్యపుత్ర
పెద్దనార్య ప్రణీతంబైన స్వారోచిషమనుసంభవం బను
మహాప్రబంధంబునందు సర్వంబును షష్ఠాశ్వాసము.

123

You're the love god himself to women.
Lord Vishnu is singularly pleased by the single-minded
devotion you show him. Like moonstones in sunlight,
the hearts of your enemies' wives grow pale
before your power.

124

Strong as the king of snakes
who bears the burden of the earth, you now
carry this glorious burden on your shoulders, as kings
like Bhoja did before you. You face your enemies openly
in battle and crush them, one by one,
Oh radiant king of kings!

The great poem called "The Birth of Svarochisha Manu" was
written by Allasani Cokkayamatya's son Peddanarya, known
to all as the "Creator God of Telugu Poetry," who comes from
a family of Nandavara Brahmans, whose mind hovers like a
bee around the lotuslike feet of lotus-eyed Vishnu, and who was
blessed by his guru Shathakopa with the ability to compose all
four kinds of fine poetry. This is the end of chapter 6 and the
end of the book.

ABBREVIATIONS

K   Kambhampati Ramagopala Krishnamurti
S   Vemparala Suryanarayana Sastri
T   Tanjanagaramu Tevapperumalayya
V   Vavilla Ramaswamy Sastrulu and Sons

NOTES TO THE TEXT

తృతీయాశ్వాసము

౧ మగిడి] మరలి V, T
౨ శిథిల] ప్రిదిలి V
౩ తీవెనంట్లుట్టిపడు] K; తీవెనట్లుట్టిపడు T; తేనెనట్టొట్లుపడు S, V. We read *tinen aṇṭlu*, with Kambhampati Ramagopala Krishnamurti. *tīvenaṭluṭṭipaḍu coṭa* (Tevapperumalayya) is incoherent. Various emendations, not much clearer, have been suggested: *tene naṭṭoṭlu paḍu coṭa* (Tevapperumalayya, note; Vemparala Suryanarayana Sastri; Vavilla), apparently "where honey drips continuously."

చతుర్థాశ్వాసము

౧ కొట్టికానిం] కొట్టుకానిం K
౨ గౌక] పరక V
౩ లేటినల్లలు] వేఁడినల్లలు V

పంచమాశ్వాసము

౧ కాళి మాగధ] S; ధూళి మాగధ V, T. We follow Vemparala Suryanarayana Sastri, who emends *kāḷimāgādha** for *dhūḷi-māgadha*, that is, "black, deep flow."

షష్ఠాశ్వాసము

౧ Added verse:
క తపనోదయాస్త సమయము
లిపు డని కాలప్రమాణ మెఱుఁగనితమి న
చ్చపలాక్షిఁ గూడి రతిసుఖ
విపులైశ్వర్యంబు లనుభవించుచు నుండెన్. T, V

౨ Added verses:
ఉ ఆ సమయంబునం బొగులు చాఁకటిపెల్లున నంతకంతకున్
గాసిలి పైపయిన్వదన గహ్వర మెండఁగ నేడ్చియేడ్చి యే
మాసయుఁ గాన కంతఁ దుహినాంశుఁడు దోఁచినఁ దత్కళారస
గ్రాసవిధిన్ శరీర మమరంగ భజించితి దైవికంబునన్.

577

సీ	ఏ నవ్విధంబున మేను పెంచుచు నుండ
	నా చంద మంతయు నాత్మ నెఱింగి
	కడు సంభ్రమమున నక్కడికి నేతెంచి యిం
	పెసంగ మైనెడిన కసటు దుడిచి
	తనయురంబునం జేర్చుకొని పోయి యాశ్రమ
	స్థలమున నిజపర్ణశాల నుంచి
	వీధుకళాంశాహారవిధి వసించితిం గాన
	నాకుం గళావతీ నామ మొసంగి

తే	నయము మీఅంగం బెనుప నానాంటం బెరింగి
	శైశవము మాని యౌవనోత్సవముం జెంది
	జనకునేమైన నడుగుచు సంతతంబు
	నోపి శుశ్రూషచేయుచు నున్నచోట. T, S, V

NOTES TO THE TRANSLATION

Chapter 1

1   Sanandana, Sanaka, Sanatana, and Sanatkumara, the mind-born sons of the creator Brahma, are famous worshipers of Vishnu.

2   Vishnu has two wives: Lakshmi, goddess of wealth and goodness, who normally resides on his chest, and Bhumi, the dark earth goddess. The dark musk left on the god's chest by Lakshmi's breasts calls up the image of the earth. Note the suggestion of critical misperception or illusion—one of the major themes of this book.

3   Arjuna received the invincible *pāśupata* weapon from Shiva as a Kirata hunter.

4   Ganapati, the elephant-headed god, is nursing at the breast of Parvati, who is the left half of the androgynous Shiva-Ardhanarishvara. Again, the theme of misperception (the figure *bhrāntimat*) adumbrates the central narrative of this work.

5   Following Peddana's spelling here.

6   Legend identifies Tikkana as *yajva,* a sacrificer/ritualist.

7   Punishment, in the case of the implied real thief, is concrete and literal, but merely a matter of losing face in the case of the rogue poet (Vemparala Suryanarayana Sastri).

8   The Gajapati kings ruled Kalinga in today's Orissa.

9   On the eastern coast to the north of Andhra.

10   Or: the grandfather, *pitāmaha*.

11   Camphor and betel leaf are given to seal a contract.

12   The blue water lily or nymphea, here seen as a woman, is said to unfold its petals at the touch of moonlight.

13   All these figures—Vishnu as the turtle and the boar, the great mountains, the cosmic snake, and the elephants standing in the cardinal directions—support the earth.

14   See the previous note on v. 23. The earth was lifted up from the depths of the sea by Varaha, the great boar; it rests upon the thousand hoods of the snake Adishesha and is propped up by the cosmic mountains.

15   *Gijigāḍulu,* the weaver birds, famous for their intricate nests— hence their name. "It builds a nest of woven grass shaped like

a bottle with the mouth downwards: hence called the bottle-nested sparrow. It is used as a carrier pigeon" (C. P. Brown 1966, s.v.). These birds are here thought to line their nests with diamonds that they mistake for fireflies (another example of the figure *bhrāntimat*, "misperception," so prevalent in this book). Krishnaraya has destroyed his enemies' cities, leaving only ruins where wild elephants roam.

16 South of the Krishna River, near today's city of Guntur.

17 Simhachalam is a major temple to Vishnu as Varaha-Narasimhasvami on the outskirts of Visakhapatnam in northern Andhra (southern Kalinga). Potnuru is a high mountain some twenty kilometers to the north. Inscriptions were incised on stone, then smeared with lampblack to make them legible.

18 Each long cosmic aeon, *manvantara*, is presided over by a Manu. Their stories are told in sequence in the *Mārkaṇḍeyapurāṇa*, from which Peddana has taken the narrative frame for his story of Svarochisha Manu (the sage Jaimini is instructed by Markandeya).

19 Rama of the ax, Parashurama, is a violent avatar of Vishnu. Kubera is the banker of the gods. Shiva appears as Bhikshatana, a naked beggar holding the skull of Brahma in his hand as his begging bowl. Some commentators think the final sentence of the verse refers to a specific tree, *ciguru*, in the Rayalasima area.

20 Bees are said by poets to avoid the champak flowers.

21 The morning prayer to Vishnu is the *vāmanastuti*, a hymn to the god in the first of his human avatars, the dwarf.

22 The *sālagrāma* stone, favored by Vishnu, is free of taint, but Pravara is unwilling even to accept so auspicious and simple a gift from a king.

23 Pravara, as an *āhitâgni* Brahman, maintains the household fire that must never go out.

24 Prayaga, at present-day Allahabad, is the confluence of the Ganga and Yamuna rivers, a pilgrimage site of great importance.

25 Sandal Mountain, Malayachala or Patirachala, is in the far south, in Kerala. Snow Mountain is the Himalaya.

26 Shiva resides at Kedarnath in Uttarancal, the Himalayas; not far to the east is Vishnu's great shrine at Badarinath. The famous Tantric goddess Hingula is located to the far northwest, in Baluchistan in Pakistan.

27 Airavana or Airavata is Indra's elephant mount.

28 The siddha, an accomplished alchemist, can make mercury freeze into a solid *linga*.

29 Extempore (*āśu*), figurative (*citra*), pictorial (*bandha*), and embedded (*garbha*—one verse including another verse in it). Others list these as *āśu, citra, madhura* (sweet), and *vistara* (extended).

Chapter 2

1 Bhoja of Dhara was a famed patron of poets including, according to the tradition, the great Kalidasa.

2 Narayana-Vishnu and Nara, the first man, appeared as a closely linked pair at the beginning of time.

3 Bhagiratha worshiped Shiva in order to bring the Ganges down to earth, and indeed the god released the river, which flowed through his matted hair and struck the Himalaya at the site where Pravara is wandering. Agni, god of fire, fell in love with the Krittikas, the wives of the Seven Sages. Here, literally: the three fires (of Vedic offering).

4 The point is that Shiva became a bridegroom, his body smeared in auspicious turmeric. Mena is wife to Mount Himalaya.

5 Literally, yakshas and gandharvas.

6 Divine beings never blink or sweat.

7 This is the *bhramara-kīṭa-nyāya*, a proverbial statement of transformation through mental obsession.

8 Nalakubara (Kubera's son), spring (Vasanta), the moon, and the love god are all exemplars of male beauty.

9 That is, the *hayamedha* or *aśvamedha* horse sacrifice and the great coronation rite, *rājasūya*.

10 The list names the most famous of the heavenly dancers, apsarases.

11 Parashara made love to Matsyagandhi, daughter of the fisherman-king, and she then gave birth to Vyasa. Vishvamitra was seduced and distracted from his ascetic regimen by the apsaras Menaka. The gods sent five celestial apsarases to seduce Mandakarni, who had performed austerities for ten thousand years. He took all of them as his wives and lived with them in a city he created under water. Indra disguised himself as the sage Gautama in order to seduce Gautama's wife, Ahalya.

12 On bees and the champak flower, see note on 1.52.

Chapter 3

1 Night is perceived as a woman and the sun and moon as men.

2 Fire burns under the ocean in the form of a mare's head, fed by the waves.

3 The figure *mukta-pada-grastālaṅkāra,* "taking up (again) the word that has been put aside," structures the syntax of this verse. Each verb appears first in its finite form and is then repeated as a nonfinite at the start of the subsequent clause. The *cakravāka* birds are models of conjugal fidelity, but they are tragically condemned to spend each night apart—hence their forlorn calls.

4 Shiva dances the destructive *tāṇḍava* dance at night, in the cremation ground. According to Elephant Science, an elephant in rut can only quench its thirst by lying down on a bed of red earth (Vemparala Suryanarayana Sastri).

5 Parvati assumed the form of a huntress to accompany her husband, in the guise of a hunter, at the time Arjuna was performing penance. The Vavilla text reads: *kirātu,* in the masculine, in the first line; but since men don't use musk, the verse must refer to the goddess.

6 The imagined protocol for finding buried treasure required that one put a magic collyrium powder in one's eye and then make a sacrificial offering of rice mixed with blood from some hapless traveler to the *bhūta* spirit that was thought to guard any such riches. The treasure hunter usually depended upon some mark, such as a nearby tree.

7 The Vavilla commentator notes that all the subjects in this verse are in the plural except for *virahiṇi,* the woman separated from her lover—a hint at Varuthini, "a certain woman."

8 Chaya, Shadow, is one of the two wives of the sun god, along with Ushas, Dawn.

9 Moonlight, a feminine noun, is seen as a woman.

10 The moon, while studying with Brihaspati, slept with his teacher's wife, Tara.

11 This verse is built around paronomastic identifications of the moon and Yama, the god of death. *Took shape from the sun:* Yama, the god of death, is the son of the Sun. The moon gets its light reflected from the sun. *Kicked by the god:* Yama was kicked dead by Shiva, who came to save his devotee Markandeya. The moon was kicked by Virabhadra-Shiva at the time of the destruction of Daksha's sacrificial rite. *Heavy club/heavy sickness:* Yama has a club, *gadā,*

and the moon was cursed to wane from consumption, *gadā. Your eyes light up:* The moon is married to twenty-seven constellations of stars.

12   The Moon has a dark mark or stain variably identified as a deer or a hare.

13   Vatapi and Ilvala, two demon brothers, perfected a method of killing guests and sages. Vatapi would take the shape of a goat, and Ilvala would kill him, cook him, and serve him to guests. After they had eaten, Ilvala would call his brother, who would emerge from their belly, thereby killing them.

14   When Shiva went into battle against the demons of the Tripura, the Triple City, the moon became one wheel of his chariot. Along with the hole in his body from that event, the moon is ill with consumption: he married the twenty-seven daughters of Daksha but showed a special love for one of them, Rohini; his father-in-law then cursed him to suffer this illness. A Telugu folk belief says that a person with fever must not make love lest he die.

15   The day lotus closes its petals at nightfall; hence the moon is its enemy.

16   Shiva bears the crescent moon on his head. At the time of the destruction of Daksha's sacrificial rite—to which Shiva was not invited—Virabhadra kicked and stamped on the moon.

17   Arjuna's bow, Gandiva, was originally the moon's.

18   Manmatha, god of desire, was sent by the gods to disturb Shiva's ascetic meditation and make him fall in love with Parvati. Shiva discovered Manmatha as the latter was at the point of shooting his flower arrows at him; the god opened his third eye and burnt Desire to ashes.

19   Rati, Pleasure, is Manmatha's wife. See verse 46 above.

20   Snakes are said to feed on the wind. "Gentle" (*mṛdu*) in the following line is meant as an insult—the gentler the wind, the worse the torment of lonely women.

21   The sun is Brahma at dawn, Rudra at mid-day, and Vishnu in the evening (Komanduru Anantacarya). Brahma rides the goose.

22   Eyeliner is made from the soot of the oil lamp.

23   The evening raga is Nāṭa, and the morning raga is Deśākṣi.

24   See note on 3.16.

25   In Kerala, the region of the Malaya Mountain, snakes are supposed to be coiled around the sandalwood trees that perfume the southern wind.

26 See note on 1.52.

27 Rambha, one of the most beautiful of the heavenly apsaras dancers, is often sent by Indra to seduce a sage whose ascetic practice threatens the gods.

28 What follows is a *ragaḍa* series of rhyming couplets. The rhymes often seem artificial, and the *ragaḍa* as a whole diminishes the poetic tension that has been building up; still, we have tried to mimic something of the effect of these couplets.

29 *Jaṭā* recitation—where syllables are recited forward and backward as if to weave them together in a thick mnemonic braid.

30 The love god is imagined as so angry that he bites the tips of the arrows he is about to shoot.

31 The washerman Revadu took clothes to wash in the river; he put the freshly washed clothes out to dry on a rock and the still soiled clothes on another rock. A flood came, and he ran first to one batch of clothes but then, as the waters rose, he rushed over to the other batch—and in the end lost both. Another story, cited by Vemparala Suryanarayana Sastri, tells of four Sanskrit students of Purva Mimamsa. Umbeka studied the *kārikā* texts; Prabhakara studied the Tantra part; Mandana studied both; Revana studied neither.

umbekaḥ kārikāṃ vetti tantraṃ vetti prabhākaraḥ/ maṇḍanas tv ubhayaṃ vetti nobhayaṃ vetti revaṇaḥ //

32 Most commentators think that she is twisting his upper cloth.

33 Travelers separated from their lovers or wives are particularly vulnerable to the attacks of desire.

34 Pregnant women are said to crave and to eat earth, which imparts a fragrance to their breath.

35 Vemparala Suryanarayana Sastri takes exception to this verse and declares it an interpolation, adducing its absence from the text that C. P. Brown had copied and that was commented upon by Juluri Appayya Pandita in the mid-nineteenth century.

36 *Prāḍvivākulu,* glossed as *akṣadarśaka.* The dictionaries, following the dharma texts, say this means "arbitrators," but we have taken *akṣa* to mean "dice."

37 By poetic convention, bees avoid the champak flower (see verses 1.52 and 3.76 above). The usual explanation is that they have a natural aversion to its smell (*sahajavirodha*). In Peddana's verse, however, it seems that the bee keeps away from the champak because the flower exerts a fatal attraction. By implication, the

love Varuthini shows the gandharva is so overwhelming that he fears he will never free himself from it.

38 *Hindū-rājya,* "land/kingdom of the Hindus," from Arabic al-Hind as a name for the entire subcontinent.

39 Yavana, in this period, is a term for Muslims in South Indian languages.

40 The Mahabharata hero Karna was famed as an exemplar of generosity.

Chapter 4

1 *Nakka-kŏmmu:* apparently a horn growing on the head of a certain variety of fox; known from later sources such as Tarigonda Vengamamba's *Ceñcu-nāṭakamu* as auspicious. The *Śrīharinighaṇṭuvu* (Hyderabad, 2004, s.v.) records the expression, current in Nellur, *nakkakŏmmu tŏkku,* "to step on a *nakka-kŏmmu,*" meaning: "If you've stepped on a *nakka-kŏmmu,* it's your lucky day."

2 All of these wilderness products are unusual and unfamiliar.

3 In dialect in the verse: *sīrāmu-sena.*

4 *Pūja-vāruvambulu:* in Kannada, *pūjāvāji* is a "greatly respected royal horse" (F. Kittel, *Kannada-English Dictionary* [Madras: University of Madras, 1970], s.v.); Vemparala Suryanarayana Sastri notes the parallel.

5 Muka is the wild boar that attacked Arjuna and was slain by Shiva as the Kirata hunter.

6 *Eku:* raw cotton rolled into an extended mass to be fed into the spindle.

7 Following Vemparala Suryanarayana Sastri's gloss of *pāru-gavulu.* Other commentators: if they (the animals) got a whiff of the leather belts (*vāru*) tied to the hunting dogs or other animals.

8 *Kŏṭṭikāḍu:* a hidden watchman or spy. *Sūryarāyândhra-nighaṇṭuvu,* s.v.

9 Juluri Appayya, in the *editio princeps,* notes that the textual variations in this long and difficult passage were too numerous to be noted.

10 According to the commentators, these tough archers used decoys as cover.

11 Vemparala Suryanarayana Sastri states that the *cĕmaruṅgāki* crow never stays still for more than a few seconds, so that it is hard to aim at it.

12 Vemparala Suryanarayana Sastri: according to popular belief, a hunter who has killed a tiger must immediately burn away its whiskers to prevent any magical use of them by enemies.

13 Women of the vidyadhara class of demigods.

14 During a twelve-year drought, the sage Gautama fed Brahmans by sprinkling rice that would ripen at once. The Seven Sages asked him to come with them, but he refused to leave his ashram. They created a magical cow and let it loose on the crop Gautama was growing. Gautama tried to drive it away by throwing *darbha* grass— and the cow died. The Sages then accused him of *gohatyā*, the murder of a cow. To revive it, Gautama went to Nasik, worshiped Tryambakeshvara, and brought the river Ganga to flow over the dead cow. That river is now called Gautami or Godavari.

15 Vavilla commentator: the Rakshasa praises his opponent's courage ("This is really something!").

16 Most versions of this story do not give this role to Vishnu but say that the gods and demons pulled the snake Vasuki, the churning rope tied to Mount Mandara, that rested on Vishnu as the Tortoise.

17 Some interpret *sekariñcu koni* as "neighing."

18 Dadhica or Dadhici gave his spine to Indra so the latter could use it for his diamond weapon.

19 The moon, however brilliant, feeds the gods with his body, which thus diminishes for half of each month.

Chapter 5

1 Bali, a demon king, gave suppliants whatever they wanted— including the land covered by Vishnu the Dwarf's famous three steps (thus, the entire cosmos). Karna, the epic hero, is another exemplar of unstinting giving.

2 Students in medieval Andhra would attach themselves to a teacher and beg each day for food from different Brahman houses.

3 In the wedding ceremony, the bride steps on the grinding stone, *sannikallu.*

4 Indivaraksha interprets the curse to include eating human flesh, though this is not stated by the sage in v. 19.

5 *Āmu* or *nāmu.* Vemparala Suryanarayana Sastri glosses the former as "poison," but the dictionaries do not support this meaning. *Nāmu* is a well-known word meaning small sprouts growing in a field after the harvest; such sprouts, especially of millet, are said to be poisonous.

6   The *cakravāka* birds are separated at sunset each evening. But *cakra-* here also means the kingdom.

7   There is an untranslatable pun on *varṇa* as "color" and "class of people."

8   All the statements in this verse also apply to a king who rules the whole world, is intent on collecting taxes (*kara*—homonymous with "rays"), and so on, as if Peddana were quietly focusing the reader's mind at this point on kingship in the context of Svarochi's impending marriage and entry into the royal setting. The verse is also a meditation on time as ruling the king *and* human destiny; the sun too is subject to time. The *Manucaritramu* as a whole leads to the birth of Manu, the ruler of time.

9   Jayanta is the son of Indra, the regent of the east; here he is playing with a *billa*, a flat, round piece of wood.

10 We follow Vemparala Suryanarayana Sastri's reading of *maṇḍapamu* as a tent.

11 Mandara is so high that the sun can illuminate only its lower slopes.

12 At the time of the churning of the milk ocean, Mount Mandara was placed on the back of Vishnu, the Tortoise, to serve as the churning rod.

13 Vasuki, serving as the churning rope coiled around Mandara Mountain, the churning rod.

14 Mainaka, hiding in the ocean, was the only mountain to escape Indra when the latter cut off the mountains' wings. Mandara encountered him during the churning.

15 The graphic symbol for *Śrī* in Telugu is a flowing curve.

16 As in the previous verse, the *tamāla* buds exemplify darkness.

17 The following verses comprise an *ulā*, that is, a description of the hero in procession and the turbulence his appearance causes among young women who rush to see him. Well known from passages in the great Sanskrit poets Ashvaghosha and Kalidasa, *ulā* became a popular genre in Tamil and other south Indian literatures (see Wentworth 2011).

18 The geese are attracted to the jingling of the anklet, which sounds to them like one of their own.

19 One way to take a strong vow is to stand in wet clothes, after a bath, and utter the binding words.

20 Sarasvati and Lakshmi naturally belong to the king, who is articulate and wealthy. Shiva's left, female half here escapes the right, male half to join the king.

21 We follow the interpretation of Vemparala Suryanarayana Sastri. Others read: So that bees focused on the temples of elephants in rut took them for their own kind (Komanduru Anantacarya).

22 *Madhuparka* today is a mix of curds, jaggery, honey, water, and ghee.

23 In Andhra weddings the son-in-law is seen as Vishnu at the time of giving away the bride.

24 *Mĕṭṭu-brālu*. Vemparala Suryanarayana Sastri proposes, on the basis of this term, that the bride was perhaps made to stand in heaps of rice before the curtain between her and her new husband was removed. However, like other commentators, he glosses the term as equivalent to the *talambrālu* rice the young couple pour over each other's head.

25 Sweat is one of the eight *sāttvikabhāvas*, or psychophysical reactions, and indicates, in this case, aroused desire.

26 In Telugu weddings today, the tying of the wedding string *precedes* the *talambrālu* pouring of rice.

27 We agree with Vemparala Suryanarayana Sastri's gloss on *viḍambimpagān* as "deceiving" the bright rubies, that is, not entering into a competition with them, since they are brighter than his fingernails. This interpretation has the merit of depicting the natural folding inward of the fingers while tying the knot. Others, such as Komanduru Anantacarya, gloss simply as "equal to the rubies."

28 A standard feature of the Hindu wedding service is the moment the groom makes his bride step onto the grinding stone. See v. 17 above.

Chapter 6

1 Images of defeated foes were engraved on a hero's anklets.

2 Modern commentators such as Komanduru Anantacarya and Vemparala Suryanarayana Sastri attach the final phrase to the next verse, so that it is Svarochi's mind that is stirred up.

3 A paste made from the *goraṇṭa* leaf was applied to fingernails and left overnight to produce a red color.

4 The baby cuckoo starts cooing in spring—so that the crow, who has brought it up, realizes it is not one of its own and drives it away. Some species of cuckoos are brood parasites, laying their eggs in the nest of an innocent host.

5 This verse, like 3.16, is built around the trope called *muktapadagrastâlaṅkāra,* in which the final word of one line becomes the first word of the next one.

6 Here two additional verses, precisely narrating the substance of the prose passage (39), appear in some editions. See notes to the Telugu text.

7 Syntactically the verse as it stands is awkward; the nonfinite *salpucun* has a plural subject and thus does not fit the finite verb *kāñce.* The commentators pay no attention to this problem. We could solve it by emending *salpucun* to *salpaga.*

8 *Svāroci* in Telugu—an irregular form of *Svarochi?* (Thus Vemparala Suryanarayana Sastri.)

9 Juluri Appayya, the commentator in C. P. Brown's edition, regarded this verse as interpolated; Vemparala Suryanarayana Sastri disagrees, though the narrative content of vv. 85 and 86 is the same. We have followed the standard editions and retained it.

10 Vishnu as Vamana, the Dwarf, asked the demon king Bali for the land he could cover with three steps; Bali granted this request by pouring water into the Dwarf's hand. Vishnu then swelled as he took his three steps to reach the limit of the cosmos.

11 This verse celebrates the violent avatar of Parashurama, Rama with the Ax, who repeatedly wiped out the warrior class.

12 Rama shot an arrow through seven *sal* trees to demonstrate his prowess to his newfound friend, the monkey king Sugriva.

13 Hair, skin, flesh, bone, sinews, marrow, and breath, according to one list. Others list blood, seed, fat, flesh, marrow, bone, and subcutaneous tissue (*vasa*).

14 Komanduru Anantacarya and the Vavilla commentator claim, illogically and without explanation, that this verse relates to the Buddha avatar.

15 See v. 102 above (and *Bhāgavatapurāṇa* 10.37).

16 *Muṅgāmurāri** (T) is unintelligible. Commentators derive it from *mundu kai muruvu,* a bracelet.

17 The future Kalki avatar will destroy all barbarians in order to usher in a golden age.

18 The Pancharama shrines to Shiva in the Godavari-Krishna Delta: see Narayana Rao and Shulman 2012: 74, 96-97.

BIBLIOGRAPHY

Editions and Translations

Svārociṣamanucaritra of Allasāni Pĕddana. 1851. Edited by Juluri Appayya as commissioned by C. P. Brown. Madras: Bhuvanagiri Cinna Rangayya Setti (*editio princeps*).

Svārociṣamanucaritramu of Allasāni Pĕddana. 1863. Edited by a group of scholars. Madras: Sankara Venkatrao.

Svārociṣamanucaritramu of Allasāni Pĕddana. 1919. With commentary by Komanduru Anantacarya. Edited by Tanjanagaramu Tevapperumalayya. 2nd ed., Madras: R. Venkatesvara and Company. (Base text for our edition; 1st ed., 1909.)

Manucaritramu of Allasāni Pĕddana. 1960. Edited by Kambhampati Ramagopala Krishnamurti. Vijayawada: Kalyanigranthamandali.

Manucaritramu of Allasāni Pĕddana. 1966. Edited by Timmavajjhala Kondadaramayya. Hyderabad: Andhra Pradesh Sahitya Akademi. 2nd ed., 1984.

Manucaritramu of Allasāni Pĕddana. 1968. Edited with commentary by Vemparala Suryanarayana Sastri. Vijayawada: Venkatrama and Co.

Manucaritramu of Allasāni Pĕddana. 1969. Madras: Vavilla Ramaswamy Sastrulu and Sons.

Other Sources

Adhyâtmasankīrtanalu of Annamayya. 1998–1999.Vol. 2. Tirupati: Tirupati Tirumala Devasthanam.

Āmuktamālyada of Kṛṣṇadevarāya. 1964. Edited by Vedamu Venkataraya Sastri. Madras: Vedamu Venkataraya Sastri and Brothers.

Brown, Charles Philip. 1966. *A Dictionary, Telugu and English*. [1852]. Hyderabad: Andhra Pradesh Sahithya Akademi.

Kāvyâdarśa of Daṇḍin. 1981. Edited by Pullela Sriramacandrudu. Hyderabad: Andhra Pradesh Sahitya Akademi.

Kittel, F. 1968. *Kannada-English Dictionary*. Revised and enlarged by M. Mariyappa Bhat. Madras: University of Madras.

Laksmikanta Sastri, Sista. n.d. *Vijayanagarāndhra kavulu*. Vijayawada: Nirmala Publishers.

Mārkaṇḍeyapurāṇa. N.d. Bombay: Venkatesvara Steam Press.

Mārkaṇḍeyapurāṇamu of Mārana. N.d. Hyderabad: Telugu Vijnapitham.

Narayana Rao, Velcheru. 1978/2008. *Telugulo kavitā viplavāla svarūpam.* 1st ed., Hyderabad: Visalandhra pracuranalayam. 3rd ed., Chicago: TANA.

Narayana Rao, Velcheru and Hank Heifetz. 1987. *For the Lord of the Animals: Poems from the Telugu. The* Kāḷahastīśvara Śatakamu *of Dhūrjaṭi.* Berkeley: University of California Press.

Narayana Rao, Velcheru and David Shulman. 1998. *A Poem at the Right Moment: Remembered Verses from Premodern South India.* Berkeley: University of California Press.

———. 2002. *Classical Telugu Poetry: An Anthology.* Berkeley: University of California Press.

———. 2005. *God on the Hill. Temple Poems from Tirupati.* New York: Oxford University Press.

———. 2012. *Śrīnātha: The Poet Who Made Gods and Kings.* New York: Oxford University Press.

———, and Sanjay Subrahmanyam. 2011. "A New Imperial Idiom in the Sixteenth Century: Krishnadevaraya and His Political Theory of Vijayanagara." In *Forms of Knowledge in Early Modern Asia: Explorations in the Intellectual History of India and Tibet, 1500-1800,* ed. Sheldon Pollock. Durham and London: Duke University Press, pp. 69-111.

Pollock, Sheldon. 1995. "In Praise of Poets: On the History and Function of the *Kavipraśaṃsā.*" In *Ānandabhāratī: Dr. K. Krishnamoorthy Felicitation Volume,* ed. B. Channakeshava and H. V. Nagaraja Rao. Mysore: DVK Murthy, pp. 443-457.

Sewell, Robert. 1900. *A Forgotten Empire (Vijayanagar).* London: Swan Sonnenschein & Co.

Shulman, David. 2001. "First Man, Forest Mother: Telugu Humanism in the Age of Kṛṣṇadevarāya." In *The Wisdom of Poets: Studies in Tamil, Telugu, and Sanskrit,* by D. Shulman. Delhi: Oxford University Press, pp. 323-350.

———. 2012. *More Than Real: A History of the Imagination in South India.* Cambridge, Mass.: Harvard University Press.

———. 2012. "Tampering with Nature." In *Aux abords de la clairière. Études indiennes et comparées en l'honneur de Charles Malamoud,* ed. Silvia D'Intino and Caterina Guenzi — Turnhout, Belgium: Brepols, pp. 137-153.

Śrīhari nighaṇṭuvu: Sūryarāyāndhra nighaṇṭuśēṣaṃ of R. Śrīhari; Jayanti Rāmayya Pantulu. 2004. Hyderabad: Sri Gopal Publications.

Śṛṅgāranaiṣadhamu of Śrīnātha. 1985. Hyderabad: Telugu Vijnana-pitham.

Viswanatha Satyanarayana. 1967. *Allasāni allika jigibigi.* Viyayawada: V. S. N. and Sons.

Wentworth, Blake. 2011. "Yearning for a Dreamed Real: The Procession of the Lord in the Tamil Ulās." Ph.D. dissertation, University of Chicago.

INDEX

ABOUT THE BOOK

Murty Classical Library of India volumes are designed by Rathna Ramanathan and Guglielmo Rossi. Informed by the history of the Indic book and drawing inspiration from polyphonic classical music, the series design is based on the idea of "unity in diversity," celebrating the individuality of each language while bringing them together within a cohesive visual identity.

The Telugu text of this book is set in the Murty Telugu typeface, commissioned by Harvard University Press and designed by John Hudson and Fiona Ross. The type is inspired by those of the Swatantra Type Foundry in the shaping of the counters and the relatively high degree of stroke modulation for Telugu letterforms.

The English text is set in Antwerp, designed by Henrik Kubel from A2-TYPE and chosen for its versatility and balance with the Indic typography. The design is a free-spirited amalgamation and interpretation of the archives of type at the Museum Plantin-Moretus in Antwerp.

All the fonts commissioned for the Murty Classical Library of India will be made available, free of charge, for non-commercial use. For more information about the typography and design of the series, please visit *http://www.hup.harvard.edu/mcli*.

Printed on acid-free paper by Maple Press, York, Pennsylvania.